Typhoon

Typhoon

The Inside Story of an RAF
Fighter Squadron at War

MIKE SUTTON

WITH CLIFFORD THURLOW

MICHAEL JOSEPH

MICHAEL JOSEPH

UK | USA | Canada | Ireland | Australia
India | New Zealand | South Africa

Michael Joseph is part of the Penguin Random House group of companies
whose addresses can be found at global.penguinrandomhouse.com

First published 2021
001

Copyright © Mike Sutton and Clifford Thurlow, 2021

The moral right of the authors has been asserted

Picture credits: pp.x–xi © Mike Badrocke. Endpapers: © Michael Rondot.
Insets: p.4, bottom © Michael Rondot; p.5, top & upper middle © Eurofighter – Geoffrey Lee, Planefocus Ltd;
p.7, middle © Gary Eason / Flight Artworks, www.flightartworks.com; bottom © Eurofighter;
p.10, bottom © Matt Cardy / Getty; p.12, middle left & right, & p.15, bottom left
from Russian Defence Ministry; p.16 © Keith Campbell, Capture A Second Photography

Every effort has been made to trace copyright holders and to obtain their permission for the use
of copyright material. The publisher apologizes for any errors or omissions and would be grateful
to be notified of any corrections that should be incorporated in future editions of this book.

Set in 13.5/16pt Garamond MT Std
Typeset by Jouve (UK), Milton Keynes
Printed and bound in Great Britain by Clays Ltd, Elcograf S.p.A.

The authorized representative in the EEA is Penguin Random House Ireland,
Morrison Chambers, 32 Nassau Street, Dublin D02 YH68

A CIP catalogue record for this book is available from the British Library

HARDBACK ISBN: 978–0–241–53599–8
TRADE PAPERBACK ISBN: 978–0–241–53600–1

www.greenpenguin.co.uk

Penguin Random House is committed to a
sustainable future for our business, our readers
and our planet. This book is made from Forest
Stewardship Council® certified paper.

Dedicated to the families of pilots everywhere

Contents

CONTENTS

Cutaway Illustration of the Typhoon
and Map of the Squadron's Region
of Operations

EUROFIGHTER TYPHOON CUTAWAY.

(Mike Badrocke)

1 Glass fibre reinforced plastic (GFRP) radome, hinged to starboard for access
2 ECR-90 multi-mode pulse-doppler radar scanner
3 Scanner tracking mechanism
4 Retractable flight refuelling probe
5 Instrument panel shroud
6 Forward-looking infra-red seeker
7 Radar equipment bay
8 Air data sensor
9 Port canard foreplane
10 Foreplane diffusion-bonded titanium structure
11 Foreplane hinge mounting
12 Hydraulic actuator
13 Rudder pedals
14 Instrument panel with full colour multi-function head-down displays (HDD)

15 Head-up display (HUD)
16 Rear view mirrors
17 Upward-hinging cockpit canopy
18 Pilot's Martin-Baker Mk 16a 'zero-zero' ejection seat
19 Control column handgrip, full-authority digital active-control technology (ACT) fly-by-wire control system
20 Engine throttle levers, HOTAS controls
21 Side console panel
22 Boarding steps, extended
23 Boundary layer splitter

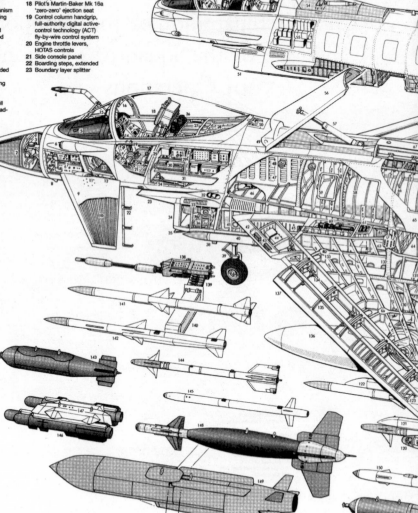

100 Tailpipe sealing plates
101 Brake parachute housing
102 Rudder hydraulic actuator
103 Parachute hinged door
104 Variable area afterburner nozzle
105 Nozzle actuator
106 Runway emergency arrestor hook
107 Aft fuselage semi-recessed missile carriage
108 Port elevon all-CFC structure
109 Inboard elevon hydraulic actuator
110 Elevon honeycomb core structure
111 Outboard elevon all-titanium structure
112 Outboard elevon hydraulic actuator
113 Actuator ventral fairings
114 Outboard pylon countermeasures dispenser
115 Aft ECM/ESM antennae
116 Wing tip electronic-countermeasures/electronic surveillance (ECM/ESM) pod
117 Formation lighting strip
118 Port navigation light
119 Equipment cooling ram-air intake
120 Forward ECM/ESM antennae
121 Outboard missile pylon
122 Port wing leading-edge two-segment slat
123 Intermediate stores pylon
124 Pylon mounting hardpoints
125 Port wing integral fuel tankage
126 Wing panel multi-panel structure
127 Cable conduits
128 Elevon hinge fairing-mounted countermeasures dispensers
129 Port main wheel –
130 Mainwheel shock-absorber leg strut
131 Hydraulic retraction jack
132 Undercarriage leg mounting stub spars
133 Wing root pylon-mounting hardpoint
134 Leading edge slat operating screw jacks and torque shaft
135 Slat guide rails
136 330 Imp gal (1,500-litre) external fuel tank
137 Wing leading edge slat extended position
138 Mauser BK27, 27mm cannon
139 Ammunition feed chute
140 Ammunition magazine, 150 rounds
141 AIM-120 AMRAAM, advanced medium-range air-to-air missile
142 Meteor FMRAAM, future advanced medium-range air-to-air missile
143 BL-755 cluster bomb
144 AIM-9L Sidewinder, short-range air-to-air missile
145 IRIS-T, close-range air-to-air missile
146 Brimstone air-to-surface anti-armour missiles
147 Three-round missile carrier/launcher
148 GBU-24/B Paveway III, 2,000lb laser-guided bomb
149 MBDA Storm Shadow, stand-off precision-guided attack weapon
150 MBDA ALARM, air-launched anti-radiation missile
151 454kg (1,000lb) HE bomb, No 117 retarded version

62 Cannon ammunition magazine
63 Titanium wing panel attachment fittings
64 Main undercarriage wheel bay
65 Carbon fibre composite (CFC) centre fuselage skin panelling
66 Machined wing attachment fuselage main frames
67 Anti-collision strobe light
68 TACAN antenna
69 Dorsal spine fairing air and cable ducting
70 Centre section integral fuel tankage
71 Secondary power system equipment bay, engine-driven engine-mounted accessory equipment gearboxes
72 EuroJet EJ200 afterburning low-bypass turbofan engine
73 Forward engine mounting
74 Hydraulic reservoir, dual system, port and starboard
75 Engine bleed-air primary heat exchanger
76 Heat exchanger ram-air intake
77 Starboard wing panel integral fuel tankage
78 Wing tank fire-suppressant reticulated foam filling
79 Starboard leading edge slat segment
80 Wing CFC skin panel
81 Starboard wingtip EW pod
82 Starboard navigation light
83 Towed radar decoy (TRD)
84 Decoy housing (2) in rear of EW pod
85 Starboard outboard elevon
86 HF antenna
87 Upper UHF/IFF antenna
88 Rear position light
89 Fuel jettison
90 Rudder
91 Rudder honeycomb core structure
92 Fin and rudder CFC skin panels
93 Electro-luminescent formation lighting strip
94 Fin CFC 'sine-wane' spar structure
95 Heat exchanger titanium exhaust shield
96 Fin attachment joints
97 Rear engine mounting
98 Engine bay thermal lining
99 Afterburner ducting

37 Canopy external release
38 Lower UHF antenna
39 Aft retracting nose undercarriage
40 Forward fuselage semi-recessed missile carriage
41 Pressure refuelling connection
42 Fixed inboard wing leading edge section
43 Missile launch and approach detection antenna
44 Missile warning sensor equipment
45 Leading edge slat drive shaft from central motor
46 Intake ducting
47 Forward fuselage fuel tank
48 Gravity fuel fillers
49 Airbrake hinge mounting
50 Canopy hinge point
51 Centre and forward fuselage section of two-seat combat-capable trainer variant
52 Student pilot's station
53 Instructor's station
54 Dorsal fuel tank
55 Relocated avionics equipment bay
56 Dorsal airbrake
57 Airbrake hydraulic jack
58 Centre fuselage integral fuel tankage
59 Tank access panel
60 Auxiliary power unit (APU), cannon bay on starboard side
61 APU exhaust

24 Air conditioning pack beneath avionics equipment bay
25 Cockpit sloping rear pressure bulkhead
26 Pressurisation valves
27 Canopy latch actuators
28 Canopy rear decking
29 Avionics equipment bay, port and starboard
30 Electro-luminescent formation strip
31 Forward fuselage strake
32 Air conditioning system heat exchanger exhaust
33 Intake ramp bleed-air spill duct
34 Port engine air intake
35 Variable capture area articulated intake lip
36 Intake lip hydraulic actuators

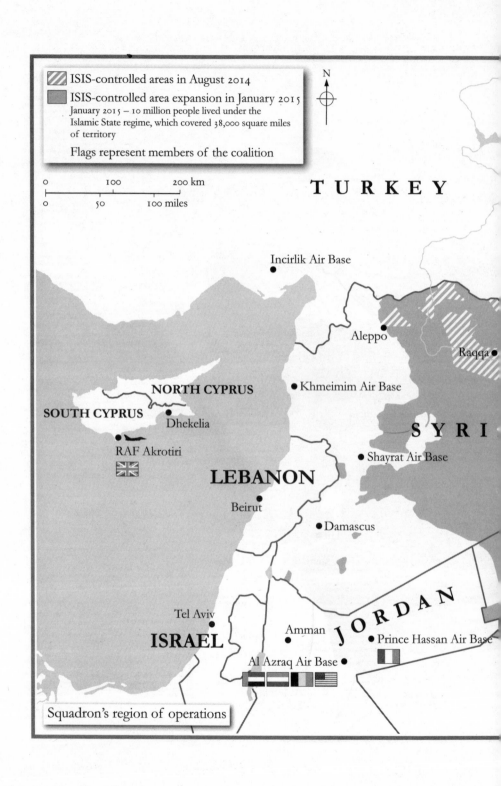

ISIS-controlled areas in August 2014

ISIS-controlled area expansion in January 2015
January 2015 – 10 million people lived under the
Islamic State regime, which covered 38,000 square miles
of territory

Flags represent members of the coalition

N

0   100   200 km
0   50   100 miles

TURKEY

Incirlik Air Base

Aleppo

Raqqa

Khmeimim Air Base

NORTH CYPRUS

SOUTH CYPRUS

Dhekelia

SYRI

RAF Akrotiri

Shayrat Air Base

LEBANON

Beirut

Damascus

Tel Aviv

JORDAN

Amman

ISRAEL

Prince Hassan Air Base

Al Azraq Air Base

Squadron's region of operations

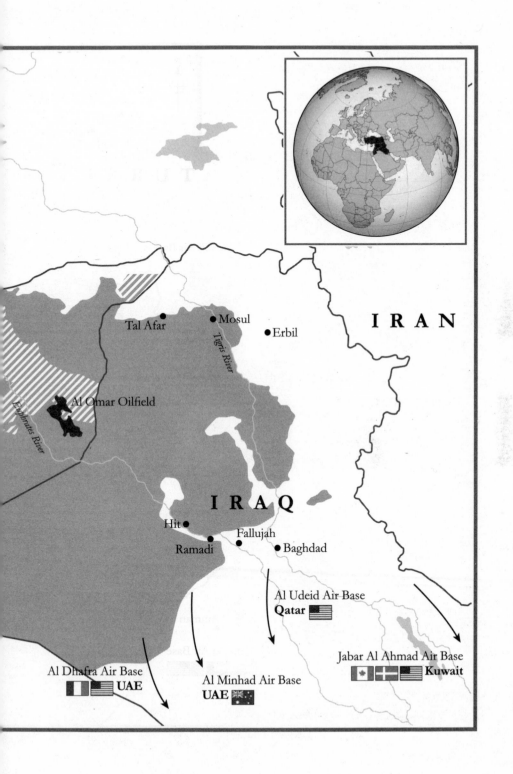

Prologue

The soldier's voice burst onto the radio.

'Dragon. Are you visual with three ISIS fighters running to the east?'

'Affirm.'

'Roger. They have been engaging friendlies and are now repositioning to attack the flank. They pose an imminent threat. We need a strike on these targets immediately. How long will it take you to set up?'

The American accent requesting air support was doing his best to disguise the urgency in his voice.

'Copy. About sixty seconds.'

It needed the lightest touch on the controls to ease the Typhoon into a left turn, staying high over the advancing ISIS fighters. I trained the targeting camera into the middle of the fight and looked down through the canopy.

Below, a huge battle was raging on the outskirts of Ramadi, to the west of the capital, Baghdad. Coalition troops were bogged down by enemy fighters who fired automatic weapons as they dodged in and out of trenches carved deep into the ancient bedrock. Soldiers were running in all directions. All around them were puffs of dust kicked up by rounds as they smashed into the ground. Smoke from an RPG spiralled over the trench line and slammed into a compound wall.

We had to keep emotions under control and work out who was who.

I could see on the Litening pod camera three ISIS fighters race across a field, protected from the Iraqi forces' sight line by an extended patch of scrub. They separated. Two ran to the north and set up a new firing position. The third continued along an irrigation channel, stooped with rifle in hand, then threw himself down against a bank of earth and opened fire once more against the coalition troops.

We needed to split the Typhoon formation and strike both groups. I glanced across at my wingman Cal, Nick Callinswood. He was about a mile away and slightly high, his jet appearing like a grey dart against the chalky blue sky. The Typhoon looked ready, menacing. Cal had flown close air support missions on Tornados in Afghanistan. I was glad of his experience.

'Dragon 2, are you visual with the individual who just broke from the three?'

'Affirm,' Cal answered.

'Your target. We'll prosecute simultaneously. Deconflict laser codes. We'll strike on a heading of 060 degrees, from battle formation.'

'Dragon 2. Copy.'

We could not release a GPS weapon against mobile targets. If they moved at the last moment, the weapon would likely miss and hit the programmed coordinate. By using the laser spot and slewing the camera to put the target in the cross hairs, the weapon entered a home-on-laser attack that would be more accurate.

'Dragon cleared to engage.' The soldier's voice was

rushed, pressing. He was a specialist, our eyes on the ground trained in coordinating air support. A joint terminal attack controller (JTAC).

I settled the targeting camera, fired the laser and pressed down hard with my thumb on the red weapon release button on the stick. I felt a small thud through the airframe as a Paveway 4 laser-guided bomb was unleashed into the airflow.

'One away, thirty seconds,' I called on the radio.

I stared back into the cockpit and made constant minute adjustments to the targeting system. I could hear my breath racing through the oxygen mask. I heard Cal release too, moments later.

The earth erupted. The three fighters were killed outright and instantly. I felt nothing. No elation. A numbness.

There was no time to dwell. In a fast jet, there's never enough time.

'Troops in contact,' the radio screamed once more.

Cal was immediately retasked onto another group of ISIS fighters engaging the Iraqi troops. He carried out another direct hit. It was relentless.

We had struck multiple targets across the region. An anti-aircraft gun, an ammunition storage building, a sniper and now direct support to troops badly outnumbered. It had been such an intense fight we were running out of weapons. Beneath us, the fighting raged on.

The attack controller was straight back on the line.

'Dragon. Confirm you have the 27 mm today?'

'Affirm. We have 27 mm.'

'Roger that,' he replied. 'I've got a gun target for you. Standby for the talk-on.'

Holy shit.

A gun target. Three enemy fighters hidden in a scrappy bush pinning down friendly troops.

This was something I had trained to use for years in the Jaguar and Typhoon but had never been required to fire it in anger. Strafing was risky. We were almost clean out of bombs and such was the severity of the situation on the ground, they wanted to resort to fast jet cannon fire. It would be the first operational use of the Typhoon's gun.

My throat had become dry and I could feel the sweat streaming down my neck. To fire the gun, I would need to get really low, right on top of the fighters involved in this contact. My heart quickened. I could feel the pistol resting against my chest. The last captured airman had been brutally killed by a screaming mob. Ejecting in these circumstances was a horrific prospect. This thought and a thousand others reeled through my mind and were instantly wiped like raindrops from a windscreen. I needed total, complete and absolute focus.

In the head up display, I selected the gunsight. It showed a single dot, which had to be placed on the target, surrounded by a range countdown circle. During a strafe attack, you need to point the aircraft, not the gun. There was no guidance or precision homing to assist. The cannon was fixed to the boresight of the airframe. I had to line up the aircraft nose and physically aim the 27 mm rounds at the mark. The aircraft computers could take into effect the force of gravity on the rounds as they left the cannon at almost 4,000 feet per second. This was my only assistance.

I threw the Typhoon into a right turn to generate some

distance and line up for the attack. As I did so, I turned my head as far as I could over my shoulder to keep sight of the target. In the moments as I flew away, the target turned from a sizeable bush to a tiny speck vanishing to almost nothing. To make the picture more confusing, my target stood in undistinguishable scrub in miles of open desert. The potential to lose sight of that exact piece of under-growth or confuse it with another was huge.

Christ, it was hard to keep eyes on. I strained my neck and took mental snapshots of the surrounding features.

From the ground, the jet would have been heard as a faint rumble, like an airliner, largely masked by the noise of ongoing gunfire. If the fighters had spotted me at this stage, I would have appeared as an indistinct dot high in the sky, several miles off and flying away from them. I hoped they were fixated on something more urgent. This gave me the edge I needed to make the attack a complete surprise.

In order to fire the cannon with accuracy, I had to dive from height to low level, right into the mix, at risk from every single weapon on the ground. My finger rested on the countermeasures switch, but no aircraft has protection against bullets from high calibre rifles. Given our activities over the last hour, I imagined they would be delighted to turn their guns skywards.

The JTAC was pressing for immediate action.

With a flick of the wrist, I overbanked the Typhoon onto the line of attack. Almost inverted, the jet spun effortlessly. I pulled the nose down through the horizon, settling into a thirty-degree dive, bang on the heading, and rolled the wings to level. At the same time, I brought the throttles back to idle, to keep the engine heat and noise signature low. I wanted to arrive silently out of the sun. The speed was building. A growing speck in the dazzling sky. The Typhoon would be on them from three miles away in less than thirty seconds. Through 350 knots, accelerating fast.

'Dragon cleared live.'

My heart felt like it was going to burst through my flying suit. Sweat stung my eyes.

Do. Not. Fuck. This. Up.

1. Night One

RAF Akrotiri, Cyprus, 3 December 2015

The air was warm and muggy. We were a long way from our Scottish home. I could see towering cumulus clouds building into thunderstorms on the horizon. If talking about the weather is a hot topic for the British, it's an obsession for pilots.

I now stood with my wingman Jonny, wearing our flying suits and each clutching a brew, as we pored over the information pack detailing the target. We were in what was grandly called the squadron planning facility: a small, stuffy room with maps on the walls, a few old chairs, two computers and an electric kettle. The RAF never goes to war without plenty of tea.

The base consisted of a rudimentary series of brick buildings clustered at one side of the runway. Through the window, I could see six Typhoon fighters precisely parked like reflections of each other, their wings glowing in the dipping sun. It was late afternoon. We'd been on the ground for less than twenty-four hours.

Forty-eight hours earlier, I had got 1 Squadron together in our hangar in total secrecy. Surrounded by the jets sitting poised for action, I briefed the final preparations while we waited for the outcome of the House of Commons vote on air strikes in Syria. If the motion were passed, we would be deploying on operations at first light.

Throughout 2015, the world had looked on in horror as terrorists in convoys of pickup trucks crossed Iraq and Syria killing everyone who stood in their path. They had seized an area of territory the size of France, killing tens of thousands, taken control of Mosul, a cosmopolitan city of two million, and planted their black flags over what they called the Islamic State.

The Middle East was collapsing. ISIS gunmen and suicide bombers had crept west into Europe. On 13 November 2015, 130 people were butchered and another 416 injured on the streets of Paris in the worst violence seen in France since the Second World War.

On 2 December, television screens played a live feed from the Houses of Parliament. The debate was noisy and ran late into the evening. Hilary Benn, the Labour Shadow Foreign Secretary, gave an impassioned speech about the urgency for action and the need to stop ISIS.

'They hold us in contempt. They hold our values in contempt. They hold our belief in tolerance and decency in contempt.' He paused and added. 'What we know about fascists is that they need to be defeated.'

We now had an hour before our first mission, sixty minutes for the mind to waver back and forth between fear and excitement. Even after all the training, dropping live bombs is hugely risky and a lot of things can go wrong. They say conflict is a failure of politics. Having seen the human horror of ISIS brutality in the preceding months on our television screens, this was decisive action and, no matter what your political allegiance, it felt like a greater good.

We wandered outside. The smell of rain carried on the warm air. I heard a rumble of thunder and the darkening sky lit up with a streak of lightning.

'Fly all the way from Scotland and it's bloody raining,' Jonny said.

It made me smile. Rain was the least of our worries. I took a quick glance at Jonny Anderson and wondered what god I ought to thank for having him as my wingman. He had started his career in the Parachute Regiment and had fought street battles in Fallujah in 2003. He then switched to the RAF, earned his pilot wings and was now one of the flight commanders on 1 Squadron. Jonny was a man of few words, as hard as rock, incredibly bright, greatly respected and had an inner stillness that gave me the extra layer of confidence I needed. The operation before us had so many moving parts I couldn't help recalling Murphy's Law, or Sod's Law, that anything that can go wrong will go wrong, and at the worst possible time.

Jonny shaded his brow as he looked up. 'A lot has got to come together if it's going to work.'

'Both weapons will need to be inch perfect,' I reminded him.

He nodded and shrugged his shoulders.

We needed to drop two 500 lb bombs with long fuse delays at a steep angle, with sufficient velocity to burrow through a dense layer of ancient rock into an oil pipeline. The second device had to enter the cavity made by the first impact one second earlier – a bullseye followed by a bullseye in the same restricted space.

The scientific study had assessed that the blast from

both warheads exploding in precisely the same location provided a fifty-fifty chance of blowing the pipeline.

I wondered if all the squadron commanders in the past had felt the same way as I did right now, before the first mission in a new conflict. It was a special moment, the culmination of everything. Full of nerves, already emotionally drained, hoping and believing that the training would be sufficient, but uncertain about what secrets lay waiting in that dark night ahead.

It must have been the same since the earliest days of aviation, with aircrews thinking the same types of thoughts, experiencing the same anxious feelings. I wondered how the heroes of the past would have responded to the conflicts of today: the Battle of Britain pilots, the Dam Busters.

Jonny returned to the office and I strolled over to Operations in the adjacent building. Engineers with tense expressions stretched cables around the walls, unpacked metal boxes, and shouted over the top of each other in ripe RAF lingo. A pair of size eleven boots stuck out from under a table as one of the team connected computer leads, and screens bleeped and buzzed as they blinked to life. They were still setting up the IT network to coordinate the dispatch of the jets with less than sixty minutes before the off. It was insane.

Ross Wherry – known as Wez – normally the most mild-mannered engineer, was effing and blinding down the phone. He paused as I entered and glanced over.

'You hang on a minute,' he said, and turned to me. 'Spares and tools still haven't arrived, boss,' he explained. 'I think the Warrant is looking for you, by the way,' and he went back to his harangue.

Daz Williams, one of our Operations team, stopped in front of me and I followed his eyes down into the cardboard box he was carrying.

'All checked and good to go, sir.'

Inside the box were two Glock 9 mm pistols and ammunition. We were going to be wearing them under our G-suits. I wasn't sure what good our small arms might be if we had to parachute into hostile territory. The last airman captured by the jihadis had been shoved in a cage and burned alive, the video of his murder uploaded for the world to see on the internet.

I imagined all the pilots had thought about how they might actually use their pistols if the worst happened. I know I had.

Daz made himself scarce as the squadron warrant officer approached with a fiery look in his grey eyes. Dave Bowman, always known to me as Mr B, was a tough Glaswegian who had spent the best part of three decades keeping RAF fast jets in the air. I had a rare affection for this no-nonsense Scot, knowing that he was in charge of the engineers caring for the aircraft.

'Fucking BBC's outside sniffing around the jets. Want to film the take-off. What the fuck is this? It's not a fucking air show!'

'Public interest, Mr B. They'll be gone tomorrow.'

He looked unconvinced. 'Public ought to keep their fucking noses out of our business, if you ask me.'

Media attention was the last thing we wanted, but it's not that often a Prime Minister sends the military on operations and a bit of flag-waving at home wasn't such a bad thing. Mr B sucked breath through his teeth.

'Deployed yesterday, air strikes today. It's an absurd timeline. The spares haven't even arrived yet.' I did know this but didn't interrupt. 'They're due in tomorrow on the C-17s. Only two jets are ready to go. No spare aircraft, I'm afraid . . .'

'Fully armed?'

'Aye, thanks to Ken working his magic. The weapons tools didn't get here either, but Ken brought his special rucksack full of odds and sods. He's sorted everything.' He was referring to Ken Gray, the engineer in charge of the Typhoon weaponry. Like Mr B, Ken had served extensively on operations in Iraq and Afghanistan and was no-nonsense. Mr B lowered his voice. 'Trust me, boss, you don't want to know the half of it. Just waiting on the crypto.'

A chill ran down my spine. No spares, no backup aircraft. I glanced at my watch. In thirty minutes we'd be walking out to the jets and we were still waiting on the crypto – the radio encryption software. After all the months of contingency training, the parliamentary vote, the hundreds of people involved in getting us to this stage, if that single email containing the digital crypto did not ping into our base computers in the next half hour, we would have to abort the mission.

I glanced around Operations. 'You've done a great job, Mr B,' I said, and a wry grin cracked his stern features.

'I wonder if the BBC crew know they're standing next to eight highly explosive bombs?'

'Feeling compassionate, Mr B? You'll be taking them out mugs of tea next.'

'Jesus H. There's me and my big mouth.'

'Last thing – can one of the guys test the ground radios? Would be nice to know they're working before we taxi.'

'Got it in hand, sir.'

He nodded and rushed off shouting instructions. Jonny, Mr B, Wez, Daz and the rest of the team were under enormous pressure. No one wanted to let the side down. I could feel the strain, having survived on minimum sleep for several nights.

Before a mission, there's normally time to coordinate tactics, consider targeting options, brief formations and discuss what's frequently a critical aspect of the operation: fuel. The Typhoon has a maximum flying time of about two hours. We did not have enough fuel to make it to the target and back and would have to air-to-air refuel before and after the attack. The irony was not lost on me that, if the strike were a success, while oil gushed from the punctured pipeline, we would have to gas up mid-air from a flying tanker on a moonless night littered with thunderstorms, over hostile territory.

The refuelling tanker would be flying an orbit over Iraq, eighty minutes' flying time and several countries away from our base in Cyprus. If we had a problem before the strike, it would take thirty minutes to fly out of Iraqi airspace to a diversion airfield. We would be operating in unfamiliar skies for the first time, with the threat of ground fire and stray aircraft belonging to Syria, Russia and Turkey. Just nine days before on 24 November, a Russian Su-24 jet had been shot down by an air-to-air missile fired from Turkish F-16s on the Turkish–Syrian border close to Latakia, where ground combat was taking place between Syrian government and rebel forces. The pilot was killed.

I returned to the squadron planning room where Jonny had been joined by three other pilots, Callum, JT and Weasel, all drinking coffee and considering the mission ahead. The guys wanted to study the brief and prepare themselves mentally for their own first sorties in the coming days.

Jonny and I huddled around the dusty computer as we read through the briefing notes. For twenty minutes we covered the basics: flight plan, routing and formation, air-to-air refuelling procedures, rules of engagement, escape and evasion. Then the strike itself. We would each launch a single GPS-guided weapon at the same time from a formation which put us at exactly the same distance from the target but on an attack axis that differed by a few degrees.

Dropping weapons from both jets would militate against weapons failures from a single aircraft and provide mutual support. By flying 'battle formation', in line abreast at approximately one mile apart, we could check each other's tails and see beneath the aircraft using night vision goggles (NVGs).

We would be flying close to two hotspots: Russian-occupied Syria, with its array of sophisticated weaponry; and the badlands of Islamic State, armed with infrared-guided missiles procured on the black market with its stolen oil money. We would stay high, out of the range of small arms, but no aircraft can fly high enough to avoid all the different types of surface-to-air missile. Battle formation provides mutual support, an enduring military tactic born in the Second World War and as relevant today as ever. Good formation flying and our onboard counter-measures were the two essential parts of our plan to defend ourselves if we were engaged by a missile.

After dropping our weapons, we would turn away from the target to ensure that we avoided the guided bombs in flight and didn't overfly the explosion. We would focus the night-sight cameras – embedded in the Litening targeting pods – to observe for weapons impact. We would then egress the area and make our remaining weapons available for any reactive tasking across the region.

'What can possibly go wrong,' Jonny said as he came to his feet.

2. Strapping In

The clock was running down. Ten minutes before the off. As we stepped out of the planning room and into the humid evening air, I knew what was on Jonny's mind by his focussed expression. I had the same thought.

'It's that time,' he said.

I strolled along the outside of the building and into the lavatory, and enjoyed a few seconds of calm standing before the aluminium trough of the urinal. There wouldn't be another chance for eight hours and there's nothing worse than a full bladder in a G-suit travelling at 500 knots.

Next stop, the flying-equipment room, a quiet space with our kit laid out by a specialist team. Jonny arrived, via the engineers.

'Any news on the crypto?' I asked.

'Still nothing.'

Dressing is a ritual, an essential part of the mental preparation and rhythm of a flight. First, I sanitized myself of all personal items, credit cards, driving licence, phone. I took the photo of my daughter from my wallet. She was on the beach in a blue T-shirt, blonde hair in a braid, with the toothy smile of a contented seven-year-old. Feeling more upbeat, I tucked the photo back in the wallet and placed it with the other items that I had to leave behind. I reached for my G-trousers.

Pilots have to parcel themselves into a G-suit to

counteract the G-force: the acceleration of an object relative to the earth's gravity. On the ground, we occupy a one-G environment with gravity pushing against you as it should. While turning in a jet, the G-force increases. The trousers have to be a tight fit over your flying suit. They zip up from the ankle to the waist and are secured by clips. Next, I stretched into the G-jacket which, when inflated, squeezes your chest and counters the pressurized air forced through the oxygen mask, ensuring your lungs receive enough partial pressure for oxygen transfer.

When pulling G, both the trousers and jacket inflate, squeezing your legs, abdomen and chest tightly to increase the blood pressure. If the G-suit doesn't fit or inflate properly, the blood can pool in your lower extremities and your brain can be starved of oxygen. The effect is a blackout called G-LOC (loss of consciousness) and is lethal.

The jacket also carries an auto-inflate life vest, should you eject into water, as well as an emergency locator beacon and radio to transmit your position.

I left the jacket unzipped, checked my NVGs and grabbed my flying helmet. Jonny gave me one of those nods that are meant to convey that all is well in the world, and we walked silently in step over to Operations. It was muggy still. I was hot in the G-suit and I could already feel a damp layer of sweat forming on my back.

'Hey boss, hey Jonny.'

It was the voice of Bobby Winchester, the squadron executive officer. He was in charge of operations for the evening. He looked us up and down, checking all the zips, buttons and clasps on our G-suits, an essential part of the pre-flight checklist.

'Here are your Glocks,' he said, handing us both the matt black military pistols with a couple of magazines. I snapped a ten-round mag straight into the gun and listened for the satisfying click as it lodged into place. I slipped the pistol into the canvas holster and adjusted the weapon so that it sat snuggly across my chest. I dismissed my earlier doubts about the weapon's practicality. Better to carry a gun, and not use it, than not to have it, and need it in an emergency. I zipped the G-jacket tight over the weapon. I felt the metal dig into my ribs.

In front of us were a couple of bottles of water, a stack of aircraft flight documents and the mission data cartridge, something we called 'the brick' – a device that transfers critical information to the aircraft computers. We signed the authorization sheets – the formal record of what we were about to do. It read: 'Operation SHADER Sortie 1'.

Bobby ran through the pre-step checklist to make sure we had considered all the possibilities: airspace, fuel, weather, emergencies, threats, escape and evasion. The last item was a personal check that we had sanitized properly.

'No phones, family snaps, receipts from Stringfellows?'

'Ha, all good,' Jonny replied.

'Yep, me too.'

'You're all set. Jets are ready. Good luck. I'll be on the radio.' That meant Bobby would be available on the ground radio during take-off and landing. If we had any issues, we could talk to the engineers or HQ.

We had to electronically sign for the aircraft as if they were two hire cars. It ran through my mind that all the effort was going to be a waste of time without the crypto, when Wez darted through the room shouting at the top of his voice.

'Thank fuck, the crypto's arrived.'

He grinned as he bolted past me and ran out to the jets clutching a CD.

The Typhoons were fully armed and equipped: a cannon loaded with armour-piercing 27 mm shells, four 500 lb precision bombs, long-range radar-guided missiles, short-range infrared heat-seeking missiles, a laser designator pod, and two external fuel tanks, giving the jet 6,400 kilograms of fuel in all.

I finished the login and signed for the jet. Jonny did the same. As we left Operations and walked out to the aircraft, we were joined by Mr B.

'Everything's sorted, sir. The boys and girls have done an awesome job. We're good to go.'

'I never doubted it for one minute. Thanks, Mr B.'

We walked together towards the flight line for a few moments, then he paused.

'Hope it's not bad luck to say good luck, but you know what I mean . . .'

With that he turned immediately and marched back to Operations, barking some indistinct orders at a couple of the junior engineers.

We continued out towards the jets. A shower had just passed. The ground was damp, with small pools of water on the concrete reflecting the lights of the aircraft line. The air had the smell of wet dust and aviation fuel. Our aircraft, like film stars in the spotlight, stood below a halo of luminescence created by the portable lighting. Engineers carried out last-minute checks, their shadows stretched and distorted.

I could just make out the hazy shadows of the BBC camera team off to one side. When the media reported UK combat over Syria, it would sound like the action of governments, but that action is carried out by individuals. Never before had I felt so much part of a team and so utterly alone at the same time.

'Take it easy, boss,' Jonny said.

'And you, buddy. See you in a bit.'

For whatever the next eight hours had in store, we only had each other. We exchanged nods – no more words – the British way. Jonny walked purposefully towards his jet and I walked towards mine. We would check in on the radio in about ten minutes.

The coast was a few hundred yards beyond the airfield perimeter. I could see in the far distance the street lamps of Limassol. It was surreal to think that just a few miles away people were leading completely normal lives, talking about what they'd done that day, putting their children to bed. I wondered what my daughter was up to. It would have been late afternoon back in the UK. Time for homework. A glass of squash. A treat.

I focussed, squeezing the thoughts out of my mind, and continued to stride towards the jet. As the familiar silhouette of the Typhoon took shape, I began to relax. It is, I have to say, a beauty of an aircraft, balanced with fine lines and carved like a post-modern sculpture. Now armed to the teeth with missiles and precision weapons, she had come of age. I felt an emotional connection and trusted her with my life. As I approached from the tail, Jamie

Robson, the engineer who would be conducting the air-craft see-off, walked towards me.

'Evening, boss. The crypto's in. She's all good. Ready for the pins?'

'Nice one, Jamie. Yes, thanks.'

He systematically pulled the safety pins from the air-craft and weapons. I made my way up the cockpit steps to drop off my helmet, NVGs and mission equipment: maps, attack plans, communication frequencies, airfield informa-tion. Thunder rolled in from the distance, the sound all but drowned out by the hum of the ground power unit plugged into the jet.

Leaning into the cockpit, I did the usual checks. The ejection seat and weapons switches all safe, the parachute harnesses correctly set. I flicked the battery switch to on. The power from the ground unit lit the cockpit screens and the aircraft systems immediately began to hum and whir. As she came to life, I started to feel at home. For years I had gone through the same pre-flight process. It is drummed into pilots to follow the same procedures, every time. It was memorized, automatic, robotic.

Dew had gathered on the metal steps and I almost slipped going back down to the ground to do the custom-ary walkaround. Under the nose of the jet, the panels were buttoned up, decent tread on the tyres, brake indicators good. Under the right wing, the missiles were correctly installed and secure, seeker-heads undamaged, laser codes on the bombs, the fins tight and immobile. Flares and countermeasures secure. I moved around the tail fin. The brake parachute door was fastened, the hook correctly stowed. Now the left wing, careful of the missile fins, which are razor sharp. I bent over to take a peek beneath the belly of the beast: no leaks; laser designation pod correctly armed.

The engineer held up the correct number of pins as I made my way back towards the cockpit. 'Nice one, thanks, all good.'

'Good luck, sir.'

It requires scores of skilled engineers and support staff to get one jet ready to launch. It's the ultimate team effort. I was fortunate to have what I considered the best squadron in the RAF.

'Thanks, Jamie.'

I climbed the ladder to the cockpit, eased myself into the seat and pushed the G-suit connector into its slot on my left side. It coupled firmly with a reassuring clunk. I pulled on my helmet and slid the leads into the housing on the jacket. With the oxygen mask in place, I switched on the microphone and heard the familiar rush of air, the crackle of the radio. I nudged the transmit button to check it was working, then pulled the ejection seat lapstraps tightly over my legs to marry them in the central clip. With the shoulder straps attached, but slightly looser, I shuffled in the seat to check everything was connected properly and none of the straps or leads were snagged.

The engineer withdrew down the steps and rolled them off to a safe distance. I was unable to see Jonny's jet due to the way the aircraft were angled. Ahead of me and all around in the darkness, Typhoons and Tornados sat in rubber hangars, temporary shelters erected quickly for the operation, that glowed orange in the harsh lighting.

I checked all the aircraft systems. Hydraulics, fuel,

electrics. All good. The navigation points had downloaded correctly from the mission brick. The laser designation pod unhoused perfectly, giving me a clear night image ahead of the aircraft and the coastline beyond. I could slew it around, zoom in and out, and change the optics settings to get the clearest image.

Next – critically – the secure radios. The crypto had been loaded into them. But if they didn't work, there would be no way to communicate once in Iraq. There were no spare aircraft, and no time for even the briefest delay. It was literally now or never. I selected the correct channel and waited for the check-in time.

Five seconds to go. Three, two, one. I held my breath and pushed the transmit switch.

Beep.

Relief. It was working.

'Dragon check.'

'Two,' Jonny responded.

He could hear me. He was ready. If Jonny was having any issues, he would have let me know right away.

I let my breath out. Another small hurdle jumped. Across the pan of parked aircraft – fuelled and rearmed between sorties – two Tornados roared to life. During my career as a pilot, I had been on detachments across the globe, and the RAF had been on continuous operations. I now felt part of something intangible and much bigger than myself. As I waited the last few moments before it was time to taxi out, I couldn't help a wry smile. To think I had once wanted to study law.

3. Dreams

When I was sixteen, travelling home from a family holiday in France, one of the cabin crew on the British Airways 737 asked if my brother Peter and I would like to go up to the cockpit and see how the pilots flew the aircraft. This was in the days before terrorist threats put an end to that sort of thing and we rushed along the aisle, thrilled by the opportunity.

'We're at 35,000 feet,' the first officer said. 'The auto-pilot's doing all the work.'

The sky was tinged with red as the sun went down in the west and I could see the lights of Paris flickering to life through the cockpit window. In the distance, the English coastline stood out sharp against the grey of the sea. The flight deck was a complex of hundreds of lights, switches and dials.

'So, what are your plans?' he continued. 'You must be leaving school soon?'

'I was thinking of becoming a solicitor.'

'Very sensible,' he said. Resting his hand on the control column, he pressed a switch and muttered some inaudible words to air traffic control.

The visit was brief and we made our way back to our seats.

'How was it?' Dad asked.

'Amazing,' I replied.

'Michael was embarrassing,' said my brother, just to be different.

I gazed out of the window along the line of the wing and beyond, to the horizon. I could see the big murmuring engine, the silver-white glow of the wingtip edging up and down in the evening air. The sun slid into the dark waves of the Atlantic, leaving a purple haze that fanned out as far as the eye could see.

Becoming a solicitor was not a dream, but something I knew would meet with my dad's expectations. John Sutton was an accountant, a man from a past age who polished his shoes every evening and always wore a collar and tie. A couple of weeks later, I found him hiding at the bottom of the garden reading the *Telegraph*. As I approached, he lowered his paper.

'Dad, I've come to a decision,' I announced. 'I'm going to become a pilot.'

'A pilot?' he repeated. He thought about that. 'But I've organized your work experience at the solicitors.'

'I know . . . I'm sure I mentioned it.'

'Yes, but your mother and I didn't think you were serious.'

He went back to his newspaper, but my dream of flying had taken root deep inside me. It became an obsession; my eyes always turned skywards to watch the Hercules transport aircraft flying into RAF Lyneham and the Chinooks thumping over my school at low level on their way to Salisbury Plain.

What I didn't know was that my father, that Sunday in the garden, had taken me seriously. On Christmas Eve, six months after our summer holiday in France, he beckoned me to take a phone call at home.

'Hello, is that Mike?'

'Yes.'

'My name's Jim. Your old man said you were interested in flying. Do you want to come out for a quick pint?'

'Yes, I'd like that, but . . .'

'I'll pick you up in ten minutes.'

I was still only seventeen, but Dad didn't seem to mind and Jim didn't care. We drove to the Carters Rest in Wroughton and sat at a corner table with two pints of 6X. James Gosling, known as Jim, was an RAF Jaguar pilot whose parents knew mine. He leaned across the table as he told me scary tales of flying at low heights – 100 feet at 500 knots by day and night – to practise evading enemy radar sites.

He talked about exercises in Oman, Norway, the United States, and operational missions enforcing no-fly zones and assisting soldiers on the ground with reconnaissance and air support. It was mind-blowing, terrifying and hugely appealing.

'Is this what you're looking for?' he asked.

'I had been thinking of becoming a solicitor,' I replied.

Like the first officer on the 737, he roared with laughter.

'They're useful people to know for house purchases and divorces.'

In the spring of 1995, while I was studying for my A-levels, I applied to join the RAF as a pilot. A week later, I received a manila envelope stamped 'On Her Majesty's Service' and felt like a spy as I ran up to my room to open it. The form inside was divided into sections for me to show evidence of my leadership skills (deputy cricket captain), flying experience (none), air cadet record (none). I was a blank sheet like the blank sheet in front of me. I didn't even have a model Spitfire hanging on a string from the ceiling.

A few weeks later, in July, I caught the train to the Officer and Aircrew Selection Centre at RAF Cranwell, the RAF's equivalent of Sandhurst, with its own long history and traditions.

Thirty of us, dressed awkwardly in suits, climbed off the train at Grantham and onto a waiting coach for the twenty-minute journey to the selection centre. Enough time to size up the competition. Some spoke of their fathers who flew Victor tankers, grandfathers who remembered Cranwell from the war; others spoke about the type of radar on the Tornado F3. One lad with curly ginger hair spoke continually, without the slightest interest as to whether anybody was paying attention or not.

The aptitude tests began the following morning after a solid breakfast at 7 a.m. The selection centre was a modern, purpose-built building, standing alone behind a wire fence, that backed onto a grass airfield for gliders. We filed into a classroom and sat at desks facing the wall.

For the rest of the morning, we performed hand–eye coordination and non-verbal assessments. Using a joystick to simulate flying, we concurrently did mental arithmetic tests, reorientated three-dimensional objects on the screen, carried out tracking exercises where the computer inputs were inverted, and a host of other hideously complicated skill tests.

Following this was a medical. We were as silent as prisoners as we shuffled through a maze of corridors with walls filled with images of iconic aircraft and portraits of

RAF officers with warrior moustaches and eyes that followed you as you passed. No one spoke. We were aware that we were under constant evaluation.

We entered a changing room, stripped off and dressed in blue towelling robes that were paper thin from countless washings and had shrunk so much they were close to indecent. Like guests at a low-end spa. We nervously chatted, but there was nothing much to say. When my name was called, I tightened my robe and prepared myself for the medical: eyesight, hearing, balance, blood tests, ECG. A nurse pressed my shoulders back against the wall and measured the length of my arms and legs.

These anthropometric measurements were essential for cockpit ergonomics and ejection seat restrictions. If your thighs are too long, you might lose your kneecaps on the way out. Too tall and you wouldn't be able to close the canopy wearing a helmet. With so many limitations, by the end of the afternoon, several grim-faced men and women had picked up their overnight bags and left their dreams behind at the gates on the way out.

Next day, we had the interview.

We sat in our suits, waiting to be called. One chap with a ready smile and floppy bronze hair seemed particularly confident. He was twenty-two and had already graduated from Durham University. He talked about his grandfather who had flown Lancasters during the war and how his own ambition was to be a fighter pilot. He gave us unsolicited advice on what they might talk about during the interview. Most of it went over my head. What did I know about the Nimrod MRA4? Did the RAF need the Eurofighter? Had I heard of JP233?

'Michael Sutton.'

A corporal ushered me down a corridor and into a room where two officers in meticulously ironed uniforms sat behind a desk. The door was closed behind me and they gestured for me to sit down.

'Mr Sutton?'

'That's right. Hello, sir.'

'Now, do tell us why you would like to join the Royal Air Force?' As the man on the left spoke, the other jotted down notes.

I hesitated. It sounded like a trick question. I knew why. But it was a feeling, something deep inside and difficult to articulate. I felt my cheeks redden.

'Well, I'd love to be a Jaguar pilot,' I blurted out. 'It's the best training in the world and I'm patriotic. I'd love to serve my country.'

'You must believe in the curvature of the earth if you want to fly Jaguars. They take an age to get airborne and need all the help they can get.'

The two officers looked at each other and smiled. Then he continued.

'The RAF is a fighting force. The Jaguar is a strike air-craft. How would you feel about dropping a bomb that potentially kills people?'

'I imagine that would be the last resort . . . and I think I would be up to it.'

It must have seemed like an off-the-cuff response to a very serious question, especially as it was answered by a seventeen-year-old schoolboy who had never flown an air-craft in his life. I then answered a string of quick-fire questions for what felt like an age.

It was a blur. Then it was over. I was escorted back down the corridor and remained in the waiting room until the last of the interviews had finished. One of the interviewing officers then entered. He thanked us for attending selection and we sat on the edge of our chairs as he read out a list of names. 'Mr Walker, Mr Hughes-Smith, Mr Goodborn . . .'

My name was not among them and my throat felt constricted. What did that list mean?

'If your name has been called, please follow the corporal.'

They filed out. The rest of us remained seated. Maybe life as a solicitor wouldn't be so bad after all.

'Congratulations, you have all made it to stage two of selection. Get some lunch and we will see you back here at half past one sharp.'

My mind was spinning. I was still in the game. Once we were thirty. Half were already back at Grantham railway station.

Next up was a group exercise. Dressed in green boiler suits, we had to solve complicated problems using planks, barrels and rope while showing that we had leadership potential and were team players, the two roles at odds with each other. The age range for applicants was seventeen to twenty-five. I was the youngest, a boy still among fully grown men. All the time we were working, RAF assessors stood alongside, observing and making us nervous as they scribbled away on their clipboards. Still in our boiler suits, we rushed off to a different classroom for a maths test. That was it. We all shook hands, and with a sense of relief I picked up my kit and boarded the coach back to the station.

Ten days later, when I came home from school, a letter On Her Majesty's Service was waiting for me in the kitchen. I weighed it in my hand. Mum and Dad were both there. Dad, still in his suit, had just returned from the office.

'Come on then, open it,' Mum said.

I slit open the envelope, unfolded the page, and read the brief message inside.

Dear Mr Sutton,

We regret to inform you that your application to join the Royal Air Force has not been successful. We wish you every success in the future.

4. Airborne

I applied to Southampton University to study philosophy, assuming the course would be stacked with hot bohemian girls. On my first day I walked into a lecture hall full of bearded men. One of them was wearing a red T-shirt emblazoned with the face of Karl Marx and the legend: 'Told you so'.

The upside was that the course required a lot of reading and self-study, which left me time to learn to fly with the University Air Squadron. Failing RAF selection had been the worst blow of my life, but a good performance on the University Air Squadron would allow a second application. That's what I set my heart on.

Thirty of us had joined the UAS based at Boscombe Down in Wiltshire that autumn. Most evenings I tried to keep up with Kant and Schopenhauer, but when Friday came I abandoned the philosophers for happy hour at the UAS bar in town. This was a vital bonding exercise, the perfect launch pad onto Jesters nightclub and essential training for learning how to deal with a hangover.

The first week, while we were being kitted out with our flying equipment, I had met Andy Booth. I had liked him immediately. Boothy was self-effacing, with a quick wit and plenty of warm northern banter. He had already passed selection and had a job waiting for him in the RAF after university. We stood at the bar, straight glasses in hand, watching a boat race – the downing of a pint as fast as humanly possible.

The winning captain was a chap named Milli – Nick Millikin – a third-year student who also had his place booked in the Royal Air Force. 'Spooling up,' he announced, spinning his index finger in a circular motion as if giving the signal to start an engine, and grabbed a fresh beer off the bar.

The following week, I had my first flying lesson. The instructor was Daz Erry, a larger-than-life Hercules pilot with a Brummy accent who had the patience of the Dalai Lama. I felt out of my depth in this alien ecosystem of flying order books, authorization sheets, technical logs, meteorological data and 1:500,000 scale maps. A few of the students were studying aeronautical engineering and had their private pilot's licences. Compared to me, they were already experts.

'The aim of your first flight,' Daz said, 'is to get upside down without puking.'

'Upside down,' I repeated.

'That's right, Mike, it puts the world in focus.'

A few months earlier, I had told the officers at the selection interview that I felt I could drop a bomb from a fast jet. Now, as I set off to walk to a tiny training aircraft without the first clue of what was about to happen, I felt in equal measures excited and rather stupid.

Daz showed me around the Bulldog and, critically, how to jettison the canopy if we had to bale out.

'When the canopy's gone, you need to climb over the wing and jump,' he said.

I got the feeling he had said the same to lots of eighteen-year-olds before me.

'Oh, yes, and don't forget to pull your parachute.'
Bloody hell.

We donned parachutes, eased our way into the cockpit, strapped in side by side and clipped into the four-point harness. Daz ran through the start-up checks and cranked the propeller. A puff of white smoke rose into the air as the engine coughed into life.

Near by, a Harrier jet hovered noisily before landing vertically like a helicopter. We lined up for take-off. It was a perfect autumn day with a light wind and the sun had broken through the clouds. Daz opened the throttle and the Bulldog vibrated like an angry lawnmower as we motored at full power down the long Boscombe Down runway, lifted off and climbed away to the west.

We headed about ten miles away, did some aerobatics and then a couple of circuits – practice take-offs and landings. The lesson lasted thirty minutes. I told Daz I loved the aerobatics, but in truth I felt sick. My first flying experience was too overwhelming to really enjoy, but something about it was strangely compelling. A week later, I couldn't wait to get back for the next trip.

It was a whole new language: ailerons, rudder trim, altimeters, turn and slip, vertical speed indicators. Every flying skill was learned the same way: a ground brief, followed by an airborne demonstration. Then you have a go. I tried to remember the advice and refine the task through practice. Most times, I made a mess of it.

Every training flight introduced new skills. Even something as simple as a turn needed back pressure on the stick, a flick of power on the throttle, and a compensating squeeze on the rudder pedals. Hands and feet needed to move in synch, and mine certainly did not, as Daz keenly pointed out.

'Jesus! Smoothly, Mike, feel the aircraft, guide her. Lightly on the stick. Stop grabbing at it like you're pulling a pint.'

Aside from the pure flying, there were instrument scans, navigation, fuel planning and talking to air traffic control. Then endless simulated emergencies: engine failures, electrical faults, diversions. Flight reference cards listed hundreds of system checks that had to be memorized and, at the appropriate time, repeated back quickly and accurately, word for word.

With my head ringing with flight checks, I went to bed exhausted and tried to remember some of the tedious philosophy I was meant to be studying. Schopenhauer. What a miserable bugger. Life, he wrote, swings like a pendulum back and forth between pain and boredom. Whether that was true or false, I had already decided that I did not want to be a philosopher.

Two months after we started, our UAS numbers had started to deplete. I met Boothy for a post-flight game of pool.

'Have you heard? Reynolds has been chopped.' He brought the side of his hand down on his palm.

'Reynolds? I can't believe it. I thought he was doing well.'

'That's all bravado. Nothing,' he said, 'is ever how it seems.'

'You sound like Schopenhauer.'

'Who?'

'Never mind.'

It was sobering. Two of the students had withdrawn,

unable or unwilling to cope with the balance of flying and university. Reynolds was out. Jez Williams packed his flying gear a week later, quit university and was never seen again. The guillotine hid in the shadows of every training flight. Being chopped felt like a death sentence. It created an intense atmosphere that fostered powerful friendships and, at the same time, fierce competition.

With few exceptions, we all wanted to join the RAF and would be streamed according to our performance into multi-engine transport, helicopter or fast jet training. I had set my heart on fast jets and would need good reports all the way to stand a chance.

One chilly afternoon in November, I flew a couple of half-decent circuits and landed with barely a bump. I taxied back and parked up. Daz released his harness and opened the canopy.

'Amazingly, you haven't killed us yet,' he said, and I felt myself tense. 'I'm going to jump out while I have the chance. Off you go, Mike, and don't balls it up.'

Christ, he was sending me solo.

Soon I was up at 1,000 feet, alone in the aircraft with no one to help get the thing back onto the ground. I turned downwind, looked past the empty instructor's seat on my right-hand side and glanced at the Wiltshire countryside below.

I flew along the length of the huge runway at Boscombe Down, then turned onto the final approach, holding seventy knots, and aimed at the piano key markings at the start of the runway. With twenty feet to go, I pulled gently back on the stick, brought the throttles to idle and lowered the little Bulldog onto the tarmac. It landed with a tell-tale squeak as the wheels made contact. I was down. Whatever happened in the future, I had flown solo. I strutted back into the Operations room carrying my parachute. The feeling was off the charts.

Boothy was standing with Adam Collins, a natural pilot who would sail through his tests. I kept a straight face.

'Well, come on then, how did it go?' Boothy asked.

I shrugged modestly. 'Just glad not to stack,' I replied, and he slapped me on the back.

For the first time since I had arrived in Southampton I felt confident about my future – always a dangerous feeling to have.

With another twenty flying hours after the high of my first solo flight, I went up with a new instructor, the A1-qualified Geoff Kennedy. The sortie was a consolidation of basic handling skills. I took off without a hitch, but then got distracted. I allowed the altimeter to drift up and down. I had a problem holding the aircraft straight and level. When I entered the turns, I applied either too much rudder or not enough. I felt so tense that I missed the radio calls from air traffic. As I descended in a left turn, I wasn't looking out properly and flew too close to another aircraft. Geoff grabbed the controls to take us back.

His face was red as he stepped out of the aircraft.

'You weren't looking out. You missed calls from air traffic. You could barely fly in a straight line.' He paused before giving me the killer blow. 'With a performance like that, you aren't fit to be a pilot, or any other RAF trade for that matter.'

He turned and marched off. I felt crushed. I couldn't work out why I had done so badly.

That night, as I lay in my bed with a tree branch tapping the window, I had a vision of myself packing my flying gear into a bag and handing it in. I thought about Boothy, Adam and the others. I would probably never see them again. Milli had completed the syllabus already and the rest of us envied his breezy self-assurance. I imagined hearing them shout noisily over the music in the cellar bar.

'Did you hear? Sooty was chopped.'

'Nice chap, shame.'

And the rest of the gang would feel as I would have felt: sad that a teammate had gone, and relieved that it wasn't them.

After thirty-five hours' flying time, I took what's called the 'spin-aeros check', the first official review of my progress and potential. I had prepared. I was ready.

It was one of those grey dismal days with rain in the air and low clouds shuffling along like a fleet of ships. The test was conducted by an instructor I had never seen before. He looked stern and was wearing a large Central Flying School badge on his arm; he must have been visiting from the headquarters at Cranwell. During the aircraft walkaround, he asked a couple of technical questions I couldn't answer. We took our seats in the aircraft, closed the canopy and buckled up.

'Right, as we briefed, off to the west and climb to 10,000 feet,' he said and glanced away.

I rolled down the runway, took off smoothly and forgot during the climb-out to turn the fuel booster pump off. He did so.

'Do keep a lookout in the turns,' he reminded me.

This had been drummed into us from day one. I'd been

careless. He now told me to display my aerobatics skills by performing a sequence of spins, loops and barrel rolls. After a nervous turn to the left to clear the airspace, I pulled into a stall turn and the instructor grabbed the control column.

'You have not completed the pre-aerobatic checklist,' he said. 'You're making basic errors. Run through the checks and then I'll give you back control.'

My nerves had got to me. I was sweating as I tried to maintain my composure. In response to my aerobatics, the instructor mumbled, 'That's good enough', in a tone I took to mean that it wasn't quite good enough.

After shut-down, we walked back to the squadron building together. The rain had come again, spitting down like tiny nails. I had a knot in my stomach and it was several minutes before the instructor broke the silence.

'Mike, overall, that was underwhelming. I think you know that.'

He sucked in his cheeks and nodded thoughtfully. I knew by his expression that he was torn about his decision.

'I'm going to give you a pass. But only by the skin of your teeth. There is a great deal for you to work on.' His stern features relaxed for the first time. 'Fortunately,' he added, 'there are plenty of aircraft in the RAF that don't need to be flown upside down.'

Friends gathered around when the news leaked out that I had passed.

'And? How did it go?' Boothy asked.

'Badly. I scraped it.'

'Well done, mate, a kill's a kill. Central Flying School as well. He looked tough. Probably flew in the Falklands.'

They disappeared down the corridor to Operations. I should have felt elated. I didn't. I felt like a reprieved man who did not deserve his acquittal. I dropped down into a chair and stared blankly out of the window.

'Are you all right, Mike? You look terribly down in the dumps.'

It was the voice of John Butterley, fondly known as Utterly Butterley, an instructor on the Air Experience Flight, which gave introductory flights to school cadets. He was the archetypal RAF old boy, tall with a slight stoop, charming and confident; he didn't give a damn. He had flown Hunters in the RAF, then Concorde for British Airways. According to the legend, he once missed London on the way back from New York as the crew were absorbed in the Sunday papers.

'No, not really, sir,' I replied. 'I passed the spin-aeros check today, but only just.'

He sat down opposite me and, before I knew it, my feelings and doubts all spilled out.

He listened patiently, then leaned forward across the table. 'This is all a game, young man, and you seem rather underconfident,' he began. 'Flying isn't like a university course, where you can just attend a few lectures and show a passing interest to your tutors. You need to eat, sleep and breathe this stuff. Being an RAF pilot isn't a job. It's a way of life. Give it everything you've got. Learn all of it backwards and show that you know exactly what you're doing. Then they'll think, "Ah, Sutton, now there's a good prospect."' He broke off, then asked, 'Do you like cricket?'

'Very much, as it happens.'

'Before each flight, think everything through in your

41

mind. Every single detail. Then you'll show 'em. Flying is like cricket. Stop thinking about getting a bloody century, just play the next ball with all your focus and effort and attention.'

Utterly Butterley was no-nonsense. No feeling sorry for yourself, no teen angst. Just play the next ball.

The next phase of instruction was instrument flying, followed by navigation. The sorties began to click. I prepared for each flight days before it took place. After being apprehensive of low-level navigation, it came a little more naturally. I couldn't wait to take off, climb into the distance and descend over the countryside, skimming over the tree-tops at 250 feet and diving among the Dorset hills.

My confidence was growing. One morning I was called for a meeting with the CO. Squadron Leader Steve Jarmain was an ex-Buccaneer, Tornado and F-111 pilot who had flown in the Gulf War. Like my dad, he was an old-school gentleman. His initial courtesy didn't put me at my ease at all, though.

'Sit, sit. Hello, Mike, thanks for coming up.'

I sat stiffly in the chair facing my commanding officer, his expression unclear in the shadows. It was late afternoon, with grey light slanting across the desk on which stood a single closed file.

'I see that you went for selection back last summer.'

'That's right, sir. It didn't go so well.'

'Well, that's not entirely true. I took the liberty of giving Cranwell a ring this morning to find out a bit more. You gave a pretty decent account of yourself. You just need to put a few more hairs on your chest. It's a serious business, and you're very young.' He paused, then added: 'They said they would welcome another application in the future.'

I let out all the dead air I'd been holding in and came to my feet. 'Thank you, sir, thank you. That's really kind.'

A few days later, we were in the crewroom, which was littered with flight safety magazines and accident reports. Daz placed a recent crash investigation report in front of me.

A Bulldog from Liverpool UAS had suffered an engine failure on take-off from RAF Woodvale and crashed, killing the student and her instructor, a squadron leader. This sort of information was tough to read, but it was shared so that we could learn from the mistakes and experiences of others. The cover of the report carried a photograph of the crash site.

Military aviation was not a safe career choice. This was the evidence.

Later that week I was flying another low-level training flight with Daz. The Bulldog has no alert systems – just a few steam-driven instruments and no means of indicating the position of other aircraft in the vicinity. I had launched from Boscombe Down and dropped into low level, flying over the countryside to the west of the airfield and looking ahead for my turning point.

Out of the corner of my eye, I saw a black dot to the right of the aircraft nose in the two o'clock position. I thought at first it must be a bug splat on the windscreen. I took a closer look and realized to my horror that the black dot was exploding in size. A Tornado jet at precisely the same height as us was closing at 420 knots.

We were on a collision course. In three seconds we were going to be swatted out of the sky. In a Bulldog we couldn't out-climb or out-turn it. The Tornado clearly hadn't seen us, or it would have manoeuvred. Instead, it continued to motor along its low-level path directly towards us.

'I'm bunting.'

I didn't wait for Daz to agree. I shoved the nose down and we floated in our harnesses as the aircraft dropped like a shot bird below our minimum height of 250 feet and we literally skimmed the treetops. The Tornado roared directly overhead, missing us by barely a couple of aircraft lengths and disappeared with a thin sooty exhaust trail left behind it.

'Well done, Mike. Non-standard, but good thinking. Climb us back up and let's carry on.'

5. Cranwell

I used my savings to buy an old red Peugeot 306 that took me, with a suitcase full of socks, through the hallowed gates of RAF Cranwell. It was 9 August 1999 and I had been summoned by Her Majesty's letter to begin officer training. I had slipped through the net. I was in.

The sun gleamed on the white stone façade of College Hall. At seventeen, when I failed the initial selection, I thought I would never return. It made that warm August day all the sweeter.

I tried to swing the car into the grand drive leading up to the college and was met by a set of massive locked black gates. As I parked up and wondered what to do next, there was a knock at the window. I turned to face a sergeant with a clipped moustache and a curious expression. I wound the window down.

'Unless you are the Chief of the Air Staff, I'm afraid you're heading in the wrong direction, Mr . . . ?'

'Sutton. Afternoon. I'm here to start officer training.'

'A new cadet. How nice. May I be the first to welcome you to Cranwell.'

'Thank you so much . . .'

He cut me off, shaded his brow and pointed across the base. 'Can you see that building over there?' he asked and didn't wait for a reply. 'There's a flight sergeant dealing with all the new arrivals. I hope you remembered your ironing board.'

I found my way over to what was misleadingly called the Number 1 Mess, a red-brick building thrown up without style or grace which smelled of ironing and hard work. I copied the other officer cadets by rolling out a sleeping bag on top of the ironed sheets. As I was soon to learn, room inspections were far easier to pass with immaculate unslept-in beds. A chap with dark cropped hair poked his head around the door.

'Tennant,' he said.

'Sutton,' I replied.

'Well, this all sucks. Ex-UAS?'

'Southampton,' I replied.

'Good lad. Yorkshire.'

Reality kicked in at 6 a.m. the next day. Thirty of us stood rigidly to attention in three ranks of ten in our brand-new uniforms.

The drill sergeant was stocky with highly polished shoes and held a drill stick with a metal end. It clicked on the ground with every other step as he paced along the ranks, staring at each and every one of us until we lowered our eyes, and straightening a few berets with a sharp twist.

'Bloody shambles.'

There were 150 of us on the course, including a dozen women. Five of us had made it into the RAF as pilots from Southampton UAS; it was considered a good year. Andy Booth had been pulled at the last minute when a pre-Cranwell medical said he needed to wear glasses. RAF pilots must have 20/20 vision in order to start training.

The fight to fly is aggressive, the odds long, the competition passionate and intense. 'Tens of thousands striving for a handful of places' – that's what we'd been told. The stress demands Herculean commitment.

After two months of drill, service lectures and a lot of PT, we began to learn leadership skills by running around the fields at the back of College Hall dressed in military fatigues. On that same patch of grass, we cleared simulated minefields, crossed rivers, created bridges and set up helicopter landing sites. It was amazing what you could do with a bit of rope, some pine poles and rusty jerry cans. There were times when leaders exploded in anger at their subordinates, the perfect example of failed group dynamics. As the weeks went by, I had an overwhelming feeling of belonging, that the RAF was exactly where I wanted to be.

The corridors of College Hall tell the story of the RAF. There are sepia images of college sports teams through the decades and formal shots of new officers at their graduation. The large, framed paintings of historic moments were stirring: Lancaster bombers taking off into the setting sun to strike deep into German territory; Hurricanes and Spitfires leaving contrails over London during the Battle of Britain; Tornados greeted by hails of white-hot anti-aircraft munitions as they approached Baghdad.

In one photo of the college football team, staring assertively into the camera lens, was Douglas Bader. I wondered if he had any inkling of the immense personal battles he would face. He lost both legs in a flying accident, then famously was a Hurricane squadron commander at the height of the Battle of Britain. The portrait of the group captured expressions of resolve as much as confidence, and I had a strong sense of what they were thinking as the photograph was taken.

Two weeks before graduation in February 2000, it was streaming day, a nervy experience for former UAS pilots. We had no idea what had been written on the confidential report that had been produced on our performance, with its recommendation for the next stage of training. Helicopters, multi-engine transport or fast jets? The decision would determine the rest of our lives.

We gathered with tense shoulders in a large lecture hall. I made a point of sitting at the back. Without warning, one of the Cranwell officers marched in. He closed the door and stood before us with a sheaf of papers, his face pale and drawn in the cold February light.

'Good morning. I know you lot are nervous, so I will crack on. The following have been selected for basic fast jet training: Chisholm, Peterson, McLean . . .'

My heart thumped like a bass drum.

'Tennant, Stewart, Strudwick . . .'

I was going over my university flying in my head. Had my struggles in the early part of the course come back to bite me? Did one of the instructors not like the look of me? Was this system fair anyway?

'Heasman, Collins, Riley . . .'

'. . . and Sutton . . .'

My own name had never sounded so good. It was one of those moments in life when you feel such utter relief that you are aware, even at the time, that you will remember it for the rest of your days.

My parents came up to Cranwell for the officer training

graduation parade. They sat among the other families in smart winter coats, watching us march up and down in front of the college in the chilly bright February air. Dad had a proud, stoic outlook and I had rarely seen him express emotion. After the parade, we walked across the square together and turned to look back at College Hall. Dad was quiet and had a shimmer in his eyes.

'Your mother and I are going to head off now. Have a lovely evening, and well done,' he said, with a crackle in his voice.

Sixteen new flying officers with shiny single blue stripes on their shoulders became course number 183, and we saw ourselves in the contented faces of each other, self-important and cocky as we swaggered around in our flying suits with a sense of invincibility.

I had scraped through the UAS flying course, slipped into the air force and made it by a whisper into fast jet training. Looking enviously at my course mates with degrees in aeronautical engineering, and in one case literally rocket science, I felt underprepared for technical lessons, armed with little more than the wisdom of Socrates, most of which I had already forgotten. *Per ardua ad astra* – 'through adversity to the stars' – the official motto of the RAF, seemed very appropriate indeed.

I was full of apprehension as I watched the grandeur of College Hall disappear in the rear-view mirror and headed north to RAF Linton-on-Ouse to begin twelve months' basic fast jet training on the Tucano. The base was set in North Yorkshire, Emily Brontë country, where Heathcliff roamed the moors long before the RAF came and built their runways in 1937. Linton housed two squadrons of

trainee pilots and was the home of RAF navigator training. After Cranwell, Linton was the Wild West.

The Tucano had entered RAF service in 1988, but had
an old-fashioned look, more like a Battle of Britain fighter
than a modern training aircraft. The pointed nose supported four big propeller blades, and the wings were wide
and sturdy. The sleek, narrow cockpit housed ejection seats,
and the aircraft delivered more than 1,000 horsepower –
five times as much as our previous training aircraft.

After ten hours' flying time on the Tucano, I was let loose
on my first solo flight. I accelerated down the runway and
felt the power beneath my seat as I departed the airfield.

The Bulldog couldn't do more than 120 knots. The
Tucano reached 240 knots with ease. If you turned off the
air conditioning, you released more thrust and could get
her up to almost 300 knots, the standard drill on the first
solo. It felt like reaching the speed limit on a motorway,
then accelerating by another 200 mph. Everything in the
distance was instantly behind you. Clouds darted by like a
meteor storm.

One of the guys on our course couldn't get the aircraft
past 220 knots. Back on the ground, he explained why.

'The thing just wouldn't accelerate. I had full power. I
turned the air con off, but it just seemed really sluggish.'
He sighed. 'Then air traffic came on the radio and told me
I still had the wheels down.'

It was a basic error – one of the many we were all
doomed to make – and it qualified for an entry in the 183
course line book, an anthology of after-hours antics, banter and flying cock-ups illustrated with sketches and comic
strips. The chief instructor finally confiscated the book

after the foot of a dead crow fell from between the pages into the lap of a visitor.

Aside from learning the maths, geometry, geography, physics and spatial awareness, and developing the faculty to make decisions quickly under pressure, we routinely had to undergo medical training from specialist doctors based at RAF Henlow. One of those doctors was an assured American colonel.

'I've been doing this for twenty-five years,' he began his lecture, 'and don't be put off by the accent. I love Brits – I've been married to two of you.'

We laughed courteously.

'Flying is not a natural activity for creatures that crawled out of the sea and evolved to have two feet planted firmly on the ground.'

Flying presented physiological risks such as hypoxia (oxygen starvation) at altitude, as well as barometric trauma, causing acute sinus pain as a result of the rapid pressure changes. Pilots can also suffer dangerous sensory illusions when the brain is unable to reconcile the difference between what you see and what you sense. This can cause a feeling of nausea and an overriding impulse to make a false correction; to roll to the left for example, because you feel like you are tumbling to the right. All pilots experience these illusions to some degree. The threat presented by the G-force, however, was the most immediate danger.

The Tucano for some reason did not have G-protection systems, despite the aircraft being able to pull up to seven G. In practical terms, pulling seven G means that your body weighs seven times what it normally does; in other words, it is seven times heavier. Your five kilogram head, with a two kilogram flying helmet, no longer weighs seven kilos, but forty-nine, which puts enormous strain on your neck muscles.

The other problem under high-G is that the blood is forced down into your legs, where it pools. If you relax, your blood pressure is insufficient to ensure an adequate supply of oxygen to the brain, causing G-LOC, a G-induced loss of consciousness. The hazard is insidious, rapid and often fatal. Tragically this would happen to Jon Egging, a friend from the UAS, following a Red Arrows aerobatic display at the Bournemouth Air Show in 2011.

We were taught about the onset of G-LOC at the Farnborough Centrifuge, a dedicated facility built in the 1950s and legendary for having featured in the James Bond movie *Moonraker*. This archaic device, relatively unchanged for sixty years, was a mock-up cockpit on the end of a sixty-foot scaffolding arm that spun around in a circular room like an out-of-control Ferris wheel.

To counter the onset of G-LOC you can perform the G-strain manoeuvre. This involves holding your breath after an inhale, while tensing your stomach, thigh and buttock muscles. Each breath of air is grabbed rapidly, then held again.

The G-force causes the skin on your face to sag, adding twenty years to your age, and where the blood pools at joints, such as your elbows, the skin capillaries break into a set of harmless red spots called G-measles. Beyond wearing the occasional pair of mirrored shades, there is little place for vanity in fast jet training.

6. Per Ardua ad Astra

On my first flight shortly after the centrifuge, my instructor and I climbed through about 3,000 feet of cumulus cloud and started a lookout turn to the left to ensure the airspace was clear of other traffic. Beneath, I could see glimpses of the North Yorkshire countryside, the array of pastel colours like a Monet landscape.

The flight was a precursor for air combat training, which we would learn on the next course. I needed to do only one lookout turn, but I did three in order to put off the inevitable, in much the same way that you might make polite conversation with a nurse to delay a nasty-looking injection.

'OK then, Sooty, all looks clear around. Follow me through.'

This meant letting the instructor fly, with my hands lightly on the controls to feel the movements and pay attention to his demonstration.

'We're going to roll into the turn; let the nose drop a few degrees. Get that G-strain on,' he said. 'Here it comes. Push the throttle up to full power; hold 150 knots. There, the speed is increasing. OK, pull back on the stick, increase the G, increase the G. Now squeeze it to five and a half, and hold it. Keep the nose position. Keep the G on.'

The turboprop engine wailed as the Tucano turned in a tight, descending, never-ending spiral. My upper torso rammed back into the seat and my head became insanely heavy. Even a slight movement caused a piercing pain in my neck. It felt like I had a ton weight pushing into my chest and legs. I was supposed to have one hand on the control column and one on the throttle, but all I could feel were my wrists and elbows being forced into my legs. I tensed my stomach and thigh muscles as I had been taught, but clearly not enough. My sight began to go almost immediately, greying and closing in from the edges. At one point, while I was aware that I was fully awake, I momentarily lost all sight. Everything had turned to black. I strained with all my might.

Like the gradual opening of a theatrical curtain, a sliver of grey vision slowly returned as my blood pressure increased and I could vaguely see the instruments through the fog. I watched in horror as the G-meter needle hovered and settled at 5.5 G. The hands of the altimeter spun down rapidly. Clouds whizzed by the canopy and the Impressionist painting of North Yorkshire tumbled around in a blur of green, brown and grey. Christ, we were dropping like a brick. I felt sick.

Then the calm voice of the instructor in the back seat woke me from the nightmare.

'OK. Easing off and rolling out. When you're ready, you can take control and show me one to the right.'

Jesus Christ, not again.

By the time I finished the flight, I wasn't sure if I needed a beer, a bucket to be sick in or a new profession.

I was pleased to see Alex Tennant in the mess.

'Blimey, Tenno,' I said. 'You look worse than me.'

His skin had a yellow tinge and I wasn't sure if it was

due to his own max rate turns flight, or a leftover from the Olympic-themed happy hour the day before when he had dressed as a Chinese marathon runner. He had bronzed himself in light-tan boot polish that had proved stubborn to remove.

'How was it?' he asked, and I couldn't sum up the energy to be inventive.

'Horrendous.'

'Me too.'

As with every new activity, there were some in the crew-room who boasted how great it was and how much they enjoyed it. All nutters.

Next was instrument flying, then formation, and then low-level instruction over the Yorkshire Dales and Lake District, ten minutes flying time to the west. On departure from Linton, I levelled the Tucano at about 1,500 feet, accelerated to 240 knots, and stared ahead to find my low-level entry point.

There were no GPS or computers in the aircraft and it was forbidden to stare constantly at the chart to see where we were. You had to maximize the time looking out for other aircraft. The key to a successful low-level sortie was in the planning. We learned to identify in advance verti-cally significant turning points that were big enough to see from the air: a large mast, for example, or an irregular-shaped clump of woodland on rising ground.

The aim was to fly a route of several legs to a 'target', which you had to fly over to within ten seconds accuracy. Fine in theory, but tricky in practice, and it was easy to end up hideously off track. Getting lost happens for any number of reasons. A hasty plan with an incorrect heading written on the map could send you spearing off on the wrong course, or a crosswind calculation applied in the incorrect direction could mean a substantial navigation error. Covering more than a mile every fifteen seconds, errors accumulate quickly.

On one occasion, I skirted around the high ground of the Lake District in poor visibility and low cloud. Without warning, the outline of Sellafield emerged rapidly from the gloom directly in front of me. I would get – at best – the bollocking of my life flying right over a nuclear power station and swung the Tucano away, cursing myself that I had become horribly lost. It was a lucky escape which didn't result in a phone call from the nuclear site to the chief instructor, for which I counted my blessings.

It was the custom to reveal your brushes with disaster, in the mess over a pint with course mates who shared a supportive fascination with every cock-up. Mine was a talking point for a few days. But then attention moved on one dark afternoon the following week, when Tom Edwards staggered ashen-faced into the crewroom.

'I just bonged RAF Scampton. A proper bong,' he blurted out.

We gathered round, sympathetic and intrigued.

'There was a massive shower on the leg. I had to turn to avoid the cloud,' he explained. 'I aimed off to the right and tried to work out how much distance I had covered, using the stopwatch and headings. I kept going, but the cloud was endless. I was miles off route.'

He paused for a moment.

'Eventually the cloud ended, so I made a heading correction in the other direction. I tried to get back on track, but I couldn't recognize where I was. It's all so flat in Lincolnshire.'

Tom had applied the correct technique. It hadn't worked. As an inexperienced pilot, if you find yourself in an unusual situation on your own in an aircraft, you've got nothing to fall back on and the best course of action might not be obvious. When things go wrong, they can go wrong quickly. The only answer is experience. That was something we didn't have.

He continued. 'I thought if I eased up a bit I might be able to get my bearings. Then, out of nowhere, a bloody huge runway suddenly appeared in front of me. I overbanked to pull away. I was almost upside down.' He glanced down at his feet, then looked up, shrugging his shoulders before the unexpected twist to his story. 'At that exact moment, the Red Arrows flew right underneath me in Diamond Nine trailing red, white and blue smoke. They had to stop the display.'

It was a funny event, but no one laughed. We all knew it could have been any one of us.

That failed sortie put Tom Edwards on formal review. Another incident like that at low level and the axe would be sharpened.

The extremity of life in the air was matched by the socials. A formal dining-in night was a smart affair in which everyone looked their best in the RAF dress uniform blandly referred to as 'No. 5s'. The mention of mess dress, however, we associated like Pavlov's dogs with extravagant parties and outrageous hangovers.

Wine with each course oiled the banter. Voices rose, and one evening a particularly cutting comment was answered with an apple strudel flying back across the table. The pilot who had made the wisecrack moved like a lynx, dodging the Austrian missile. The station commander's wife, who was wearing a lavish ball gown with a plunging neckline, gasped as the strudel landed on her chest.

The station commander, Ken Cornfield, gave her his napkin and glared across the room. An icy hush fell while his wife carried on talking to her companion as if nothing had happened.

The following day, the guilty pilot bought a bunch of flowers from a garage forecourt and took them around to the station commander's house to say sorry to his wife and attempt to repair the damage to his fledgling career. He was sure his apology had cleared the air. He got back into his car, reversed down the drive and ran over the family cat, killing it instantly. He then had to go back to the house and say that he was sorry for that as well.

I bumped into him when he returned to the mess.

'How did it go?' I asked.

'It did not go well,' he replied.

But for all the pressures and disappointment, none of us would have changed it for the world.

A few weeks later, on a Friday in June, I was flying solo and descended to 250 feet over Lake Windermere. It was a warm, cloudless English summer morning. The sort of glorious day that lifts your soul. I now knew the Lake District well and barely needed the map as I raced along just above the deep blue shimmering water. To my left and right were wooded hills, stretching up and away into jagged peaks. On the eastern shore of the lake was a bustling market town, full of people, spilling out to the water's edge. Some of them looked up as they heard the approaching noise of the aircraft.

All I could hear inside the cockpit was the steady hum of the turboprop engine and the faint crackling of the microphone in the oxygen mask as I drew breath. Ahead, I saw a thin, glistening, silvery trail in the water, at the end of which was a two-masted yacht in full sail. I altered course and flew right overhead the boat. As the crew waved, I waggled the wings to wave back. I continued up the lake and into the hills, rolling away over the crest above a valley and down over the fields below. I was twenty-one. Life, I thought, does not get any better than this.

The day after completing the final handling test, I was unexpectedly called into the chief instructor's office. This was unusual. No one else had received this 'invitation' and I was wondering which of my misdemeanours had finally caught up with me. Pete Round was sitting at his desk making a spire from his fingers.

'Do take a seat and relax,' he said. I did the former and tried to obey the latter.

He leaned forward and rested his elbows on the desk.

'I've been told to nominate two pilots to go to NATO flying training in Canada. It's an alternative to the regular route of advanced training at RAF Valley in Wales. It will help clear the training backlog. This is a new set-up with new Hawks.'

He paused, and I noticed his lips turn up in the faintest of smiles.

'You would be there for a year and do all your tactical training. If you pass, you would be straight to a frontline jet afterwards. You need to leave in ten days. I'm sending you and Matt Peterson. That is, if you're interested?'

It did not need a second thought.

7. Canada

The NATO flying school at Moose Jaw was ringed by rivers, lakes and expanses of mature coniferous forest in Saskatchewan, a vast province almost three times the size of the UK. The sky was made for aircraft, icy blue and infinite. The air tasted clean and fresh, as if it had just been taken from the refrigerator.

The flags of all nations hugged the entrance to the shiny new glass building which housed the Hawk squadron. A jet flew low overhead, skimming the runway at 500 feet and 420 knots, breaking up and away into the circuit to land. The noise was loud, guttural.

We dumped our bags, signed registers, met a few senior officers, and sneaked off to the hangars to look at the brand-new Hawk 115. Supine in the shadows, it gleamed as if with an inner light. It was painted a glorious shade of deep blue, with a Canadian roundel on the tail. It reeked of hard work.

'Look at that beast,' Matt said.

It had a mean, business-like appearance, with a pointed nose and a thin fuselage just big enough to accommodate the two ejection seats, fuel tanks, and a Rolls-Royce jet engine kicking out 6,000 pounds of thrust. Old pilots say, 'If it looks right, it flies right' – and boy, did this thing look right. Just the thought of getting to grips with this multimillion-pound machine in front of me was overwhelming.

'Christ, it looks fast,' I finally responded.

We strolled back through the chilly afternoon to the mess, with its cocktail of trainee pilots from Canada, Italy, Singapore and a couple of Danish guys standing in front of a mirror chatting about their social plans for the weekend.

After ten hours, it was time for a solo flight in the Hawk. I experienced a whirl of competing emotions. A feeling of euphoria that I was about to strap myself into a fast jet and blast off over Canada, tinged with the lingering anxiety of making a cock-up. Fear of failure was a major motivator. Equally, given my inexperience, there was a constant dread about coping if something went wrong. What if the engine cut out miles away from an airfield? What if I ejected and the parachute failed to open? What if the electrics gave out and I got completely lost?

It was a roasting day. The high bright sun glinted off the wings and they were baking to the touch. Before I knew it, I was belting down the runway, feeling as if I had lost control as the Hawk accelerated rapidly and climbed quickly. In two minutes I was up at 15,000 feet, flying south with a groundspeed of 400 knots. The airfield vanished behind me and I was soon forty miles away, at the edge of the base's radar coverage.

The first thing I had to do was some aerobatics. I took a long breath, tensed my stomach muscles, and pushed the throttle forward. The jet gained speed so quickly I felt as if I were hanging onto the tailplane. I looked directly up above, through the canopy and high into the sky that I was about to disappear into, and pulled back on the stick. Instantly I felt the G-trousers inflate and clamp tightly around my legs. In the HUD I saw the G reading increase to 4 and the altimeter whizz around as the jet raced upwards. As the world disappeared beneath me, I glanced to the left and right to check the wings were level and kept up the back-stick pressure to keep the nose tracking higher and higher into the sky.

Soon the world was upside down at 300 knots. My feet pointed directly towards the sun and the horizon approached from above as I looked up through the canopy. Inverted at 10,000 feet, I eased back on the throttle as the Hawk accelerated downwards under the force of gravity, the G increasing as I pulled back harder on the stick to counter the rapid descent.

The altimeter was plummeting: 9,000, 8,000, 7,000, 6,000. It took only a few seconds to slice through 5,000 feet of air as the increasing G-forces hammered me into the ejection seat. I felt hot and slightly sick as I levelled at 5,000 feet and brought the speed back down to 300 knots.

Wow.

When the solo flights were behind us, Matt and I entered an intense period of instrument flying, low-level sorties, formation practice, night flying and long evenings after dinner in the mess studying procedures in textbooks and practising in the simulator.

The hardest thing to grapple with was the speed at which everything happened in the cockpit. You had to be constantly thinking ahead. There was no autopilot, no time to relax and gather your thoughts. You had to be fully engaged with every passing second. Switching off, even for an instant, put you 'behind the jet' – an easy thing to happen when you're racing along at seven miles per minute.

It was a draining, unremitting calendar of study and of restless nights thinking about the next trip and worrying that I was not going to be good enough. At times my mental capacity and situational awareness were at the edge of their limits and my brain simply felt as if it had run out of RAM, like a computer freezing. Recovering back to an airfield twenty miles away took just 180 seconds. Three minutes to sort the navigation, radio calls, formation, air traffic and run the systems checks. It was utterly consuming, and slowly, incrementally, beginning to take over life itself.

Every flight was ruthlessly evaluated against key objectives. It was like taking your driving test every day for years on end. After landing, there would always be a nervous wait while your instructor wrote up a tick-sheet assessing each element of the trip: checks, take-off, airmanship, capacity, low-level flying, formation, landing. Only those pilots with consistently good scores would be sent to the single-seat jets, the Jaguar or Harrier, the ultimate goal we shared.

After five months, we received our wings and the right to wear that revered badge on our uniforms for ever. I was now an RAF pilot. Whatever happened from here on, no one could take that away. That little set of swift's wings, with all the history behind them, became my prized possession. Five years after my first solo in a Bulldog with the University Air Squadron, getting to the RAF frontline had become a tiny light at the end of a tunnel sixty months long.

After Moose Jaw, the tactical weapons unit at Cold Lake was the final hurdle and the toughest to pass. The course had a fearsome reputation and a massive failure rate. But that was a worry for next week. Now it was time to celebrate. The Rocking Royal was a bar in Moose Jaw where the girls wore cowboy boots and knotted their plaid shirts above the waist, the men wore Stetsons, and everyone line-danced to country rock – including us, badly, after a couple of jugs of Pilsner.

We soon had a cluster of locals around our table, as fascinated by us 'talking funny' as we were by them trying to pronounce 'Edinburgh' as 'Edin-bor-row'. They found it incredible that we didn't line-dance in Britain and drove tiny cars: 'How do y'all haul wood without a truck?'

We transferred up to the Canadian forces base at Cold Lake, aptly named as the sweltering summer receded and the bitter temperatures signalled the approach of the Alberta winter. The lakes in the region froze with such thick ice that they were a viable option if the single Hawk engine failed and you had to make an emergency landing.

It had now been six months since I had seen my new girlfriend, Kate, a teacher from London. We had met at a family Christmas party and I had been instantly enamoured by this pretty blonde full of wit and charm as she smashed down the Prosecco. She asked me when I would be back and where I would be based, and on both counts I had literally no idea. It was an early indicator of the innate strains of service life on relationships.

Our course had grown to four, with Chris Folkes and Ben Spoor joining from the UK. On the second morning, a tall instructor with a booming voice and a diamond-shaped Tornado badge on his arm marched into the room where the four of us were waiting and stared at us with a challenging, seen-it-all expression. We went to stand and he waved his arm to tell us to sit back down again.

'Good morning. My name's Vinny Brown. Welcome to Cold Lake,' he said abruptly. Brown looked terrifying. 'Congratulations on getting your wings. But I'm afraid to say life's about to get quite a lot tougher.'

He took a breath. We sat there like statues, immobile and silent.

'What we are looking for is controlled aggression. We're going to teach you how to fight the aircraft. We want to see tactical hunger, an ability to operate the jet throughout its flight envelope. We will immerse you in air-to-air combat, defending against missile threats from the ground and air, and how to strike ground targets.'

There was another pause and his expression changed.

'And just in case any of you haven't thought about it, we are going to train you to drop bombs and fire missiles. This isn't about ego trips and air shows. You will be trained to kill people. If you haven't reflected on that, you need to do so. Grab a coffee. We're back in ten minutes. First up is a brief on 1 v 1 air combat.'

With that, he left the room.

Some people, even at this late stage, did have a crisis of conscience. A pilot on my Cranwell intake withdrew under exactly these circumstances and was redeployed. Up until the time that I arrived at Cold Lake, learning to fly fast jets had felt more of a challenge than a career. I hadn't allowed myself to think about anything other than passing the next trip. One ball at a time.

All through training, I concentrated on the journey, not the destination. I didn't ignore the possibility that my role might one day involve extreme violence, but I didn't think about it too deeply either. That might seem naïve, even heartless; but with zero experience, I had no idea how I might feel if I made it all the way to offensive operations.

Another reason for not overthinking potential war situations was the relative peace in the world at that time. The course at Cold Lake took place before the hostilities in Afghanistan and Iraq. At Cranwell we had received a classified briefing which stated that the primary threat to UK security was from animal-rights activists. The RAF had not seen major action since the Balkans and the Gulf War, when I was still at school. Tales from those conflicts felt distant, historical, no more tangible or real than the Falklands War or the Battle of Britain.

With my shiny new wings I was full of the breezy self-confidence that gets young men into trouble. The following weekend, after an intense programme learning how to defend against surface-to-air missiles, that's exactly what happened.

A couple of guys on the senior course, Oli Davis and Andy Knight, had been invited to take a group of us to a hen-night party in Calgary, a twelve-hour round trip by road.

Andy reached into his pocket and waved his civilian pilot's licence.

'Squared this away last weekend. If we all chip in, we can rent a Cessna . . .'

We piled into a car first thing in the morning and raced out to the municipal airport. Waiting for us outside a tired-looking hangar was a 1960s Cessna 172 Skyhawk. The single-engine, fixed-wing, four-seat trainer was like a large moth speckled in brown rust marks. I wondered how reliable it was. At least, if the engine failed, we could glide down onto one of the huge highways or frozen lakes.

'She's a beauty,' Oli said ironically. 'Like an underpowered Bulldog with back seats. Perfect hen-night transportation.'

We shoved our rucksacks full of overnight kit into the tiny baggage compartment and I climbed into the narrow back seat beside Matt. It had been a long week and I thought it would be a good chance to catch up on some kip. Matt had already closed his eyes.

'Oi. Wake-up bells. You two are navigating,' Oli growled.

I opened my eyes as the 'co-pilot' threw something backwards. It landed on my head.

'You are joking. This is a bloody road atlas.'

'Well spotted. We've got the air traffic frequencies for the airport. We had a look on Friday. It's about 300 miles – about three hours. We need to make a heading of about 200 degrees after take-off. She's full of fuel.'

Andy fired up the machine – it sounded like a tumble dryer – and made no apology for his scant planning. I shouted over the noise.

'Did you check the weather?'

'Ginners, mate. Stop bleating.'

Ginners as in 'gin clear', excellent weather. We bumped over the grass onto the tarmac taxiway and headed out towards the runway.

'Calgary will stand out like a dog's knob,' Oli said. 'We'll see the skyscrapers from about sixty miles away.'

I opened the atlas. Forests, roads and coffee stains. I had a bad feeling for some reason, an intuition. Perhaps it was just a hangover kicking in. Matt had closed his eyes again.

The runway was a short strip surrounded on all sides by towering pine trees of the sort that live for 800 years and feature on David Attenborough documentaries. We lined up for take-off. Andy revved the little engine to the max and off we went. The acceleration was somewhat less than we were used to in the Hawk, but after a bumpy twenty seconds we lifted clumsily into the air. I was relieved. But not for long.

'Shit. It's stopped climbing,' Andy groaned.

'Try to accelerate to get some more lift,' Oli shouted.

'I can't. It's not accelerating or climbing.'

We were flying at eighty knots, fifty feet above the runway, at max power with the ancient pines closing fast. There was not enough runway remaining to land again. The blue sky above was tantalizingly close, but it was impossible to get any altitude. Matt had opened his eyes and raised his brows as he looked at me. I was holding my breath. Having almost made it through fast jet training, my life was about to end in the back of a rusty Cessna on the way to a hen night. The trees were getting nearer.

'Lose the flap,' I yelled.

'We need it to climb,' he yelled back.

'It's our only option. Bring the flaps up. Bring the fucking flaps up!'

He reached forward and I watched him move the flap selection lever to zero. The aircraft immediately juddered and began to sink, losing what little altitude it had gained.

'Shit,' he said.

'Don't change it!' Oli, Matt and I all shouted in unison.

He ploughed on. I heard a faint change in the engine sound as the drag reduced and the airspeed bumped up.

Eighty knots . . . eighty-five knots . . . ninety knots. We sunk a little, but with the speed increasing, Andy pulled back on the control column and the Cessna slowly climbed. We gained some precious height and in a horrific slow-motion sequence the sweeping branches brushed beneath the aircraft, missing us by inches. I turned around and peered through the window towards the receding trees that had almost spelled our final moments.

We limped off to Calgary to a hen night that was not worth almost dying for.

Flying can kill you in a heartbeat. We had been drilled in the best techniques to operate complex aircraft in dynamic situations – many of those lessons learned after someone had paid the ultimate price. We had ignored our training when taking off for Calgary and had behaved like a bunch of amateurs who believed that a simple aircraft posed little threat. We were lucky to walk away in one piece.

Back at Cold Lake, the daily assessments on the Hawk continued and the write-ups became more direct, full-on, unforgiving. After each flight, we piled straight into the debriefing room to analyse the trip in minute detail. The instructors were focussed, the debriefs intense.

That was the wrong manoeuvre.
I'm not sure you've got the capacity for this.
You don't understand the lift vector at all, do you?
You're shying away from it.
That was the wrong call.
Your friend got shot down because you weren't looking out.

I sat silently in a chair. The instructor, Vinny, remained standing. Like a judge, he explained the gravity of my mistakes. The whiteboard in front of him was covered in red pen highlighting tactical execution errors. I knew better than to speak. A debrief is not a debate. Sit, and absorb. My wingman had been 'shot down' by an instructor flying an aggressor aircraft because I wasn't looking out properly and had not spotted him dart out of the clouds towards the formation. It had all been over in ten seconds.

'In flying you'll ride your luck sometimes. But remember, you've only got to be unlucky once. And it's all over.' Vinny's wisdom was hard won and well meant. The significance of his advice settled on us as we walked back to the mess and my thoughts turned again to the pine trees brushing inches below the Cessna.

The instructors were there to squeeze you through the wringer until you were ready to fly a frontline fighter. At Moose Jaw we had still been learning the basics. At Cold Lake we were inducted into a culture and a way of working that was non-negotiable.

In the debrief room, we spoke with unrestrained honesty about our own performance. There was no sugar coating, no spin, no rank. Critical lessons were identified, shared, studied. When the debrief was over, these tense exchanges were left behind the closed door of the room and personal friendships reinstated.

Advanced fast jet training was physically exhausting and I would invariably climb out of the jet at the end of a sortie drenched in sweat. Fighting against another aircraft is both an art and a science. Like all skills, it begins with a process that has to be understood and mastered. During air combat, there is no time for analysis. Responses must be instinctive; a fight can be won or lost in a fraction of a second.

Pulling sustained G in a combat mission stresses the body. It's painful. Blood pools near the joints, causing your legs and elbows to ache. The strain on your neck is immense, and injuries are commonplace, with pilots often requiring lifelong physiotherapy. A poor sortie would result in an instant fail. Three fails and the fast jet dream would be over.

Progress felt precarious and practically impossible. Our gang of four muddled through long winter evenings and it was mortifying for the entire team when Chris Folkes was sent back to the UK. He hadn't cracked the low-level strike phase and would be reassigned just a few weeks away from finishing. Gutted.

At last it was over. Almost over. The final flight of the course. The three remaining students, with a fourth air-craft flown by an instructor, worked as a formation at low level, fighting an air and ground threat to simulate striking a target. Back at Cold Lake, we raced the length of the runway at 420 knots and 250 feet, climbing up and into the circuit to land.

Without our realizing it, the skill set had started to become second nature. The final flight wasn't painful. It was enjoyable.

The last act of flying training was role-disposal, where you found out which jet you were going to be posted to on the frontline. We all knew what we wanted but weren't saying. In a way, it was unimportant. All three of us had passed. That's what mattered.

It was the end of an era. Flying training was over. My journey as a fighter pilot was just beginning. I needed to pack my kit, get back from Canada and find my way to

RAF Coltishall, home of the Jaguar Force – and to a world that had changed for ever.

A week before I left Cold Lake, just after breakfast one sunny Tuesday morning, there was a hurried knock on my door. Matt stood outside, looking flustered.

'Mate, turn on your TV. There's a terrorist attack happening in New York.'

We watched open-mouthed as the second hijacked airliner slammed into the World Trade Center. Little did we appreciate it at the time, but the horror of 9/11 would shape everything in our fledgling careers.

8. The Big Cat

The Jaguar was shaped like a dart, with a pointed nose section that closed around the pilot and was so thin at the front that it formed a spike. Protruding from the nose was the metal tube called a pitot that measures airspeed. The grey two-seater was more than fifty-five feet long and weighed in at fifteen tonnes.

It was powered by two Rolls-Royce Adour engines that produced 17,000 pounds of thrust – three times the power of the Hawk. It was fitted with afterburners, or reheat, which delivered a substantial upsurge for take-off, supersonic flight and combat. Afterburners inject additional fuel into a combustor in the jet pipe which ignites the exhaust gas. They are an alternative to using a bigger engine, with the additional weight that implies, but at the cost of high fuel consumption.

I was looking at the big cat head on, feeling completely overawed and unable to imagine how I was ever going to get to grips with it. I remembered that night out with Jim Gosling, drinking 6X at the Carters Rest in Wroughton. He had spoken with such passion about the Jaguar and his eyes had lit up when he said, 'What's life without a bit of danger?'

I moved around to the side. They say a camel is a horse designed by a committee. The Jaguar was like that. It was big and ungainly, with practice weapons canisters and fuel tanks that hung below the stubby wings. Over-wing missiles were strapped to the top surface and a targeting pod hugged the underbelly between the undercarriage. With its array of aerials and vents, the fuselage was constructed from sections of rigid panels, with gaps where they didn't quite join.

The body was stained with smudges of what looked like oil or hydraulic fluid. Along the left side was a long, ash-coloured streak made by the exhaust from the auxiliary power unit. Unlike the Hawk, which was sleek, shiny and new, the Jaguar was hardy, weather-beaten, as if bearing the scars and experience of action. It carried a bewildering array of ordnance, including guided and unguided bombs of different weights, cluster bombs, air-to-air missiles, rockets and guns. All of these weapons had multiple delivery profiles and safety considerations that had to be mastered for use by day and night.

To counter the Jag's poor turning capacity, it had to be flown fast and low, a Cold War tactic to hide behind the terrain and dodge enemy radar. It was well suited to this, flying at 450 knots, increasing to 480 knots for target runs, and up to 540 knots during evasion. That's nine nautical miles a minute: a statute mile in under six seconds. The normal altitude for day and night flying was 250 feet – less than five times the length of the aircraft. When necessary, pilots had to fly down to 100 feet. This was called operational low flying (OLF) and was practised only in less well-populated areas of the UK.

If I passed the nine-month conversion course onto the Jag, I would move to a frontline squadron. This was by no means a guarantee: pilots were routinely chopped even at this stage. It was like playing snakes and ladders. Every time you climbed up a level, there was another hissing cobra waiting to bite you in the balls and bring you spiralling back down again. Those who made it onto a squadron faced another four-month workup to gain the status of combat ready junior pilot, or JP, able to fly missions under supervision. Until then, I was colloquially known as a 'cub', and was acutely aware of my place in the hierarchy in the mess at RAF Coltishall.

The Jaguar Force had a reputation for laid-back professional excellence. Many of the senior pilots had experience flying attack sorties during the first Gulf War in 1991, operations over Bosnia, and reconnaissance and air policing missions for a decade in Iraq on Operation Northern Watch. As a cub, you weren't made to feel like an outcast by the easy-going pilots who strolled through the mess, but there was a pecking order you did well to observe.

I was grateful to have arrived on base with Matt Peterson. We'd been together for officer training at Cranwell, and at Moose Jaw and Cold Lake. He had gone through the same doubts, the same bollockings for every small failure, the same fleeting moments of despair when the struggle to become a fighter pilot was overwhelming. We had encouraged each other during the worst times and, in some respects, had each other to thank for getting this far. With another year of training and assessment ahead, our sense of achievement at passing advanced fast jet training had been short-lived.

With its friendly people and open spaces, Canada had been literally a dose of fresh air. But when I arrived at Coltishall, ten miles from Norwich, it felt as if I had reached the beating heart of the Royal Air Force. You could smell the history as you entered the gates, the resolve and sacrifice from the station's heroic past. It made me feel like a bit of a fraud, wearing the uniform and trying to join those ranks. Surely, at some point soon, I would be found out.

Coltishall's motto, 'Aggressive in Defence', was highly appropriate during the Battle of Britain when 242 Squadron, with a team mainly of Canadian pilots flying Hurricanes, was led by Douglas Bader. All RAF bases have their own feel and sense of identity, but Coltishall was special. Half hidden in the Norfolk countryside and surrounded by mature trees, it was like a time capsule preserving the past. When the Jaguar was introduced in 1973, it was one of the most advanced strike jets in the world and became the last of the old-school RAF aircraft. It was a privilege to be selected for the Jag Force and I sensed that everyone who ever took off and landed on that runway sensed the weight of its history.

The corridors of the ground-school building were lined with photographs of seated rows of young officers from courses dating back to the 1970s. Everyone in those black-and-white days looked older than their years and there were rather a lot of moustaches. The pictures had been graffitied with marker pens: a Martin-Baker tie added to someone who had ejected, an axe sketched over someone who had been chopped from training, a little gravestone with 'RIP' for those pilots who had died.

The Martin-Baker tie – dark-blue silk, patterned with the red triangular warning sign – is worn by members of the Ejection Tie Club: the 7,000 pilots whose lives had been saved after an emergency ejection from an aircraft using a Martin-Baker ejection seat. The first proper use of the seat was in May 1949, when a pilot named Jo Lancaster survived ejecting from an early jet bomber over Warwickshire. Martin-Baker seats were highly revered. We trusted them with our lives every single day. Not that I had any desire to wear the blue-and-red silk tie.

The ties, graves and axes were a chilling reminder that life on the frontline was high risk. The Jag Force had originally been set up with 165 single-seat jets and thirty-five trainers. Of those 200 aircraft, sixty-nine had been lost in accidents or incidents between 1973 and 2001. The crewrooms were littered with accident reports with cold unemotional evaluations. One three-page report that followed a fatal accident during Exercise Red Flag in 1981 concluded:

> This is the fifth Jaguar to crash because the pilot lost control. Three of the previous accidents occurred at low level. Attention was drawn to the unforgiving nature of the aircraft at (or beyond) the published limits.

The report contained no mitigating circumstances, nor – as one might expect to see from a twenty-first century perspective – did it acknowledge psychological pressures such as fatigue and work stress or failures arising from training deficiencies. The simple analysis was that the pilot had 'lost control', and that was that. In this context, the pedigree and history of the Jaguar were stark. The risks were gin clear. For a fledgling flight lieutenant at the bottom of the pecking order, it was my cue to learn fast from the veteran pilots on the conversion unit.

The Jag had been designed as an advanced trainer in the 1960s. After turning in good performances, someone high up in the food chain decided it could be modified to take on frontline offensive operations. That meant making design revisions and bolting on masses of equipment without upgrading the engines, rather like fitting a fully laden roof-rack and bicycle carrier to a rally car.

Sturdy landing gear was added to enable rough field (grass) operations for take-off and landing, drop tanks to increase range, and a suite of missiles, rockets and bombs. The end result was a much heavier aircraft. The short wings still functioned well at speed, but the jet lost energy in turns and struggled to recover with its comparatively small engines. There were also aerodynamic quirks: firm diagonal inputs to the control column and use of the rudder could cause uncontrolled roll and instability, requiring constant pilot corrections just to maintain straight and level flight.

The cockpit was cramped and intimidating. After climbing the metal ladder that fixed to the airframe, you had to haul yourself over the sill and squeeze into the ejection seat. Pilots carried nav bags containing maps, flight reference books, a velcro-backed kneeboard full of quick reference data, the metal brick with navigation information that plugged into the jet, and a couple of cassette tapes to record the head up display and navigation screen.

Having strapped yourself into the ejection seat, the nav bag had to be wedged towards the back of the cockpit on some barely used circuit breakers. The airframe sides surrounded you almost to shoulder height with a bewildering arrangement of switches and dials. There was a moving map about A4 size, and all around to the left and right were radio panels, engine, hydraulic and electrical dials, weapons control panels, electronic surveillance equipment, countermeasures switches and controllers for the targeting system.

As the aircraft matured in capability, space had to be found for new kit without losing the old. That meant equipment had to be moved and reorganized into every available cavity and gap. The relocation broke the logical flow, with fuel gauges wedged into random places and the second UHF radio installed upside down on a low panel behind your waist. It was an ergonomic nightmare. To change a radio frequency, you had to look over your right shoulder, swap hands on the flying controls, move the channel selector switch and interpret a set of inverted numbers, all while intermittently looking where you were going. There was no autopilot, not even a flying-altitude hold function, so something as simple as a radio change was one thing you tried to avoid when flying at low level.

There were times on the operational conversion unit (OCU) when I wondered if aiming for single-seat fast jets, rather than something less challenging, had been the right choice. Every sortie was stressful and it felt like we had been immersed in a culture of assessment and survival rather than learning.

I had managed to hold my own during flying training, but I now found myself in a select pool and felt distinctly average. As students, we had to prove ourselves – not only as pilots and officers, but as individuals. The frontline squadrons were only yards away, and yet there was a vast invisible barrier between the training unit and the combat units. Frontline pilots were amiable enough, but distant like strangers. Until you had made it to the frontline, you were not part of the club.

Days on the OCU were spent between the flight line and a place nicknamed 'the sub', a windowless back office where the students spent hours preparing for sorties and reading manuals the size of telephone books. The pilot checklist consisted of dozens of pages that had to be memorized precisely, in order to configure the aircraft for various phases of flight. There was, for example, no time to read the four pages of downwind checks when you were a few seconds from turning onto the final approach or flying in close formation with another aircraft. They had to be rattled off in seconds as your gaze swept around the cockpit from switch to dial to gauge and you simultaneously controlled your speed, made radio calls and maintained your position relative to other jets in the circuit.

The course was much harder than anything we had faced so far. Only slowly, as I got to know the Jag, did I begin to trust myself to fly the thing safely and enjoy the experience. Strapping into the ejection seat was like strapping into a 500 knot backpack. The big cat became a part of you. Like a second self, it told you whether you were flying well or badly, and the airframe would respond and settle with the control inputs. It would twitch and shudder if you were too harsh, a sign that you needed to back off, or risk the sort of unpredictable response that was all too clear from the accident reports. I slowly learned how to apply just the right amount of force, when to roll quickly and when to ease off. It was as if the Jaguar were a living entity, and I began to understand why the pilots loved the aircraft and displayed so much loyalty towards it.

Tenno had joined Matt and me on the conversion unit. We had gone through the same doubts, mishaps and pleasures and it felt like history repeating itself when we graduated from the OCU.

I found myself posted to 6 Squadron, a frontline fast jet squadron. It had been six years since that first tenuous flight in a Bulldog. I wondered what Daz Erry, my first instructor, would have thought of me now with a Jag badge on my arm. I had so much to thank him for.

One afternoon I had to fly a low-level route over Devon to support an exercise for the Royal Marines. It was naughty, but I told my father I could fly over his golf course on the way back as my routing took me close.

'Promise me you won't tell anyone, Dad. I'll be over at exactly 2.15 p.m. from the south-west.'

My parents had since moved to Devon. I had planned to visit them that weekend and thought it might be nice for Dad to see me at work before I arrived. I raced up the estuary at Teignmouth and dipped a wing as I popped over the golf club at 450 knots. I looked down and to my horror saw about thirty faces in a group staring back up at me. Dad had clearly mentioned the flypast to everyone he had met that week.

Christ, my new boss would have my balls for this. I hauled up, flew the forty minutes back to Coltishall and was relieved to get off the base. I drove straight to Norwich to pick up Kate and we set off on the long drive to Devon. Flypasts over families are not allowed. I was terrified that someone from the golf club posse would say something to the wrong person at the wrong time, or there would be a complaint that drew attention to my poor judgement. Being a single-seat pilot was all about responsibility and I had behaved irresponsibly.

I gritted my teeth and stared at the road.

'What's wrong, Mike? Is anything the matter?'

I told Kate what I'd done. 'I'll get a terrible bollocking if anyone finds out,' I added.

'Don't be grumpy. Your dad's just proud of you.'

'Still . . .'

'Probably nothing will happen.'

'And what if it does?'

'You'll deal with it. Take the bollocking and move on.'

I leaned over and squeezed Kate's knee. We had been going out together for two years. She had always been patient with my long absences, my obsessions, my objectives. Dating an RAF pilot can't have been easy. I cheered up and we stopped for coffee and a sandwich. When we arrived at my parents', Dad was beaming. He told us that one of his friend's sons in the forces had just deployed to Iraq and the flypast had brought a lump to his throat.

9. The Frontline

When I walked into the crewroom at 6 Squadron for the first time I was conscious of a different vibe. I would be a junior pilot for some time, and would have to go through another workup before I was combat ready, but I was nearly there. For six years – the whole of my adult life – I had felt an underlying anxiety, not severe, but ever-present, that I wasn't going to make it, that I wasn't quite good enough. The psychological change in attitude made flying easier. It was as if the pressure relief valve had opened a fraction.

The three frontline squadrons of the Jaguar Force each had their own focus: 41 Squadron led with reconnaissance, 54 Squadron with laser-guided weapons, 6 Squadron with night attack. Pilots could cross-pollinate their skill sets, while a degree of specialization was useful for generating and refining tactics.

With a year of frontline training under my belt, I entered the night shift, haring around under the cover of darkness at low level through mountainous terrain and an invisible obstacle course of radio masts on hilltops. Belting along at 450 knots into worsening weather in order to make head-way towards a target required constant quick decisions about routing, terrain, visibility and timing. You could not slow down; the Jaguar needed every pinch of speed to manoeuvre and react to threats. The airframe was not overly blessed with thrust; a hard turn at three or four G instantly bled the speed back.

The force prided itself on being overhead of its targets to within five seconds' accuracy on every strike. If you were not within this time bracket, you would abort the attack. Not only was this incredibly embarrassing, it would be judged as a personal mission failure. There would often be up to eight aircraft in your tactical formation at low level, all aiming for their targets in a similar location, with timing being the primary method of deconfliction. If you were twenty seconds late, you could arrive at the location at precisely the same time as another jet, causing the risk of a mid-air collision to rise exponentially. Tornado F3 fighters simulated air attacks which needed to be countered and avoided. We practised defensive manoeuvres and counter-measures against surface-to-air missile radars from the electronic warfare range at Spadeadam in Cumbria.

Snaking the big cat through mountain passes at low level was both exhausting and stimulating. There was always a new challenge, a new qualification to strive for, a new skill to learn, and the persistent performance anxiety was never far away. I observed new pilots arriving on the force, or pilots visiting from fast jet training. I listened to their nervous conversations about the next training event and saw my own feelings reflected back in their anxious faces. But as the months passed, I began to feel more at ease. Hitting targets, flying at low level and escaping threats had started to become second nature.

It was an ironic badge of honour that, unlike other frontline jets, the Jag had no forward-looking infrared, radar or autopilot to assist with navigation at night. As the jet zipped along at furious speeds, I sat at the controls in total darkness with a set of NVGs called Nightbirds that struggled to produce a half-decent image and belonged in an aviation museum. It was mid-winter, bleak and cold, with clouds as thick as pea soup and the moon constantly AWOL.

The force had acquired the Nightbirds some years earlier, and by the time I was using them, the technology was already past its sell-by date. They clipped onto the top of the helmet with a hinge that allowed you to bring them down over the front of the visor, and perched forward of the face like a pair of metal toilet-roll tubes. As the Jaguar cockpit was so cramped, if you turned your head too abruptly, the Nightbirds hit the canopy. Once, when that happened, they were pushed off my helmet and clattered to the floor. I was left in complete darkness, with nothing but the message on the head up display telling me that I was at 270 feet in a left-hand turn at 480 knots.

Don't panic, Mike.

I held my breath, yanked the jet away from the ground, and scrabbled around down between my legs until I found the damn things behind my left ankle. My confidence was beginning to grow, but every flight posed new challenges.

A few days later, I wandered into the crewroom and saw our new US exchange officer, Keith Derbenwick – Derbs – previously an F-16 pilot.

'How was your first trip on 6?' I asked him, and he shook his head.

'Emotional, dude. I flew with the boss. At low level, I hit a bird the size of a pterodactyl. The UK is freakin' dangerous, man.'

My squadron boss was Mike Seares, a self-assured officer in his thirties who had been the youngest Jaguar pilot during the Gulf War and had since earned an MBE. He was highly revered, always upbeat and had become my mentor and friend.

'Ah, there you are, Sooty,' he said, and he beamed at me as I entered the Ops room. 'We're outbriefing in five minutes.'

Standing at the Ops desk was Chris Plain, one of the flight commanders. 'Planko' to his peers, he was very much 'sir' to a young scrote like myself. He was the squadron 'auth', or 'authorizer' – a senior pilot in charge of the daily flying operation who could assist on the radio if there was an emergency.

'Tanking tonight,' he said, and the blood drained from my face as he glanced at me. 'Looks like a dark night for it.'

I must have appeared horrified. Planko and the boss both laughed.

'Don't worry, Sooty, this will put hairs on your chest,' the boss remarked. It was not the first time I'd heard that phrase. I fixed a smile on my lips while my stomach churned. I knew I would have to do my first night-time air-to-air refuelling, but the weather happened to be particularly foul. There was virtually no moon, and it was overcast with gusty winds, thunderstorms in the vicinity and turbulence: a grand slam of crap conditions for night flying, let alone tanking.

'Do you want the airfield lights on or off?' Planko asked. I was praying for 'on'.

'Off. We're going to do a lights-off NVG close-formation take-off,' the boss continued in a level voice. 'We'll get some gas, then head to the bombing range at Holbeach to practise some weapon drops.'

'Sounds like a fun evening in this weather,' Planko added with a raised eyebrow.

I could hear the rain spattering on the window behind me. Planko ran through a checklist before we headed to the aircraft.

It was lashing down during the aircraft walkaround. I peered beneath the jet to check that the eight practice bombs were securely housed and could see little more than the spikes of rain in the thin beam of torchlight. By the time I climbed into the cockpit, my flying kit was soaked and I was grateful for the uncomfortable immersion suit we wore under the G-suit. I closed the canopy, leaving an inch gap for some air. The glass immediately steamed up on the inside. My maps and paperwork were drenched. As I plugged myself into the seat, there was a tell-tale high-pitched whine from the radios, signalling that water had leaked into the electrics.

I grabbed the NVGs from their protective box and was all fingers and thumbs inserting the batteries into the tubes with slippery wet hands. I dropped one and cursed as I swept my hand over the floor in the narrow space, losing valuable seconds in the pre-flight checks. I glanced across the pan when I heard the APU start up from the boss's jet. He was well ahead of me. I looked down at my kneeboard to find the check-in time. The ink had smudged in the rain.

I now had ninety seconds to get through at least five minutes of pre-start checks.

Surely life would have been less stressful as a solicitor.

The Jag started up without a hitch. I taxied out to the runway behind the boss's jet. All the airfield lights were off, except for our own little taxi lights which illuminated a short stretch of concrete ahead. At the end of the runway, we manoeuvred onto the tarmac for take-off into the oncoming wind. Mike's jet was on the right-hand side of the centre line. I positioned mine to the left and fractionally behind, in echelon formation.

The aircraft wingtips were about ten feet apart. The boss's landing light went out, the signal to power up. I spooled the engine up to 90 per cent thrust. I held the aircraft on the toe brakes and I could hear the deafening roar of the boss's jet exhausts right next to my cockpit.

The NVGs function by amplifying the available luminescence, although due to their shape they provided virtually no peripheral vision. I could either look at the other jet or move my head to look down the runway. Not both together. As this was a formation take-off, my role was to remain exactly in position alongside the boss as we accelerated. To achieve this, I had to stare directly at his jet throughout the take-off roll. A minor miscalculation would add two more Jags to the scrapheap. If I glanced away, even for a moment, I could lose all situational awareness of Mike's aircraft. Staring down the runway during take-off was solely his responsibility. If I held the formation position precisely, he would rotate his aircraft at 180 knots and I would follow him safely into the air, lights out, in close formation.

As I spooled the engines up, the nose of the jet dipped and strained against the brakes. I glanced into the cockpit to check the engine temperatures and pressures. All good. I flicked the landing light on to indicate that I was ready to roll. We both released the brakes at the same instant. I slammed the throttle into full afterburner and stared at the boss's jet as we careered down the runway. I constantly made minute adjustments to the rudder and throttles in order to hold position fore, aft, left and right, and was aware of the lights of the airfield buildings whizzing past in a blur.

The nose of the other jet lifted into the air – my cue to rotate. I smoothly matched its nose position with my own. The ground began to slide away from beneath the wheels. The boss called on the radio for the landing gear's retraction, which I had to match exactly to his aircraft in order to keep the drag the same between both jets. As the gear snapped into its housing, the landing lights fitted to the wheels disappeared, and we were plunged into the inky darkness of a thundery winter night. My job now was to hold close formation as we began the slow ascent into cloud.

To maintain formation, I had to line up two references. I judged depth by keeping my head alongside the boss's tail. The side angle had to be held by lining up a dim navigation light on his left wing with a small electronic warfare display, a couple of inches in diameter, which glowed green within his cockpit. These references became my sole focus for the next thirty minutes as we bumped along in thick cloud towards the VC10 tanker waiting in a holding pattern somewhere over the North Sea. I made adjustments, instant by instant, to the thrust and control column in order to hold the precise position. These manoeuvres were like a form of meditation, requiring Zen-like concentration and the absence of all external thought.

Twenty minutes later, we changed radio frequency to an intercept controller, callsign 'Boulmer', who sat somewhere deep in a bunker in Northumberland. The controller used ground radars to vector us towards our airborne petrol station. The weather had not improved.

'Boulmer, this is Vader. We can't make contact with the tanker. The weather is too poor. We are heading back to Coltishall.'

This was another Jaguar squadron, which was supposed to be in the refuelling slot before ours. If they could not find the tanker, neither could we. They were turning course for home. I allowed myself a sigh of relief. Perhaps we could try this again, on a less horrible night.

In light of Vader's decision, the fighter controllers must have thought our formation was about to make the same choice and came onto the radio:

'Turbo, this is Boulmer. Is your formation returning to base as well?'

'Turbo' was our callsign. I listened for the boss to confirm.

'Negative. We'll have a look.'

Jesus Christ, here we go.

I clung on like a drowning man to driftwood as we weaved our way across the North Sea through thick cloud that was intermittently so dense that, every now and again, I lost all sight of the boss's aircraft for half a second. It reappeared as a ghostly outline and I adjusted the formation spacing to as close as I dared.

We were vectored around for another fifteen minutes. Then, still in cloud, I was able to make out an ominous shadow looming out of the murk just feet from the boss's jet. We had closed to the same location as the VC10, flying in the same direction and at the same speed. The boss inched the aircraft up, to reduce the height difference between us. Through the green gloom of my NVGs, I saw a faint image of the left wing of the tanker bouncing like a hovering bird in the turbulence.

'Turbo, visual, request join,' I said.

'Turbo 2, clear astern.'

The reassuring voice came from the tanker cockpit. Somewhere above the icy North Sea, with no visible horizon and surrounded by a dark cloak of cloud broken by the recurrent flash of a red strobe light, it was time to fill up.

The tanking was horrendous. I was groping and lunging for success like a teenage boy in the shadows at a house party. Somehow I plugged and the fuel began to flow. I gripped the controls with sheer bloody-mindedness and willed the jet to fill up before I fell out of the basket contraption at the end of the hose which was supposed to stabilize the whole apparatus as it bounced around in the airflow.

We called the air-to-air refuellers 'the tanker-wankers', but they are the lifeblood of fast jet warfare, the unsung heroes who place their lives in danger over enemy territory so that the fighters can get the fuel they need. The Royal Air Force is a machine with hundreds of moving parts and every part has to work for the machine to function.

With the tanking complete, the boss directed me into a one-mile trail formation. This meant easing back into the night sky and letting him accelerate away as I studied a single instrument that told me his range was increasing . . . 0.6 nautical miles . . . 0.7 nautical miles . . . There was no additional information, just a range. By flying at the same speed and in the same direction, I remained roughly at the correct distance. If I slowed, the range would gradually increase, and vice versa.

By remaining in trail formation, we would not hit each other. As we descended through the cloud, the world became darker and I prepared myself for entry to low level. A few thousand feet above the ground, the cloud dispersed and I could make out the dimly lit villages and street lights speckling the misty east coast countryside. We continued down to low level and accelerated through the hills. A few cars beamed shafts of light, like curling snakes, as they wound through the bends in the darkness. In most of the houses the lights were out and people were tucked up in their beds.

We were following a navigation route that would take us to the weapons range. My role was to stay visual with the boss, one mile behind him at 450 knots and 250 feet, as we weaved our way tactically through the terrain to simulate a low-level night bombing run.

At times the cultural lighting – the night lights of humankind, the towns and street lights, rather than the moon and stars – was so poor that I was barely able to make out the terrain through the NVGs and I eased the aircraft higher for safety. In the HUD, the radar altimeter showed me that my height was now 300 feet, a measurement that fluctuated up and down as the two jets raced across the undulating hills. An unlit mast flashed past my right-hand side at eye level.

Christ, that was close.

Mike's aircraft had a single infrared light on the tail, invisible to the naked eye. Staring manically through the NVGs, I followed this puny light with all of my concentration. When his jet passed over populated areas or lines of traffic, the infrared glow was consumed by the ground lights. To maintain trail formation, I watched for this single bulb to reappear and glanced rapidly at the minuscule distance number in the HUD. As long as I kept that at one mile, I could not hit him. And if I kept his light slightly below my aircraft, I could not hit the ground.

The light pollution fell away as we coasted out over the murky North Sea at low level and turned south towards the weapons range at Holbeach. The aim was to conduct a 'first run attack'. This required maintaining altitude, identifying the training target, and dropping a practice bomb that contained a smoke and flash charge so that its accuracy could be scored by the range controller and reported back to the formation.

I accelerated to 480 knots, selected weapon aiming in the head up display, and ran through the pre-attack checklist, arming the weapon pylons and firing a laser range finder through the nose of the jet to get an accurate fix on the target. A small green diamond appeared in the HUD to highlight the target position. If this was in error, I could modify the aiming point once I was visual with the target by taking my hand from the throttles momentarily and using a separate control just behind them. By adjusting the aircraft heading left or right, I could move a vertical green image, called the 'bomb fall line', which would indicate where the weapon would fall.

'Turbo 2, cleared hot.' It was the voice of the range controller.

Three miles out. Fifteen seconds to release. The bomb fall line was through the target. I fired the ranging laser. Suddenly the jet bumped up in the turbulent air. I cursed and eased back to 250 feet. The aiming line was drifting left and there was a slight crosswind.

Come on, Sutton, sort it out.

Five seconds to go. A quick correction back onto the target, then let the sight settle. A nice stable release was important.

Late Arm to live. Press the weapon release button. A little thud from the airframe as the practice bomb was ejected into the airflow. A gentle pull away from the ground, up to 1,000 feet, then back for another go.

'One away.'

It was 11.30 p.m. by the time we landed back at Coltishall and the rain had stopped. I walked back into Ops; the boss was already there chatting to Planko.

'Well, how did it go?' Planko asked.

I thought about the dropped NVG battery, the soaked kit, the terrifying take-off, the formation and tanking in cloud, the low level where I kept losing sight of the other jet, the unlit mast and my ham-fisted weaponeering.

'OK, I think,' I replied.

They both chuckled.

'It's late. We'll look at the tapes tomorrow,' the boss said casually. 'Well done.'

I enjoyed the calm of the late evening as I drove home. I felt content, drained, a little bit proud and relieved that I'd completed my first night refuelling. It was well past midnight when I slid into bed next to Kate, who was already fast asleep.

10. Piano Burning

Unlike airline flights, where passengers start at one point and land somewhere else, on a fast jet sortie you normally end up back where you started. When we flew somewhere else to train with another force or for exposure to different operating environments, we just crammed some overnight kit into a bag and squeezed it into the Jaguar, a jet designed for warfare not awayday excursions.

After we arrived in the crewroom with our rucksacks, it was essential to follow the old adage, 'Never get separated from your bag.' Junior pilots spotting neglected kit would stuff things in or take things out, then the owners would fly off without checking and land in Scotland in the rain with a rucksack containing women's clothing instead of a waterproof, or a shoe replaced by a textbook. On one occasion, one of the boys found he had only a Pink Panther outfit to wear. Another unpacked his bag in the officers' mess to find a 3 kg practice bomb under his jeans. This may seem immature – it *was* immature – but the intensity of training needed a safety valve and senior pilots caught up in this mischief took it exceedingly well.

Almost every day, for weeks on end, we were flying low at devilish speeds among the mountains and weapons ranges, performing strikes that, to use a dartboard analogy, had to hit the treble twenty every time. We all made errors. I certainly did. At Donna Nook range, where the fens of

Lincolnshire meet the chill of the North Sea, I misidentified a target designed to take a practice weapon no bigger than a Pringles tin and scored a direct hit with a 1,000 lb bomb, blowing it to smithereens. The range controller in a tower a mile away did not give me the benefit of the doubt. He scored it as a miss, 2,500 feet from the target. I was mortified. The rest of the formation found it thoroughly amusing.

A few days later, I passed Mike Seares in the corridor.

'Morning, boss,' I said.

'Morning, Sooty,' he replied. Then he stopped and turned about with a curious expression. 'How's the piano coming along?'

'I'm sorry?'

'The piano. We can't turn up without a piano. There's a good chap. I'll leave it with you.'

The boss marched off with his usual calm countenance. A piano was required for the Pilots' Lunch, not for a sing-song, but to wheel out of the officers' mess and set on fire. The annual revelry on the last working day of the year in the run-up to Christmas leave always concluded with pyrotechnics. It was the first I knew that it was my responsibility to provide the fuel.

The tradition of piano burning is thought to have started during the Second World War when a pilot pianist was shot down and his squadron burned the mess's old upright because they hated the silence now that he would play no more. There is another version, that pilots obliged to take lessons to improve their dexterity torched the piano to avoid them. Piano burning caught on in Canada and the United States and the ritual has prompted contemporary musicians to compose for and perform on pianos which have been deliberately set alight.

Whichever way it all started, piano burning was one of the year's highlights on fighter bases, a convention so vital that in messes with grand pianos and expensive uprights you saw signs glued to the woodwork that read: 'This piano is NOT to be burned'.

Later that day, I was catching up with Matt Peterson, when my flight commander, Chris Hadlow, stopped as he walked past.

'Have you sorted a piano yet, Sooty?' Hadders asked.

'I'm still working on it, sir,' I replied.

'Better get to it, then.' I couldn't tell whether I could see a hint of a smile or not as he strolled off with his hands in his pockets.

'Austin Powers looked a bit frustrated,' Matt remarked.

I chuckled; there was a clear resemblance.

'Where the hell am I going to find a piano?'

'A piano shop, I imagine.'

'Are you joking? It'll cost a fortune. We're going to burn the bloody thing, not play Mozart on it.'

'Try the local paper?'

'Genius,' I replied. 'Gotta go.'

I searched through the free ads in the *Eastern Daily Press* and by sheer luck found the offer of a free piano for someone who could give it a good home. I called immediately and spoke to an elderly woman. I told her I was a pilot at RAF Coltishall, and she invited me to come for tea the following day at her bungalow in a nearby village. I dressed smartly to make a good impression.

The highly polished piano stood in an overcrowded

room by the window, with framed photographs arranged on lace doilies on its top. She said it had been in her family for forty years. Her husband had been the musician. He had recently passed away but had been fond of 'those chaps down the road at Coltishall'.

'You're learning to play?' she asked.

'I am,' I lied.

'How wonderful. He would be so happy to know it was going to a young pilot who would take great care of it.'

I kidded myself I was doing the woman a service by leaving her with the belief that the instrument was going to a good home. I made arrangements with a local company to collect the piano and the kindly lady wiped a tear from her eye as I left. I gave her a cheery wave and had never felt so guilty in my life.

A few hours later, the piano was standing in the mess car park being painted up in red and blue squadron colours and stuffed with straw. I had dragged Kate along, and I watched her working away with a red paintbrush in one hand, a dab of red on her cheek, and a bottle of Belgian beer at her side. Hadders passed.

'Brilliant. Well done,' he said. 'It's mahogany – nice slow burner.'

The Pilots' Lunch was a mainly liquid affair, with the four Jaguar squadrons celebrating the festive season by competing in outrageous pranks. An area of tarmac at the front of the mess had been dug up and replaced with a concrete base for such occasions. At dusk the decorated piano was wheeled out of the mess to join a trio of others from our sister squadrons. Hadders struck a match and our piano went up like an inferno, the flames rising high into the night sky. On one memorable occasion, a small car took the place of a piano on the pyre.

A game of mess rugby followed. One of the anterooms became a temporary pitch and two teams battled to get the ball – in this case a cabbage – across the opposing team's try line. Despite the utter carnage, there was only minor structural damage to the mess and a broken collarbone for the intelligence officer.

In the early months of 2003, the Jaguar Force prepared to take part in what has become known as the second Gulf War. The force was already running reconnaissance missions from Incirlik in Turkey, and planned to launch offensive operations from the base, a sixty-minute shuttle following the River Euphrates across Syria to Iraq.

The anticipation was intense. Prime Minister Tony Blair had released information about weapons of mass destruction, and while the political effort was not without controversy, the Russian equipment operated by the Iraqi forces was very real indeed. More than fifty coalition aircraft had been lost during the first Gulf War, including seven RAF Tornados, with many more damaged.

6 Squadron's focus was on readiness and preparation. Not politics. Yet a diplomatic row with the Turks played out daily on television screens, and ultimately permission to operate from Incirlik was withdrawn. For the Jags, all operations ceased and the jets returned to the UK like a demoralized army withdrawn from the fight at the peak of its capability.

It was a huge blow. During the 1991 Gulf War, twelve Jaguars had flown 612 combat sorties against the Iraqi forces without a single aircraft loss. Three years later, in an effort to suppress the genocide being conducted by Bosnian Serb forces in former Yugoslavia, a Jag from 41 Squadron conducted the first RAF bombing raid over mainland Europe since the Second World War. The Bosnian conflict was vicious, with six coalition aircraft losses, including a British Sea Harrier shot down by a surface-to-air heat-seeking missile. The pilot, Lieutenant Nick Richardson, ejected and fortunately landed in territory controlled by friendly troops.

Throughout this time, the Jaguar had patrolled northern Iraq, flying policing and reconnaissance missions alongside US fighters. The squadron came under daily fire by anti-aircraft artillery (AAA), the operators keen to capture the huge bounty offered by Saddam Hussein for shooting down a coalition jet. The AAA would appear as puffs of black around the formation. The jet could be turned when under threat, but lacked agility at height, with the airframe responding lazily in response to inputs which were invariably cautious – stalling the Jaguar could be fatal.

The jet had been upgraded throughout its life, but performance and manoeuvrability limitations were its Achilles' heel – fast in a straight line, but poor at turning. I recall a time during a training flight over the North Sea when an F-15 simulating an enemy fighter had saddled up behind me. I strained over my left shoulder and stared directly up and into the huge square jet intakes. I banked hard and threw the aircraft into a descending turn, then reversed, pulling the maximum G available to try to shake him off. I glanced over my right shoulder a few moments later and the F-15 was in precisely the same position, stuck to me like glue. Pointless. It was like trying to evade a police motor-bike on a scooter.

Missing out on operations from Incirlik was crushing. As a force we had been totally ready and raring to go, and it felt dispiriting for our focus to return once more to a future of dropping practice weapons on oil drum targets in the Norfolk countryside. But frontline pilots must stay proficient in a range of skill sets: instrument approaches, emergency handling, tactical know-how, tanking and so on. The majority of them practised on rolling monthly cycles, and, as the months passed by, the temporary gloom that hung over the base dispersed.

I was soon back in NVGs for a low-level night trip in the Scottish Highlands. It would take in a route through the mountains and a couple of target runs. Nothing too tricky. As I descended over the Cairngorms, I was above the cloud tops, just me and the setting sun, which pro-vided a glorious view I wished could go on for ever. I then dived down like a corkscrew, twisting and turning through cloud into the hills at 500 knots, the darkening world zooming by.

I already had a couple of night seasons under my belt. My squadron specialized in that role and I was beginning to feel comfortable flying in that environment. This was a good ego boost but, as always in flying – as in life – it illus-trated the adage that pride comes before a fall.

The met man's forecast of low cloud and poor visibility was spot on. It was an overcast night besieged by showers and gusty winds. As there was negligible cultural light in the hills, the goggles did almost nothing to enhance what little illumination there was. The image had become grainy, a tell-tale sign of decreasing visibility and increased moisture; possibly some thin cloud.

To my right and left was high ground disappearing up into the clouds. Above was controlled airspace packed with airliners cruising steadily towards their destinations. I often conjured up images of cabin crew serving chilled wine to relaxed passengers as I shot through the night alone in the big cat. With bad options in all directions, the only route appeared to be onwards and I plunged ahead, winding my way among the valleys. I continued to thread a path through the weather and terrain, weaving to avoid a small village and seeking out a fork in the low ground ahead of me.

There was a mammoth cloud bank off to the left, closing down that particular option. I pulled hard to the right into less atrocious weather and rolled out on what I thought was the ground horizon. I was wrong. It turned out to be a slope descending from left to right. The level cloud base I had seen above me was in fact a low cloud layer rolling down the hill into the valley below and forming fog.

I was totally disorientated. The NVGs provided no distinct images. I leaned forward but had no time to interpret the vague green shadows that flickered before my eyes. The radar altimeter suddenly burst into life with a deafening audio warning and a flashing red light. I glanced towards the altitude and saw 200 feet. The world was a blur except for a small crop of jagged rocks with trees that had dug their roots into every available crevice. They were perfectly in focus and exactly where my flight path was heading.

I snatched back on the stick, engaged the afterburners and threw the jet into an uncontrolled climb away from the hills into thick cloud. I cursed myself and prayed that I could out-climb the terrain and miss whatever airliners happened to be flying above me. I had been at most two seconds from slamming into a rocky outcrop on a Scottish hillside and was extremely lucky to escape. Pilots had lost their lives in similar circumstances and I understood more than ever the risk of pressing on into a worsening situation. Most of the guys had similar stories and lucky escapes. Some had ejected. Just as you got complacent in this job, you were reminded of the fragility of it all.

Training deployments took us around the world and gave junior pilots the chance to grow our skills in weaponeering, precision strikes, reconnaissance and electronic warfare. On Arctic operations in the north of Norway, we operated from a snow-covered airfield and our jets slid around in comical fashion even when taxiing at low speed. We practised low-level desert flying in the burning heat of Oman and attended NATO exchanges across Europe. Since the illicit flypast over Dad's golf club, I had kept my head down and stayed out of trouble on these excursions. That all came to an end at RAF St Mawgan in Cornwall, when I was a guest on a NATO evaluation exercise with 54 Squadron.

We spent two weeks roughing it in tents on a muddy campsite. At the end of the first week, we were given a few hours off, with a strict midnight curfew. I went into Newquay, to meet a friend, and two beers led to two too many. I made my way back to camp on foot and tried to sneak by the airfield guards. I found a dark spot, climbed the fence and fell head first into a hardy thorn bush that ripped my face to pieces. I was finally picked up by the RAF police in the middle of the runway at three in the morning, the darkest hour.

I had only popped out for a quick beer, but I appeared before the boss of 54 Squadron the following morning looking as if I'd been mauled by a mountain lion. He shook his head.

'Anything to say?'

'No, sir.'

He could have thrown the book at me. Instead, with the planning room buzzing with activity, we sat for a few minutes on the grass outside Operations in the sunlight and he reminded me that if I wanted to get on in the RAF then I couldn't indulge in this sort of thing. I knew full well that I had embarrassed myself, disappointed him and let the side down. The incident was forgotten – though not by me. I learned that there were times when the best action when a member of the team goes astray is to give them the benefit of the doubt and move on.

11. Back to Reality

In the spirit of NATO unity, in 2004, 6 Squadron flew out to the Mihail Kogălniceanu air base near the Black Sea in Romania to conduct exercises with the former Soviet Bloc MiG-21 squadrons. In spite of its wonderful name, the base was run-down, with Stalinist-era huts that hadn't been painted for years and an airfield that looked as if it had been ploughed up to plant potatoes.

The Russian MiG-21 was even older than the Jag. It had been the Jag's natural enemy during the Cold War and had become the most widely produced supersonic jet in aviation history. Used extensively in conflicts across the Middle East and Asia, MiG-21s had also shot down dozens of American fighters during the Vietnam War. The success rate of the MiGs had been so high it led to the creation of the 'Top Gun' school in Miramar, California, to teach the fundamentals of air combat to US Navy pilots.

We learned on our arrival at Mihail Kogălniceanu that there was to be a joint parade to formally mark the start of the exercise. It was distressing news for the squadron warrant officer, whose job it was to lick our contingent into shape. Drill remains a part of every military officer's skill set, but it is best left to languish by fast jet pilots unless there is plenty of time to refresh. As it happened, there was none.

Fifteen Jaguar pilots trooped onto the parade square

and Warrant Officer MacTavish tried to disguise his horror at the sight of pilots trying to recall their drill moves. With a gasp of bracing Black Sea air and some equally bracing language, he reminded us which leg led off for an 'about turn' and which knee to raise high when ordered to 'halt'. We breathed a sigh of relief only when the MiG pilots joined the RAF contingent on the square and were just as bad.

We all came to attention facing two flagpoles. A senior Romanian officer marched forward and saluted his country's flag. A young conscript in a thin uniform then turned the handle on the flagpole as the national anthem played over speakers clearly borrowed from a 1980s mobile disco and the flag rose with exemplary timing to the top of the mast.

I had learned to fly with Nick Millikin on the UAS. I now stood next to his older brother Andy, a Jaguar pilot. Both brothers were noisy, and passionate about flying. Their father had been the Vulcan airshow display pilot, and their grandfather flew dangerous raids over Germany in Lancaster bombers during the Second World War.

'So far so good,' Andy whispered without moving his lips, in a brilliant piece of ventriloquism.

'God Save the Queen' crackled into life over the speakers and the same young soldier turned the handle on the second pole. This time his pace was so far off that the Union flag was barely a third of the way up the mast as the anthem drew to a close. He tried to catch up, winding faster and faster, the music accompanied by a high-pitched squeal like a cat being run over by a car.

Milli's shoulders were faintly bobbing up and down. I

was biting my lips to stop bursting into laughter when a rabid dog attracted by the screeching wheel entered the parade square. All eyes turned as it padded towards the flagpoles. He gave them a good sniff, then raised his leg and peed over the stand holding the speakers. Mr MacTavish turned as white as a sheet. Eventually the shambles drew to a close and we were marched back across the parade ground to a bus waiting to take us to our hotel. As we stood easy, he turned to the boss.

'Sir, I have never been so embarrassed. Thank God you lot can fly better than you can march.'

I climbed aboard and sat next to Harry Barraclough, another Jag pilot.

'I think it all went rather well, all things considered,' he said.

The bus wound its way back through the small villages dotted along the Black Sea coast to our hotel in Constanţa, overtaking locals on horses and carts. The former president of Romania, Nicolae Ceauçescu, had been executed with his wife Elena on Christmas Day 1989 during the revolution that overthrew the communist regime. Fifteen years later, in the computer-driven world of the new millennium, villagers in remote areas of the country were still washing their clothes in the river.

Flying began in earnest the following day. Every morning during the next two weeks there was a formal briefing with a Romanian air commodore who sat behind a large desk with an impatient expression while his nervous underlings provided information on the number of working phone lines, the serviceability of the trucks, the amount of fuel available and the reliability of the electricity supply.

It was all a show. There was, seemingly, an abundant supply of everything, and any momentary shortage would be met with apparent horror from the senior officer. Romania had joined NATO only that year and the old communist ways still reigned.

The Mihail Kogălniceanu air base provided the perfect metaphor for the decline of the Soviet Union. The hammer and sickle symbols were still discernible on the beaten-up buildings but fading slowly to nothing. From the end of the Second World War until the fall of the Berlin Wall in 1989, RAF training had been hard-wired to defend against an attack from the USSR which never came. Pilots had trained relentlessly with cluster munitions and nuclear warheads in readiness to launch east on one-way missions to save civilization itself.

Each side had spent four decades equipping itself with ever-greater arsenals of devastating ordnance that would assure mutual destruction. It exemplified what is known as 'the security paradox': in order to secure peace, each state feels an urgent need to be dominant, resulting in a continuous escalation of military forces. The fall of the Berlin Wall had brought a brief spring to the world, a moment of hope that had faded like the air base paint with the rise of Islamic terrorism. A new enemy, the same escalation.

I was tasked that morning to conduct a training sortie against a MiG flown by a stern young Romanian with dark eyes and no sign of a smile. The upgraded MiG-21 was a ground attack aircraft with new glass-cockpit avionics and air-to-air radar. The jet had evolved, but shades of Soviet thinking and doctrine had endured.

Taxiing out for take-off, I could see the rusting hulks of two MiG-29s, tyres flattened, the grass growing through the cracked tarmac and climbing between the main wheels. Ferocious as they looked, these jets probably hadn't been airworthy for years. They had once been the Soviet point defence fighter, equipped with radar-guided missiles and ready to shoot down western jets if they approached the USSR's borders.

We levelled at 10,000 feet over the countryside, the city of Constanța abutting the Black Sea a few miles to the south. To the west stood the hulks of the Carpathian Mountains: a national park with ancient woodlands, volcanic lakes, wolves and bears.

The MiG sat just over a mile to my left, both jets heading the same way. The aim was to practise air combat – dogfighting – turning the jets aggressively into the other's six o'clock to take a simulated missile shot. This was not the Jag's natural habitat, but it was an important discipline. The risks with air combat arose from over-aggression: flying too close to the other jet while turning, drifting too low and risking ground collision, or leaving the thirsty afterburners on for too long and running out of fuel.

Fights On.

The MiG rolled towards me, a smoky exhaust trail appearing as its pilot applied maximum thrust. I did the same. I racked the Jag into a left-hand turn and allowed the nose to slice downwards to keep the speed on. I aimed slightly to the MiG's left, to create a miss-distance between us, but the Romanian pilot maintained perfectly head on.

A collision course.

Had he lost sight of me against the ground? I adjusted a little left again. His wings rolled right to point directly at me once more. The MiG bloomed in size, flashing past my right shoulder at a closure speed of 900 knots and perhaps a couple of aircraft lengths apart.

Bloody hell!

I broke into him with full afterburner and the MiG dived again, this time well below the minimum height that we had agreed – the hard deck. I levelled and watched his nose track around and then up towards me. Again we passed practically on a collision.

That was two huge safety busts in under sixty seconds.

We had agreed on a safety bubble of 1,000 feet around each aircraft. But it seemed that my opponent thought it entirely optional. I was more than happy when he disappeared off to a sister base to conduct some low-level aerobatics down to treetop height.

It was a relief to be on the auth's desk the following day, monitoring the flying from the security of terra firma. I was sipping a cup of Turkish-style coffee so strong it made my eyes water, when Stuka stormed in and threw his flying jacket across the table.

'Jesus Christ!' he exclaimed.

'Stuka' Wilson, so named as he broke cloud almost vertically downwards from low level during flying training, was just the sort of man you wanted on your mess rugby team. He had set off two hours earlier for the bombing range fifty miles away for a weaponeering sortie on the wing of a Romanian. The plan was to drop a series of 3 kg practice weapons on a burned-out tank precisely twenty seconds behind the MiG-21 which led the way.

At the Fairford Airshow in 1981, aged three. Jets are always kept off the grass these days.

Fly it.

PILOT
RAF officer

1980s RAF pilot recruiting advert.

Bulldog of Southampton University Air Squadron, with Mum and Dad, in 1998. Even as a thirty-year-old fighter pilot some years later, Dad would still never let me drive his car.

Line Astern in four SUAS Bulldogs. Elementary Flying Training introduced some basic tactical flying, including aerobatics, formation and low-level navigation.

Officer training, 1999. Sutton (*second from left, top row*). Nikki Thomas (*front row far right*) became a Tornado GR4 navigator, and the first female to command a fast jet squadron in the RAF. We served on Operation Shader together.

The RAF Tucano served as the basic fast jet trainer from 1989 to 2019. Based at RAF Linton-on-Ouse in Yorkshire, the year-long flying course was much loved by the RAF and RN trainee pilots.

The brand-new glass-cockpit Hawk CT-115, which I flew in Canada. After the Tucano, it was like stepping into a Ferrari. The Hawk is primarily a two-seat jet trainer, but is also used by some countries as a light attack aircraft. In the UK the Hawk T1 is famously used by the RAF Red Arrows

6 Squadron Jaguars doing a 'flat turn' in formation on recovery to RAF Coltishall. Aircraft ED is carrying a centreline fuel tank, Paveway II laser-guided bomb on the left wing, and TIALD laser-designation pod on the right wing. The Jag carried AIM 9L infra-red guided missiles on over-wing launchers.

6 Squadron, 2004. *Back row*: Hadders, Skids Harrison, Nick Hindley, Dan Ingall, Derbs, Cutty. *Front row*: Planko, Damo, Gogsy, Mike Seares, Sutton, Staitey, Mudge.

Mess rugby, RAF Coltishall, 2005. One cabbage, few rules. The perfect way to end the carnage of the annual Pilots' Lunch.

The Jaguar GR3a cockpit. A fearful sight for a brand-new student on the conversion unit.

The Jag's natural environment. A low-level pass over a JTAC during Close Air Support training in Oman, 2004. Fuel tanks and CRV-7 rocket pods on the wings.

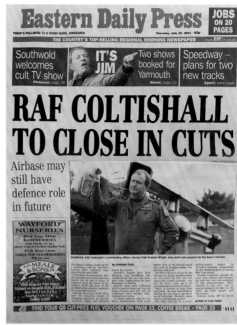

Sad times. A media report of the impact of a Defence Review and cuts; including the closure of RAF Coltishall, and with it the demise of the Jaguar Force.

East meets West: a Jag leads two Romanian MiG-21s. The old enemies playing nicely.

Broken Silence by Michael Rondot. Jaguars race at low level through Scotland en route to the Cape Wrath bombing range.

Multi-role Typhoons: XI Squadron participating in Exercise Green Flag in Nevada, 2008. The Typhoon was now ready for any air-to-air or air-to-ground operation across the globe.

Scramble! A pilot and team of engineers rush to a Typhoon on Quick Reaction Alert. Jets are on standby 24 hours a day, 365 days a year ready to launch at a moment's notice in response to an incursion into UK airspace.

An American Airlines 767 lands safely at Heathrow following a suspected terrorist incident in March 2010. Little did they know I'd intercepted them in a Typhoon twenty minutes earlier and remained hidden in their six o'clock.

glorious summer's day in June 2009 as Typhoon jets lead the Queen's rthday flypast down the Mall and over ckingham Palace.

The RAF is back. A 1 (Fighter) Squadron Typhoon stands ready for a Red Flag night sortie out of Nellis Air Force Base, *The Home of the Fighter Pilot*, 2015. Red Flag was created in response to the high US aircraft loss rate during the Vietnam War and provides an intense training environment for combat aircraft.

Four-ship over the Grand Canyon, January 2015.

An ASRAAM accelerates to Mach 3 as it is fired from a Typhoon during a weapons training event over Aberporth Range in Wales. The target was a flare pack towed by a drone. The infrared heat-seeking missile is capable of turns up to 60 'G' when intercepting targets.

o. 1 Squadron officers with SE5 biplanes, at Clairmarais aerodrome near Ypres, July 1918. 1 (Fighter) quadron is the oldest military squadron in the world, tracing its roots back to 1878 as the No. 1 alloon Company. It has participated in nearly every major conflict the RAF has been involved in, om the Battle of Britain, the Falklands War, the Gulf Wars, Afghanistan and Syria. During the First /orld War the squadron had among its ranks no fewer than thirty-one aces.

An artist's impression of a 1 (Fighter) Squadron Hunter flown by Alan Pollock flies under Tower Bridge on 5 April 1968, in protest at the government deciding not to mark the fiftieth anniversary of the RAF. Frowned on by the MOD, Pollock was dismissed from the RAF but received much public support and the British Overseas Airways Corporation (forerunner of British Airways) sent him a keg of beer.

onducting the first RAF frontline release of aveway 4, at Cape Wrath in Scotland. Note the rawing of the wasp just beneath the cockpit. rthur Clowes was a Battle of Britain Hurricane lot who painted a stripe on the wasp every time e shot down a Luftwaffe aircraft. The symbol as painted on to the Typhoon as a tribute to is heroic pilot.

Robin Olds (*front row, left*) in front of 1 Squadron Meteors, RAF Tangmere in 1948. Olds was posted to the RAF on an exchange programme, having flown 107 missions from England during the Second World War, shooting down thirteen German aircraft.

Olds is now celebrated as the greatest aerial warrior in American history. He was a revered tactician and leader during the Vietnam War, where he flew over 150 combat sortie shooting down four MiGs. Most famously he led the 'Wolfpack' during Operation Bolo, which was so successful that Vietnamese MiG operations ceased for months.

The Robin Olds Bar on 1 (Fighter) Squadron. The only place to start a Friday night!

The A400 – a tactical workhorse. The aircraft deployed squadron pilots, engineers and equipment from our base at RAF Lossiemouth to RAF Akrotiri.

The 3 kg bomblets discharged little more than a firework crack on the target, enough to briefly highlight the accuracy of their position. A twenty-second separation between the strikes would be more than sufficient to ensure safe deconfliction.

'I was set up for the run, 250 feet, 480 knots,' he said. 'I had the MiG in sight. I was in twenty-second trail. I could see the target ahead. It all looked fine.'

He paused to sign the auth sheets, a record of his flight. Then he looked back up.

'The MiG was cleared to strike. I was expecting to see him fly over the tank then ease up for my run in.' He threw up his hands. 'He didn't. Suddenly there was a massive explosion and the entire range erupted in bloody great flames and black smoke. I felt like I was in *Apocalypse Now*. I snatched back on the controls, threw the Jag into a climb and burst through the carnage.'

I went to speak and he cut me off.

'You're not going to believe this. Apparently, he dropped *napalm*! Napalm for fuck's sake. It's 2004 – who even does that?'

Stuka grabbed his jacket and went off mumbling to himself. I called the Romanian squadron to try to establish what had happened.

'Our pilot seems to think you dropped napalm?' I inquired. 'I thought we would only be using training weapons?'

'Yes, sir. Training napalm.' His English was broken. 'Just small canisters.'

On our return to the UK, I was posted to the Jaguar QWI (qualified weapons instructor) course, a six-month

thrashing designed to turn jet pilots into weapons and tactics trainers. As a student learning to be a teacher, you were
under the microscope every day and judged on your performance, tactical knowledge and ability to lead large
formations. It was tough, rigorous and stressful, and I was
glad when it was over. There was a party on graduation
day, and it had become the custom for students to gather
in the bar in their own 'vehicles'.

Matt Peterson and I discussed this tradition at great
length. We decided protocol required us to try to be
original, and we rocked up on a pair of Chinese mini-
motorbikes. We celebrated as pilots do, and were rather
the worse for wear when we had the brilliant idea of conducting speed-trials in the mess. As we were blasting down
the corridor, a figure suddenly emerged from the shadows.
Of all the people, it was the station commander, Group
Captain Wright. He stood flat against the wall as Matt
swerved to avoid him and lost control. He was flung off
his bike and slid head first across the carpet, searing his
face with friction burns that lasted for weeks.

'Well done on passing the course,' the station commander said in the same calm manner you might politely
wish a colleague good morning. He continued along the
corridor.

'Err, thanks, sir,' I replied.

He glanced back. 'Matt might need a beer – looks rather
nasty.'

The following day, with the clatter of mini-motorbikes
still circling in my skull, I swapped my red-and-blue name
badge for a crisp red-and-white one. With an instructor's
ticket – and old loyalties that would be edged out by new

ones – I headed off to 41 Squadron to run a weapons training camp from RAF Akrotiri in Cyprus.

The Akrotiri base was to play a major part in my future, but it was that summer in 2005 when we were reminded that there was a new enemy right on our own doorstep. On 7 July – 7/7, as it became known – London had suffered one of the worst terrorist attacks in modern times. Three home-made devices carried by Islamist suicide bombers exploded within the space of one minute on three London Underground trains. A fourth bomb went off on a bus an hour later in Tavistock Square. Fifty-two people died and more than 700 were hurt, many with life-changing injuries.

These events were in the front of my mind during the two weeks I spent teaching high-dive sorties: climbing in clear weather and swooping down from 15,000 feet to drop practice weapons on a target raft floating in the azure waters of Episkopi Bay. The base closed at 3 p.m. due to the high August temperatures and we spent afternoons on the beach before rustling up spicy sausages and lamb shanks for barbecues.

I had the job I had always wanted and had gone through what I considered the best training in the world. It was a privilege that came with obligations and responsibilities. Like all the senior pilots, engineers and instructors whose faces lined the walls of the long corridors in Cranwell, I was aware of my duty to square that privilege.

When we had started weapons training at Cold Lake, we had been warned that if we had a crisis of conscience about learning to kill people, then that was the time to change career. If I had experienced any doubts in the past, they had gone by 2005. In an interconnected world, terrorism, populism and fascism could grow exponentially. There was an elusive, asymmetric threat out there that killed children on buses and people on their way to work on the Underground. On the squadron we all felt ready to defend the nation's liberal democratic values, but it felt unclear how we could respond from 15,000 feet to such an enemy. Nor were the events of 7/7 the only tragedy that clouded my time in Cyprus.

One Thursday morning, with an alarm set for 0545, I was woken at 0530 by the annoying ring tone on my mobile phone. I was still half asleep when I answered, and was surprised to hear the voice of another Jag pilot, Graham Pemberton – Pembers – calling from the UK.

'Hi, mate. Hope the detachment's going well.' Unusually for Pembers, he sounded glum. 'I knew you'd be up early for met brief . . . thought I'd catch you before work.'

'Yeah, it's a bit early, but all's good. You OK?'

'I've got some sad news, I'm afraid.' He paused. 'It's Mike Seares. He died yesterday. He committed suicide. I knew you were mates. I wanted to let you know before you heard through the grapevine.'

There was a long silence before I spoke.

'Thanks, Pembers. Thanks for letting me know. You take care.'

'And you, Sooty.'

We hung up. I tossed my phone onto the table and slumped back on my bed. I could barely take the news in. What? Why? It made no sense. We had been enjoying a beer together in the mess a few weeks before and he had seemed fine. Mike was only thirty-nine. He had just been promoted, stopped flying Jags and taken up an office job at the RAF's headquarters. He was one of the youngest and most promising group captains and had been marked out to reach the very top of the RAF. He was happily married, with three young children. He had the world at his feet. He was my role model, a man I looked up to and admired.

My muscles ached as I dressed, and I was still in a daze when I headed into work. I was teaching some junior pilots how to conduct rocket attacks. After putting some briefing slides together, I needed a few moments to pull myself together and quietly slipped out of the planning room.

Being a fast jet pilot was addictive and rewarding. We were away from home for six months every year. There was an unending drive to be better, to absorb more tactics, operate the jet in more complex environments, to do well in front of your peers. But, of course, there was the inherent risk. I was aware of all the psychological pressures, but none of them had felt acute to me. I was twenty-seven – life just felt like an adventure. That's probably why Mike's suicide hit me so hard. It was totally unexpected and exposed the fragility of my own existence in a way that I had never considered.

The pressures are something you adapt to and learn to live with. Following stressful sorties, you feel physically spent but mentally charged. You don't need sleep. You want to rehydrate and chat about the tasking with other pilots. That close-knit teamwork carries us through, together, with a shared sense of unity and purpose.

After Mike's death, I lost another friend in near-identical

circumstances a few years later. Nick de Candole was incredibly bright and adventurous, the sort of man who buys a paraglider on eBay and launches himself off a hill two days later. Our courses had overlapped in Canada. He then flew Tornado F3s, Jags with me on 41 Squadron and F-16s on an exchange in the United States. You rarely saw Nick without a beaming smile, and he was expert at not showing those around him that they were intellectually light years behind. With two young children, a lovely wife and a fantastic career ahead of him, Nick took his own life.

Mental health issues in the armed forces are becoming more recognized and better treated. Not before time. The pressure on servicemen and women is subtle, constant and intense. Serving in a squadron, ship's company or army brigade isn't so much a job, a career: it's an identity. You don't want to let anyone down, so you strive to be at your best at all times. You make one error, and friends can end up wounded or dead. That's why the training is so harsh and protracted, why pilots get chopped for the smallest mistake.

All of this forges bonds, a sense of purpose, and team-work so strong that, when you leave it behind, the loss can be intolerable. Prince Harry described leaving the army as like being on a bus, driving along happily with your mates. Then the bus pulls up at a deserted stop in the middle of nowhere. You step down and watch as the bus drives off, leaving you alone. It is a neat analogy and very real.

We will never know what drove Mike and Nick to make the decisions they did on those fateful days. Their loss was tragic and felt by every member of the team.

Personal loss causes reflection, and for a while perhaps a renewed energy and a fresh perspective on what is important. It also highlighted my own fallibility in understanding the hidden battles others face and internalize, as well as the importance, ultimately, of looking after your friends and colleagues.

12. The Old and the New

Early in 2006, we deployed to Nellis Air Force Base outside Las Vegas to take part in the US Exercise Red Flag. It was by far the biggest exercise I had ever taken part in, with more than sixty aircraft launching twice a day to conduct training scenarios against potent air and surface-to-air threats. A huge stone sign at the base entrance read: 'The Home of the Fighter Pilot'.

In our 1970s jets we were outclassed and we knew it. As I jammed myself into the stuffy cockpit of my Jag, the last words of the American F-16 mission commander hung in my mind like the punchline to a bad joke.

'. . . and the Jaguars will be shaving the rocks at low level.'

Red Flag had a fearsome reputation. It had been set up in response to the enormous aircraft loss rate during the Vietnam War. An analysis at the time had shown that a pilot's chances of survival were much higher if they made it through their first ten operational missions. The aim of Red Flag was to recreate the intensity of those missions in the relative safety of the United States.

'Relative' was the word. The enemy was not real in the skies over Nevada, but still there had been multiple fatalities as the complexity of the missions pushed the crews to the very edge of their capabilities. The crash report from a sortie during Red Flag which I had read during ground school had concluded that 'the Jaguar might depart from controlled flight near to its limits'. What deadly mistake had the pilot made that I needed to avoid?

After eight hours' planning the previous day, and three hours of mission briefing that afternoon, the Jaguar pilots were the only fools crazy enough to head out at night onto the Nellis tactical ranges at low level. There would be no moon. There never seemed to be a damned moon during night sorties; and, with no cultural lighting, the gloom would cloak every contour and visual cue.

I fumbled with the little torch velcroed to my index finger and scanned my kneeboard for a precise check-in time. Ten minutes to go.

Across the base, pilots were walking to their jets. Engineers held glowing marshalling wands like characters from *Star Wars*. The smell of dust and jet fuel drifted across the pan and the roar of the engines spooling up was like a giant wave that could drown the whole world. I plugged the radio headset leads into my jacket, then with my left hand I leaned on the jacket connecter until it clicked into the ejection seat. Immediately the radio chatter of a dozen voices filled my ears, the tense communication clipped and precise.

'Viper check.'

'Two.'

'Three.'

'Four.'

'Viper cleared to taxi runway 21 right. Caution, lighting failure northside of Foxtrot, hold short of Echo.'

'Ghost cleared for take-off runway 21 left. Stop climb 6,000 feet.'

There was a rumble in the distance as two huge after-burners raced along the runway. The aircraft became a faint silhouette against the distant mountains lit by the last grain of light from the setting sun. Every second or so, the twinkle of the jet's red strobe light winked at the night. I followed its path to my right as the jet accelerated up and away, the flames vanishing as the pilot cancelled the burn-ers and the strobe light becoming lost amid the glare of Las Vegas a few miles to the south.

The Jags were taking off near the back of the sixty or so jets in the stream. While the fighters tried to clear the air-space of aggressor fighters acting as the enemy, our mission was to drop down beneath the fray, sneak through unseen and release the laser-guided bombs strapped to our wings.

Time to taxi out. I released the park brake and gave the jet almost 90 per cent thrust to get her moving off the chocks. Directly ahead of me, the airfield lights momen-tarily disappeared from view behind the vast hulk of a B-2 stealth bomber as it taxied from left to right. It had ten targets to strike by itself. My formation had two between the pair of us. The Americans had evolved low-observable technology to a point where aircraft such as the B-2 were all but unseen by enemy radars and could fly almost as if shrouded in an invisibility cloak precisely where they wanted.

I swung the big cat's nose around to the right and sat almost directly behind the B-2, its huge batwing barely con-tained within the taxiway. To my rear I could see a formation of F-117 fighters taking up position for take-off after the Jags. The F-117 stealth jet had been developed in total secrecy at the Skunk Works in California, and had made its operational debut in the skies over Baghdad during the 1991 Gulf War. It was breathtaking to see the world's first stealth aircraft in the flesh, its angular wings forming a futuristic triangle as it sat 100 feet away, poised for action. It would be the last I would see of it for the rest of the night. Pincered for take-off between a B-2 stealth bomber and the F-117 stealth fighter – two up-to-the-minute, highly capable platforms – the mighty Jag looked just a little vintage.

It was warm still, almost twenty-five degrees Celsius. Weighed down with over-wing training missiles, fuel tanks and a laser-guided bomb, the Jag struggled to get off the ground in the heat and high altitude of Nellis. I rotated the jet at 190 knots, the minimum speed to get airborne at this temperature and a fraction below the maximum speed for the tyres.

I was transfixed by the rapidly approaching lights signalling the end of the runway. I pulled back on the stick and the aircraft nose rose slowly into the air. The airframe followed – reluctantly – and the green digits in the HUD seemed to hover as the altitude gradually increased to twenty feet. I reached for the landing-gear lever with my left hand and raised it. I immediately felt the drag increase as the gear doors opened and the aircraft hung in the sky, afterburners roaring, holding just over 200 knots, neither climbing nor accelerating.

Come on. Come on. You can do it.

Below, the red runway lights flashed past beneath my feet with the jet pointing steadily at the faint outline of the mountains stencilled against the night sky. I stared at the undercarriage indications. They took an age to blink from green to black. I felt the doors close with a reassuring thud through the airframe. The speed sluggishly began to tick over and increase.

The American pilots seemed to think we were hotdogging, holding the jets low to show off. Little did they know. Perhaps that officer at Cranwell when I was interviewed half a lifetime ago was correct in his assertion: that Jaguar pilots needed to rely on the curvature of the earth to get into the sky.

Once airborne, it was a case of trying to sneak around, stay low and evade every hostile radar in the airspace. God, how I wished to be unthreatened by radars in the same way as an F-117 or B-2. The Jags didn't even have a radar of their own, let alone a cloak of invisibility. Just the curvature of the earth, what Churchill referred to as 'the Mark 1 Eyeball' – enhanced by a set of NVGs – and a determination to fly as fast and low as the night ahead would allow.

They say, 'Train hard, fight easy' – and Red Flag training was certainly hard. Not that we were getting to fight. Perhaps that was the best thing for the Jag by that time.

The RAF had once been the greatest air force in the world, but in recent decades had shrunk in size and capability. Harold Wilson's 1965 government had delivered a body blow to British aviation with the politically charged cancellation of the futuristic TSR-2 programme, a contentious decision with repercussions still being felt decades later. RAF jets since then had served a Cold War purpose. They were loved by their crews but lacked the agility and innovation of both American and Russian fighters. In a world where the technological edge would determine survival, the limitations of RAF fast jets in the late twentieth century had created a defensive mindset from the off. As a nation we were behind the drag curve.

The Americans on Red Flag respected our contribution, but it seemed to be more out of a sense of inclusion and admiration for our plucky spirit than esteem for the teeth of the aircraft. The F-15s, F-16s and F-18s we faced could knock us out of the sky using radars and long-range missiles before we could even see them. The RAF had the Tornado F3 as its air defence fighter. As a converted Tornado bomber, it was pretty quick and a decent interceptor, but poor at turning, and little match for the modern peer fighters.

A couple of weeks after Red Flag, during happy hour at RAF Coltishall with 41 Squadron, the Air Officer Commanding 1 Group made his way across the bar towards me. This was my boss's boss's boss's boss – a very senior, not entirely amicable officer.

'How was Red Flag, Sutton?'

'Very enjoyable, sir. But I think the Jaguar might have had its day.'

He stiffened, muttered something inaudible, and stormed off to find the 41 Squadron boss to complain about his lippy weapons instructor.

It was not the first time that I had to explain away my naïve honesty, nor would it be the last. When I said this in March 2006, I had no idea that the writing was on the wall for the Jaguar. Just weeks later, everyone on the station was instructed to stop work and meet together in one of the hangars for a briefing by Station Commander Graham Wright. A few hundred faces stood together in silence and stared at our group captain, who did well to contain his emotions as he delivered the devastating news.

There had been a Defence Review. RAF Coltishall was to close within the year. The move rang out the death knell for the Jaguar Force. The pilots, engineers and supporting staff would be posted away from the jet we had all grown to love. It was emotional for everyone, whatever their capacity. We were not merely pilots, we were Jaguar pilots, and were proud of that.

I needed an escape tunnel. I applied to the Red Arrows display team and was shortlisted as one of the final nine applicants. I had a fabulous few days flying in the iconic red jets and the selection week in Cyprus was made into a TV documentary hosted by Julia Bradbury. Rather sensibly, they chose two Harrier pilots to join the team that year. I was given the news on return to the UK by the station commander.

'Sorry about that, Sooty, but you've been posted to the Typhoon. You're off to XI Squadron in about six weeks. They need an air-to-ground weapons instructor to bring in the strike capability to the frontline.' He drew breath. 'You're going to have a bit of a job on.'

He was right. This would be the first RAF multi-role squadron in decades. I couldn't quite take it all in. I reacted to the news in the same casual way that it had been delivered, but that's not how I felt. I had learned what it was to be a fast jet pilot with the Jaguar Force. I had experienced the last days of a passing era and was entering a new age at its very beginning.

After two weeks' leave, I reported for duty at RAF Coningsby, ready to climb into the cockpit of the sparkling new Typhoon, the most modern, most powerful multi-role jet in the world.

Earlier in the year I had seen a Typhoon fly a touch-and-go at Coltishall. The huge delta wing lifted the jet off the tarmac almost instantly. It roared into the sky, carved through the air and swept around the airfield, flying over the squadron and departing vertically upwards like a rocket. We all stood open-mouthed as the scream of the jet made the buildings vibrate.

I was standing beside our US exchange officer, Derbs. He stared skywards.

'The RAF is back, dude.'

13. Typhoon Strike

Never let an aeroplane take you somewhere your
brain didn't get to five minutes earlier.
Anonymous

I left the battle-hardened Jaguar team and arrived on a
Typhoon Force yet to define itself. The jets had received a
thorough kicking in the press for being 'an over-budget
Cold War white elephant' – 'an air show jet' that had little
role in the peaceful modern world. I thought about the
conflicts in the Balkans, 9/11, 7/7, Sierra Leone, Afghanistan, Iraq, Iran, and wondered if I was living on the same
planet as the western media.

New Formula One racing cars are normally met with
enthusiasm and new fighter aircraft often with derision.
The Typhoon wasn't the first to have a difficult birth in the
press. The utility of the Harrier was widely doubted until
it excelled during the Falklands War. The F-15, one of the
most successful fast jets of all time with more than 100
kills and no losses, was initially criticized for being too
large and cumbersome.

Racing cars are updated annually and prepared for specific races at specific times. There is no such certainty with
fighters on operations, and the stakes are higher. With a
fighter jet, a new concept can take years, sometimes

decades, to develop. A new aircraft will need to be in service for at least thirty years and the government of the time will have no idea when or how the fleet will have to be used in anger. Imagine designing a Formula One car now, for roll-out in 2035, to race sometime between 2035 and 2065.

The European Combat Aircraft programme commenced in 1979, three years before the Falklands War. The UK, Italy, Germany and Spain worked together on the project, after France withdrew a few years into the development phase. The demise of the USSR in 1991 triggered political wrangling over the future role of NATO, and the Typhoon became a bargaining chip in that debate. Yet the requirement for a modern fast jet was crystal clear after the first Gulf War, the sustained conflict in the Balkans in the 1990s and the need to conduct no-fly zones in Iraq.

The Typhoon began frontline trials and evaluation in 2003. The birth of a new fighter normally signals the end of the road for another, so it wasn't wholly surprising that the old guard loyal to the Harrier and Tornado forces were afraid for the survival of their own fleets and joined the press in putting the boot in. The new jet had yet to earn its operational spurs, but it was a class act, unbelievably agile, a nine G threat armed with a treasure chest of advanced weapons. It was the supersonic future.

RAF Coningsby, where the first Typhoons were based, had a different character to RAF Coltishall with its cosy ambience and Battle of Britain history. The Cold War air defence station was ringed by high fences and felt austere with its series of concrete hardened aircraft shelters. The runways were flanked by the windswept Lincolnshire

Wolds, the flat landscape dotted by isolated villages offering little in the way of downtime amusement.

Despite this, the air base in 2006 was buzzing with energy as it began to take on its new role. New buildings were popping up all over the place and the tired old accommodation was being refurbished. I was one of about twenty-five pilots posted to Coningsby at the start of something new, with the chance to shape the future on our own terms. The first two frontline squadrons were XI and 3. XI Squadron was leading the ground attack and multi-role capabilities; we had six pilots at first, before we grew to the usual fifteen. 3 Squadron was initially focussed on air defence and likewise slowly grew to full complement.

There was also a test and evaluation squadron which had done the early trials needed to introduce the Typhoon into frontline service. Andy Millikin and Pembers were on this unit. I continued to work closely with them, elements of the old team together again. At any one time we had about thirty jets on base, with about half serviceable and ready to fly. The rest were lodged in the hangars and concrete shelters, being pored over by the engineers. Logistics, intelligence and admin staff made up the rest of the team.

On the training unit I also joined forces with Will Saunders. He was an air-to-air expert from the Tornado F3. With my training as an air-to-ground tactics instructor, I had been brought together with him to develop multi-role tactics for XI Squadron, the first unit that would have that capability.

Will was gruff, outspoken and built like a rugby prop forward. He was the same age as me, but had a wisdom beyond his years. He often expressed reservations about the role of aviation industry contractors, an area that until that time I had never really thought about.

Shortly after Will and I arrived on base, we had an appointment with a contractor from BAE Systems, who arrived with a laser machine to map the exact contours of our heads. Using the measurements, they planned to make bespoke helmets with mounted sights that tracked your head movement in such a way that you could target another aircraft or point the camera at something on the ground simply by looking towards it. The design was revolutionary, a leap into the future, and provided an opportunity for Will's natural scepticism to emerge.

'I wonder if the laser's safe for your eyes?' he remarked. 'It wouldn't surprise me if BAE built a helmet that fits like a glove but makes you go blind during the fitting process.'

The contractor was tall and thin and wore a polo shirt; he overheard the banter.

'No, no. No need to worry,' he responded. 'The prototype's been through every check in the book.'

We sat still in the locker room, surrounded by flying equipment, while the contractor went about his business with the head-mapping laser machine. We must have looked like old women sitting under a hair dryer.

'When will the helmet sights be ready?' Will asked.

'A couple of months, apparently.'

'That'll be three years, then,' he responded.

Classic Will Saunders. His humour made the mountain of aircraft manuals and mission briefings all the more bearable. We had already established that I knew virtually nothing of the air-to-air world, and he knew little of air-to-ground. We were going to have to learn from each other.

For decades the RAF had procured jets for either bombing or air defence. The Typhoon was designed for both and would require empathy with and an understanding of two very different skill sets. No more than a handful of pilots in the entire RAF had overseas exchange experience on multi-role jets. The Typhoon was new to us all, with different avionics, handling, weapons and performance capabilities.

Will and I, together with a few others across the new force, had to write a tactics manual from scratch. We continually challenged each other's basic assumptions. Why this? Why that? How does this work? Why can't we try it another way? Will would get frustrated.

'We always did it like that on the F3 Force,' he'd say, and pause to stroke his chin. 'I have no idea why. Let's change it.'

I was the same. With the air-to-ground, he would ask fundamental questions that challenged the basics. There was no right way, there was just a Jaguar way, or a Tornado way, or a Harrier way. Unencumbered by a stifling force culture, we had the freedom to set a new path. It was liberating, revolutionary, and not without its critics, who felt more comfortable trying to steer things back towards more familiar territory. It was a time of creative tension.

First off, though, I had to learn how to fly the thing.

Climbing into the Typhoon cockpit felt as if you were entering the space age. Unlike the big cat with its archaic dials and hidden switches, the layout was simple, almost sterile, with all the information the pilot needed on the head up display and three colour TV screens. It was well designed and intuitive. In a few minutes, pilots could get to grips with the cockpit information. After a few sessions in the simulator, I was comfortable with the basics.

The Typhoon chiefly consisted of carbon fibre wrapped around two massive Rolls-Royce engines and over six tonnes of fuel. With 40,000 pounds of thrust, it was more than twice as powerful as the Jaguar. The thrust and manoeuvrability were beyond anything I had ever imagined an aircraft could achieve. At any altitude, engaging full reheat (the afterburners) caused an acceleration that felt like a kick in the back. From a standing start, the jet outperformed a Bugatti Veyron – as screened on TV for a *Top Gear* challenge – and it would keep powering on until it reached a top speed of Mach 1.8, almost twice the speed of sound. It would climb at more than 10,000 feet a minute without using reheat. From take-off with reheat, it took you almost vertically skywards.

It had totally carefree handling. This meant you could snap the control column back as hard as you liked at any speed and it would be impossible to overstress the airframe. Once, when intercepting a formation of Tornados at low level, I merged head to head with them at 520 knots. As they raced down to the right, I turned the Typhoon onto its side and pulled fully back on the stick to slow. That allowed me to turn in a shorter distance and get behind them quickly. With the jet in full afterburner, I could feel my chest tightening. My legs became painfully heavy and my eyeballs pressed deep into their sockets as the aircraft maintained nine G and continued to accelerate like a spaceship.

Unlike any competing jet in the world, it was impossible to stall, spin or lose control. If you slowed down too much, a warning voice that sounded like Judi Dench playing M in the Bond films would rebuke you through the headset: '. . . slow speed, recover . . . slow speed, recover . . .' Judi always had the last word. If you ignored her and persisted to the point where a normal jet would spin out of control, she would simply remark, 'Override', and an autopilot system would momentarily engage, advance the throttles, lower the nose, and hand the jet back to you at a safe airspeed a couple of seconds later.

The Jaguar had a mind of its own and seemed to be constantly trying to flick, spin, and throw you into a hill-side without warning. You had to watch it at all times, adjusting power, controls and speed and speaking to her in a soft, soothing voice. The relaxed handling of a Typhoon allowed you to concentrate on fighting, while the flight control software squeezed out every scrap of power and manoeuvrability without you having to worry about over-stressing the airframe or losing control. This gave you a significant advantage over aircraft that had to be flown to strict limits and required the pilot to be constantly looking into the cockpit and making adjustments to the G loading so as not to damage the airframe. In the world of air com-bat, where a fight can be won or lost in a fraction of a second, this marginal gain was a total game changer.

The operational conversion unit was still in its infancy and began with the limited aim of teaching us the funda-mentals of air-to-air only. This, as we all knew, left wide training gaps in large-formation tactics, missile defence, radar jamming, strafing, electronic warfare, the use of the targeting pod, close air support and ground attack – all key requirements for a multi-role jet.

British forces at this time were on the frontline in Iraq and Afghanistan, with further expeditionary operations in the Middle East on the horizon. At the top levels of the RAF, the culture of what was called 'single-role thinking' was widespread, and exasperating to those who had seen first-hand the Typhoon's multi-role capabilities.

On one occasion, when I was sitting in the crewroom with Will going over our notes, two senior officers came in and began making themselves a coffee. They both looked disgruntled.

'There's a lot of Jaguar pilots kicking around. They don't understand air defence at all,' one of them remarked.

'How can they?' said the other, shaking his head. 'Quite why they are making such a fuss about bombing is beyond me.'

'This jet is a fighter, pure and simple. It takes an entire career to understand air-to-air. All this chit-chat about "multi-role" is a pipe dream. Bombing with the Typhoon would be like taking a perfectly crafted gold-nibbed fountain pen and smashing it into the desk.'

As he spoke, he brought his hand crashing down onto the table, spilling coffee onto his pristine blue uniform shirt.

Will raised his eyebrows and grinned.

I rolled my eyes and smiled back. I knew what he was thinking.

'Jeez,' he muttered under his breath. 'Didn't Confucius say that "Real knowledge is knowing your own level of ignorance", or something like that?'

'He probably did. I can't remember,' I said. 'Not bad for a *Guardian* reader, Will.'

'Have you heard of John Boyd – a US Air Force colonel?' he asked, and I shook my head. 'He said you can either "be somebody or do something". He always spoke truth to power. All assumptions should be challenged, or what starts as doctrine becomes dogma. The guy was a genius.'

Will was well read. I admired that. He was also correct. When the past and the future are in conflict, the future always wins.

As a result of the invention of the missile, Cold War procurement had been myopically focussed on speed and nuclear weapons. Colonel Boyd's vision challenged that concept. He knew that for a fighter to be truly successful it had to be highly agile and able to out-manoeuvre other aircraft. In his words, able to pull enough Gs at 30,000 feet to 'roll down your goddamn socks'.

The RAF had followed the traditional Cold War doctrine with the Jaguar and Tornado. Nukes and speed. John Boyd had fought his way through the endless layers of bureaucracy to finally convince the Pentagon to procure the F-15 and F-16, the most successful and agile fighters on the planet – as I had witnessed first-hand going up against that F-15 over the North Sea in the Jag. With the Typhoon, the air force had found itself with a world-class jet that even Colonel Boyd would have approved of. We were back in the game.

At RAF Coningsby I was exposed for the first time to the murky world of service politics, budgets, sovereign capabilities and defence contractors. To protect equities and the capabilities of other fast jet fleets, there was a huge flap about what weapons should be added to the Typhoon and when. As a young officer, I had no vote and no say on priorities, and little interest in dipping my toes into that particular tidal wave.

With just thirty-four hours of Typhoon time in my logbook, I moved across the runway as part of the new XI Squadron, which included Will and four more pilots, four spanking new jets and a team of engineers. We took over a scruffy, refurbished building with whitewashed walls and lino floors, our new home for the foreseeable future. We had been pencilled in for an eight-week bombing exercise in May 2008 in the US, initially in Arizona, then at Nellis, the place where the Jag had shown its age during Red Flag. The purpose was to declare the aircraft ready for attack operations.

'No pressure, then,' Will observed.

Milli, Pembers and I focussed on writing the tactics manual and developing the strike attack techniques. After some trials work, we then had to train the other pilots with the Litening targeting pod and the Enhanced Paveway II (GPS- and laser-guided bomb), and in the strafe profiles with the aircraft's 27 mm cannon.

It was exacting and draining work that made us close as a team, but the pranks and banter were never far away – and necessary to let off steam.

On Christmas Eve, Will accomplished a faultless night intercept of a Russian Blackjack strategic bomber. But the fact it occurred at midnight in pitch-blackness meant that there was no imagery of this historic event, and the guys were teasing him that it had never happened. To provide 'proof', I mocked up a rectangular black image in Microsoft Word and added the caption: 'Photo of Will's Blackjack

Intercept, Midnight.' He was admiring my artwork when Milli bounded in and strode purposefully to Will's desk.

'What the hell's that?' he boomed.

'Sooty made it. He's such a knob,' Will replied.

'There you go, mate, it's evidence,' I insisted.

Milli looked at me, shook his head and looked back at Will.

'You're right. He *is* a knob.'

As the Typhoon tactics manual was completely blank, we had the perfect opportunity to develop original ideas and cut through the dead wood and superfluous dogma of traditional thinking. The single-seat jet was required to play multiple roles. For the Typhoon Force to fulfil its potential, it had to make things simple and effective. Expansive, overly complex tactics needed to go.

Pilots are taught the right and wrong way to do something. In training, especially, that is non-negotiable. That means a force is conditioned in the optimum ways of operating. On the flip-side, this can constrain and fix your thinking so that it is difficult to break out of it. We were at an inflexion point; a moment of cultural change. We were attempting to sequence the genome of the newly born jet from the DNA of all the fighters and bombers that had gone before – and adding our own twist.

The pilots from the Harrier, Mirage 2000, Jag, Tornado F3 and GR4, F-15, F-16 and F-18 all had their own cultures that were, in their own minds, definitively correct. Taking the best ideas from these competing voices and forming a 'Typhoon way' would take time. Slowly we began to discover the Typhoon's own rhythm, its hidden potentials and secrets.

The strafe profiles worked flawlessly, the jet diving down from high level at 450 knots, firing accurately and pulling five G to race up again into the deep blue, away from the threat of surface fire. There were, however, teething problems with gun fails, but these were a manufacturing issue and not in our power to resolve. Even when the aircraft was loaded up with heavy weapons, fuel tanks and a targeting pod, the thrust was such that you didn't need afterburners to get airborne. At height, it was smooth and forgiving, with such great visibility from the cockpit window it was easy to see the ground – critical for a bomber. I had flown the Jaguar in this role for some years. The Typhoon beat it in every way on the very first training sortie.

Close air support (CAS) was a skill that required many hours of exercises and training to achieve proficiency. It is an intense mission which provides air support – often dropping bombs – to assist land forces when your soldiers are close to the enemy, especially when they are in trouble. A radio call for CAS is often a matter of life or death, something I had first-hand experience of during secondment in Afghanistan, working as a fast jet integration officer.

Most army units have air support teams with specialist soldiers trained in directing strikes at critical times from artillery and jets. The most highly trained are the joint terminal attack controllers (JTACs), who can coordinate air strikes using artillery, jets, helicopters and UAVs – unmanned aerial vehicles, which carry cameras, target designators, and weapons designed to destroy or impede enemy activity. In the heat of the moment, the JTACs may be required to do this under fire, using little more than a hand-held radio and a scruffy map.

Across a theatre of operation, there would be dozens – perhaps hundreds – of friendly foot patrols on a daily basis. As most would not need support, the best way to use the fast jet fleet was to put aircraft over known hotspots or hold them close enough to be able to react quickly and get to wherever they were most needed. Pilots rarely know the soldier's voice on the radio, or the task they are about to support until the last moment – normally when it has already started to go south for the guys on the ground.

After teaching the tactics instructor course on the Typhoon, I found it a completely alien world riding in the back of a Chinook at low level over the deserts of Helmand Province, wearing body armour and carrying a rifle. In the fading evening light, the compounds and villages would pass by in a blur, pockets of civilization hunched around open fires against the winter chill as the sun set in a pinky haze against the red rocky sand.

A couple of months into my tour, we had just taken off from the UK base at Camp Bastion in Helmand, when the helicopter banked sharply. I felt a thud through the airframe and saw a bright stream of flares eject from the aircraft as countermeasures against a threat. I knew exactly how potent surface-to-air missiles could be against helicopters. For a few moments I braced in my seat, praying that whatever had triggered the countermeasures had been decoyed. We continued to race away over the desert and I suddenly realized how uncomfortable and helpless I felt as a passenger. It was a hell of a difference to sitting at the controls and knowing precisely what was going on.

We were lucky that day. Not so the 454 British troops who lost their lives in the long campaign against the Taliban, or the more than 6,000 sick and wounded who were aeromedical evacuees. Time and again, our soldiers found themselves ambushed and outnumbered. Desperate calls for air support were a daily occurrence.

On one occasion, I was sitting in my own pool of sweat beside a rusting metal shipping container, waiting to get into a Chinook, with the forty-degree heat baking my skull and the fine, powdery yellow sand whipping into my eyes. An exhausted British paratrooper slumped down on the plastic seat next to me. As he dropped his kitbag to the ground he let out a sigh.

'You OK?' I asked.

'Yeah, I guess so. On my way back to the UK,' he said. 'Can't wait to get the fuck out. I just lost one of my mates.'

We both put our forearms up to our eyes as the thump of the Chinook approached and the rotors kicked up a blast of sand and debris.

'I'm sorry. How'd it happen?'

'We were out on patrol and got hit by a home-made bomb in a massive contact. One of the lads lost both his legs. He was screaming his head off. Harry, my mate, ignored orders to stay still and crawled over to help him. He put tourniquets on both his stumps to stop the bleeding, then got himself killed by a second IED a moment later.'

'Jesus.' I didn't know what to say.

'Then another contact started,' he said, and glanced at my sweaty uniform. 'Luckily there was an F-18 jet around. They dropped a bomb and the Taliban scattered.'

In the heat of battle, the JTAC often has limited visibility on an enemy firing point and may have to cope with a mix of incoming bullets and rocket propelled grenades, as well as sometimes with casualties. For the pilot flying above the contact, with multiple combatants hiding in scrub, it is not always immediately clear which are the friendly forces and which are the enemy.

A troops-in-contact mission, and the immediate risk to life, puts pilots under enormous pressure to complete the strike quickly, enabling the ground troops to break contact and regain control. The jets may have just flown a hundred miles from another attack in a different part of the country. With soldiers in extreme jeopardy, pilots have to gain situational awareness rapidly and conduct close air support without emotion, suppressing that ancient, reptilian part of our brain that surges with adrenaline and urges you to act on instinct, not rational thought.

Coordinating an attack begins when a pilot receives a '9-line' radio brief from the JTAC, normally en route to the target. The 9-line contains key information on the target's location and description, the position of friendly troops, the effect required and the synchronization with other assets. In Afghanistan, a brief was often shouted through a hand-held radio in the middle of a firefight, with rounds searing over the heads of the soldiers. The JTAC must also make sure that there are no other assets, such as UAVs, helicopters or friendly aircraft, between the fast jet and the target – clearing an imaginary line between the two.

While listening to the brief on the radio, the pilot would be flying the jet with one hand, while writing the details down on a scrap of paper with the other. This may seem archaic in our digital age, but it is the quickest and most effective way to get the information from a dynamic situation on the ground into the cockpit. It gets the soldier and the pilot talking, a vital part of the process. Pilots learn to hear from the tone of the soldier's voice how urgent the situation is, and the most effective CAS missions are when the JTAC and pilot find a rapport.

The close air support required by a JTAC isn't always a strike. Instead, they may want overhead imagery to get an idea of daily life going on beyond their view, or they may be seeking specific reconnaissance information, such as whether individuals are a potential threat and are carrying weapons. When direct intervention is necessary, the required outcome is determined and the appropriate weapon chosen to achieve the result. The decision to strike comes with clear rules of engagement. The need to minimize the risk to friendly forces, prevent civilian casualties and avoid collateral damage to buildings and infrastructure is prerequisite.

Through lectures, studying tactics, memorizing procedures and training in the simulator, Typhoon pilots learned the processes and techniques of CAS before taking to the air with a Litening pod to train with JTACs in the field. During practice, they would also learn how to cope with the weather, night operations and integration with other jets and UAVs.

The debriefs in training, as in operations, were clinical. I found myself explaining dozens of reasons why an attack might have failed: a height error on a GPS coordinate, an unsteady laser, too much surface-level wind, or taking too long for the attack. Training was a process of repetition:

keep reading, keep learning, keep practising. Eventually it would start to stick and the weapon-handling and decision-making would become timely and accurate, with errors the exception. Errors on operations could easily result in casualties.

Fast jet pilots are used to the peer scrutiny of a formation debrief. Nobody pulls any punches. All the cockpit TV screens and the mission audio are recorded, and they are replayed in real time during debriefs for all to see. Errors are shared openly among the formation and, more broadly, across the force if there are lessons to be learned. Most pilots took instruction and criticism positively, but emotions did on occasions spill over when someone had underperformed and knew it. Occasionally, a more senior pilot would sit at the back of the room, arms folded and glare: challenge, if you dare. We always did.

After an intense year of training, the Typhoon Force joined the US exercises first at Tucson Air Force Base, then Nellis, in the summer of 2008 for eight weeks of live heavy-weapons practice. The force integrated with the British Tornados and US F-16s without a hitch.

'Better to be lucky than good,' joked Milli, quoting Napoleon, as we headed home with a multi-role declaration under our belts.

The Typhoon was set for anything the world could throw at it.

14. Scramble

It was a Tuesday morning in early March 2009, a grey day with the wind slicing across the turnip fields as I followed the airfield perimeter road and entered the metal gates that led to the quick reaction alert (QRA) buildings.

For the next twenty-four hours, with fellow pilot Ian Laing and a team of engineers, our job was to protect the nation's airspace. RAF Coningsby is one of two bases responsible for the security of our skies. The other is at RAF Lossiemouth in north-east Scotland.

On the call of 'Scramble', we would sprint to the hangar and, in minutes, be in the air ready to intercept any aircraft that had entered UK airspace without permission. We had been trained to interrogate, to offer assistance to aircraft in distress and to give the unequivocal ultimate warning: if you do not comply, you will be shot down.

I parked up, grabbed a file of papers on the passenger seat and buzzed myself through a large metal gate into the compound, the only access point through the razor wire fencing. I made my way into the small single storey brick building, where Ian was sitting staring at a computer. Today I was number two, and more than content that he was running the show. He stood and stretched his muscles.

'I've spoken to Ops. Nothing expected from the Russians. Should be a quiet day,' he said and hit the switch on the electric kettle. 'Fancy a brew, Sooty?'

'Thanks, sir. White, no sugar,' I replied. 'I'll just go and fluff the jet. Back in a tick.'

Ian Laing was a wing commander, tall with blonde hair, and in charge of running operations on the base. I was now a squadron leader, with another bar on my shoulder and a lot more admin, running the Typhoon qualified weapons instructor course. We had four students on the course, and if there was no call to fly, my day ahead consisted of generating tactical scenarios, writing sortie reports and planning a weapons exercise later in the year.

I walked across to the aircraft shelter, a substantial, thick-walled bunker next to the Ops building. My breath made icy streamers that were swept away by the wind blowing from the north-east. Low cloud hung over the airfield. The bunker inside was bare concrete with a GPS location painted on the wall in large white letters. Faintly glowing in the shadows, a Typhoon sat poised, fuelled and ready to launch with eight live air-to-air missiles and a loaded cannon.

The quick reaction alert role is the very lifeblood of the RAF. It harks back to the Battle of Britain, and for decades fighters have been held on high alert, ready to scramble twenty-four hours a day, 365 days a year. The Russians, for their own national reasons, strategic posturing and intelligence gathering, frequently approach UK airspace and quickly receive an armed reception. Since 9/11, QRA has been expanded to assist or escort hijacked civilian airliners or, if intelligence suggests the aircraft posed a strategic threat, to take the ultimate action. Having to shoot another aircraft out of the sky was unlikely. It wasn't something anyone would want to do, but there is a process in place should it need to happen.

Andy, one of the engineers, stood next to the jet and tapped away at a screen housed behind an aircraft panel.

'Morning,' I called, as I climbed the aircraft steps. 'Everything all right?'

'Morning, sir, just sorting a crypto load,' he replied. 'All good.'

One pilot. Five engineers. I was spoiled rotten.

'Thanks, Andy,' I returned, and he ducked back down again.

Looking at that armed fighter, I had the familiar feeling of imposter syndrome, that I was somehow going to get found out, that I had slipped through the net.

I dumped my flying jacket and helmet at the top of the metal steps next to the jet, did a quick walkaround to check everything looked in order, and wandered back to the Q building, more worried about the amount of paperwork I had in front of me than a Russian incursion, particularly as they normally came from the north and were hosted by our sister base in Scotland. I sat down in front of one of the computers and Ian put a brew down beside me.

'There you go, mate,' he said. He glanced at the file I had placed next to my computer. 'The QWI course?' he asked, and I nodded. 'Rather you than me. I'll let you get on with it.'

A pilot on Q mostly sits around waiting for the call that never comes. It makes you feel terribly proud and patriotic when you are first assigned to the role, but being confined to a small room with a couple of chairs and misted-up windows soon becomes monotonous. When the phone rings, you leap for the handset, but it's usually someone trying to get hold of one of the pilots to discuss a routine matter. Once I answered the phone and it was a lady from Lincolnshire trying to get hold of her aunt. How she had managed to get through to the Ops room for QRA I never found out.

'I'm terribly sorry, you have the wrong number,' I told her.

'Are you sure? I call her at this time every Tuesday.'

'Perhaps she's out,' I suggested.

'Very well. I'll try again later.'

For scrambles, a classified phone would ring, or a voice would sound on the telebrief speaker – a direct line to the fighter controllers.

I was idly scrolling the cursor down my computer inbox and could hardly believe my own ears when the telebrief snapped into life. Ian and I both stood instantly and I'm sure I had the same look of surprise on my face that I saw on his.

'QRA south, this is RAF Scampton. Are you receiving, over?'

It was the GCI (ground control intercept) controllers. They provided tactical command and control for the fighters.

'RAF Scampton, this is QRA south,' Ian replied. 'Go ahead.'

'We are getting reports from civil air traffic of a reported terrorist incident on a flight from the United States. A passenger has tried to break into the cockpit. The aircraft is currently over South Wales, descending towards Heathrow. We may need to launch you. Standby. Acknowledge.'

'Copy.'

My pulse raced. I instinctively tightened my G-suit ready to dash out of the building. There was an anxious pause as the seconds stretched. Ian had remained by the speaker and turned to me as I zipped up my immersion suit.

'Sooty, my jet's still unserviceable. It's going to need another hour to fix. If this goes, you are on your own.'

Before he finished speaking, the same voice on the telebrief burst back into life.

'QRA Scramble. Scramble. Scramble. Vector 210, climb flight level 450, contact London control. Scramble. Scramble. Scramble.'

I darted from the Ops room, head spinning, and slammed the scramble alarm as I ran past. The green button set off a siren that wailed through the Q building and all across the site. Engineers with panicked faces appeared from all corners and raced down the corridors and out to the hardened shelter.

A klaxon blared and a huge red light flashed above the concrete doors as they began to open automatically, slowly peeling back like a vast curtain. I ran through the gap towards the jet, which bristled with missiles and gleamed in the widening shaft of daylight. I shot up the metal stairs to the cockpit, pulled on the flying jacket over my immersion suit and grabbed my helmet. I zipped the jacket up as I climbed on the ejection seat and Andy pulled the steps away from the aircraft.

The klaxon continued to echo about the hangar as I slid down into the seat. I connected my G-trousers and radio leads, then strapped myself in. A quick flick of the APU and, with my left hand, I advanced the throttles to idle. The engines roared to life, producing a deafening noise in the cramped shelter. The adrenaline rush from charging out to the jet began to subside, and I caught my breath as

I brought the canopy down and went through the cockpit checks. With a quick thumbs up to the team, I rolled out into the grey morning light.

I relaxed into the normal rhythm of taxi checks and radio calls as I sped down the taxiway. I was cleared for take-off. I felt composed, energized, prepared for anything. I swung the aircraft onto the runway, made sure the ejection seat was live and threw both throttles straight into full reheat. The world became a blur as the jet screamed down the tarmac, the engines booming like rolling thunder. The air conditioning hummed in my helmet. Within seconds I was airborne. The airfield disappeared as I shot skywards like a bullet and all the blurred world turned white as I vanished into the cloud.

I set course to the south-west and was soon up at 45,000 feet, above most of the flotilla of airliners crossing the spine of the UK. The fighter controller's voice was female and focussed.

'Set course heading 210. Intercept my contact bearing 240 degrees, eighty-five miles, heading 095 degrees, flight level 180. Mission VID.'

VID: 'visual identification' – my first instructions were to find the airliner and report back to the fighter controller.

I set the auto-throttle to Mach 0.95, a fraction below the sound barrier. There was just enough time to make the intercept without shattering windows on the ground with a sonic boom.

The radar screen showed dozens of aircraft on the display, the little orange symbols merging together and overlapping in places across the black background. I had no idea what to expect after the VID had been completed.

Identifying the aircraft wasn't going to be easy with all the cloud about, but once I was behind the airliner the fighter controller couldn't provide much more help. My priority was to conduct a safe intercept. Different scenarios surged through my mind and I just hoped that whatever upheaval had broken out on board had been suppressed.

I had been airborne for ten minutes and had not been called off, the most frequent outcome from a scramble. I listened as civilian air traffic control moved other aircraft out of the way to clear a space for my intercept. It would have appeared as a routine deconfliction and the airline pilots sitting back on autopilot would have suspected nothing.

The fighter controller's voice broke in.

'Contact now bears 210 degrees, fifteen miles, you are cleared for descent and intercept. Report the aircraft type.'

The controller would have known exactly what aircraft it was but wanted me to radio it in to make sure there was no doubt or confusion. I descended through layered cloud and brought the speed back to Mach 0.8, eight miles a minute. As I stared through the gloom, I caught intermittent glimpses of something without being exactly sure what.

Then I became aware of a shadow emerging out of the murk. It was an airliner passing from right to left, directly in front of me. I rolled the Typhoon into a left turn to stay below and behind the aircraft. I wanted to make sure I wasn't seen by anyone on board. Once directly behind, I inched towards the jet, its outline becoming clearer as I got closer.

My palms were clammy and I was extra cautious with the controls. I was conscious of the devastating power at my fingertips and repeatedly made sure that all the weapons switches were safe.

Creeping forward through the intermittent cloud, I slowly closed up behind the airliner. I could make out that it was an American Airlines 767, probably carrying some 200 passengers into London from the United States. I had no idea what they would have seen on board, and they would have no idea that an armed fighter jet was just feet away, escorting them into Heathrow. I reported what I could see to the fighter controller, then slipped silently back and away, taking up a position further behind the airliner.

'New mission. Remain in trail of the contact, and report anything unusual.'

I acknowledged the controller's instructions and remained in trail, locking the airliner up with my radar in case it disappeared again into cloud. I took a deep breath.

This was a Tuesday morning. How could it be that I was shadowing a 767, by myself, in a Typhoon, hoping to God that it was a false alarm or the incident had been contained? Why didn't I have a more normal job?

We continued to cruise to the east, descending. Ahead, the cloud cover began to break. I could see the grey outline of suburban London stretched out before me, then the parallel runways of Heathrow. There were airliners all around. At least the 767 seemed to be coming to a safe landing. With about ten miles to run, I was instructed to turn north at 4,000 feet, and return to RAF Coningsby.

That was a close one.

I could sense the calm easing through my limbs. I breathed normally and the tension drained away. I just wanted to get back onto the ground now. Ten minutes later,

RAF Coningsby materialized from the gloom. I got the speed back to 220 knots, lowered the landing gear and turned onto the final approach. Nice and steady all the way down, with a quick check back on the stick with twenty feet to go. A little bump, and throttles back to idle. I was down.

Once clear of the runway, I taxied back to the QRA shelter and was met by the engineers and a fuel bowser. They immediately went about their tasks, checking the airframe and connecting the fuel. They would fill her up, kick the tyres and she'd be ready to go again in no time at all. I opened the canopy and removed my helmet. I could hear the clank of the compressor blades slowly turning as the engines wound down. The cold air tasted good.

Ian was waiting with a hot cup of tea as I walked back into the Q building.

'Two cups of tea from a wing commander today,' I joked. 'I could get used to this.'

'Nice work, mate, you're on *Sky News*.'

He pointed at the television. It had a live report of the scramble against a possible terrorist hijacking. How the news outlets had got the information so fast, I had no idea. I slumped down in a chair. As soon as the jet was refuelled, we'd call to say we were again ready on alert. Until then, I watched the pundits and experts speculate to reporters.

I thought about how, when you get airborne, you leave the normality of life on earth and enter a little personal cosmos. Every flight has its own quirks and peculiarities, but there is a recurring rhythm, like the flow of a story with a beginning, middle and end. That's why life as a pilot is so engaging. A career is made up of a bookshelf of diverse stories. When you close your eyes in bed at night, you reflect on the chapter of that particular day. It is a moment of completeness. Tomorrow a new page will be turned, and you never know how the tale will unfold.

Fate, though, had decided that my Typhoon would make a second appearance on TV.

A couple of months after the scramble, I was sitting in the boss's office with the other flight commanders waiting for the weekly planning meeting. Milli had everyone roaring with laughter as he recounted a story about a recent squadron night out in Edinburgh. The theme had been fancy dress, and one of the guys had crammed himself into an old wedding dress he'd bought from a charity shop.

The boss, Wing Commander Johnny Stringer, ambled in and we quietened down. There was nothing exceptional about the meeting. We were about to leave the room, when he stopped us.

'Oh, by the way,' he said casually. 'There is one more thing. The Queen's Birthday Flypast is coming up. It's going to be our job to lead it. Six Typhoons at the front, about thirty aircraft in all. Red Arrows at the back to finish, down the Mall . . .'

'Red, white and blue smoke,' Milli added.

'Indeed. All very British.' The boss paused, and glanced at me. 'Sooty, would you mind doing the honours?'

'Errr, yes, sir.'

Blimey, I thought, as we shuffled out. Here was a good opportunity to publicly mess up if ever there was one. I had no idea when the first Birthday Flypast took place, but there had been decades of them. All executed perfectly. As we left the office, Milli wasted no time in reminding me of the risk.

'Don't miss Buckingham Palace, mate, that would be embarrassing.'

'You'd be live on the BBC with Huw Edwards peering into the distance,' added James.

They laughed together.

'Wankers!'

Was this a poisoned chalice or an opportunity? My stomach was doing somersaults. If the jet worked, the navigation kit behaved, the thirty aircraft flew their formations perfectly, civilian aircraft stayed outside our corridor of airspace and the weather was glorious, it would be a cakewalk. What could possibly go wrong?

The moment I opened my eyes on Saturday 13 June 2009, I was straight onto the BBC weather app. A fine English summer's day was forecast. I breathed a sigh of relief, made Kate a cup of tea and tried to leave the house quietly without waking our one-year-old daughter. Kate and I had married in the summer of 2006, a lovely traditional ceremony in Devon under deep blue skies, and two had become three soon after. I closed the front door and stepped into the warm morning air. Time to get a lot of jets over the capital.

The formation was broken down into seven distinct elements which gathered in separate holds just over the Norfolk coast. They slotted into line, separated by thirty seconds' timing, as we set off towards London. All around us, dozens of light aircraft were airborne to catch a glimpse of the formation as it weaved its way southwards like a huge metal snake.

We had been allocated a corridor of airspace just for our use. My radar showed a thin, vacant flight path with all the sightseers staying clear. Our biggest risk was a mid-air collision with a lost Cessna that had strayed into the wrong piece of sky; easily done when there aren't any road markings, or signs to warn where airspace began and ended.

Buckingham Palace is enormous and the Mall is easy to identify, but you cannot see them from a distance because of the forest of surrounding high-rise buildings. Approaching at low level from the north-east at 300 knots, I crossed the M25 and pointed the Typhoon towards the heart of London's amorphous mass. I could see the Millennium Dome, the Barbican and the angular silhouettes of Canary Wharf off to the south.

Ahead and to the left was the iconic London Eye and I flew the speed, height and headings as accurately as possible. I kept checking the navigation kit to make sure it didn't let me down. With six Typhoons in close formation keeping a perfect V-shape, I tried my utmost to fly smoothly and to make heading and height changes gentle so that the rest of the formation could hold their positions.

As I looked ahead, the Mall suddenly eased into view, the crowds filling every space. The Union flags rippled and swayed in the breeze. Multitudes of cameras and smartphones were pointing up towards us and the television cameramen had us in their sights. At the far end of the Mall, the palace was dead ahead. With the aircraft camera, I could see the Royal Family standing on the balcony. We were bang on track. Thank God for that.

Twenty-nine aircraft flew over the palace, with the iconic red, white and blue smoke from the Red Arrows finishing the spectacle. We then swung to the right, passing into Heathrow's airspace, where all air traffic had been stopped for ten minutes to let us through. Next stop was RAF Halton for another flypast, then a left turn for the families day at RAF Brize Norton, before heading back to Coningsby. Job done.

I was greatly relieved after the palace. Having ticked that box, I allowed myself to relax a little and tried to enjoy the rest of the flight. Not for the first time when flying, I was reminded that you can't stop focussing until you climb out of the jet.

Near Oxford, at 1,200 feet, I noticed a faint blip on the radar in a place where a blip should not have been. I strained to look ahead but couldn't see anything. But there it was, a blip on the radar a little higher than us, a few miles away. We were closing fast. Then I saw something: a dot in the windscreen, dead ahead. To the right and left were a number of light aircraft. Whatever was just ahead, it was still a little higher than us, so we couldn't climb out of the way.

Bugger.

The dot suddenly bloomed in size. We were now about ten seconds away and needed to get clear immediately. The only route was down towards the ground.

'Windsor formation, *bunt*! Unknown aircraft on track at 1,500 feet.'

As I pushed forward on the stick and eased the formation down, a tiny microlight skimmed overhead, unwittingly right in the middle of the flypast airspace. Whoever it was hanging there precariously in the flimsy flying machine was about to have the shock of their life as Typhoons, Tornados, a Nimrod, a Sentinel, a VC10 and the Red Arrows whizzed directly beneath at 300 mph.

15. In Omnibus Princeps

Fighter pilot is not just a description, it's an
attitude; it's cockiness, it's aggressiveness, it's
self-confidence. It is a streak of rebelliousness and
competitiveness. But there's something else; there's
a spark. There's a desire to be good, to do well in
the eyes of your peers and your commander, and
in your own mind.

Robin Olds

My dream as a teenage boy was to fly. I knew that pilots
had ground tours in the RAF, but I had put it to the back
of my mind and quietly hoped that the day would never
come. But it had. I had spent six months hopping from
helicopter to helicopter around Afghanistan as a fast jet
liaison officer, working with the JTACs and trying to
nudge along the integration of the army and the air force.
It was an opportunity, if that's the right word, to see close
air support from the soldier's perspective. Hugely humbling it was, too.

I then became submerged in administration, working as
the personal staff officer to Air Marshal Sir Richard Gar-
wood, the deputy commander of the RAF. I was a kind of
executive assistant, a job that required endless meetings,
taking notes, organizing workflows and writing emails. It

was seen as a step up, but sitting in an office chair was rather less fun than strapping into an ejection seat. 'Staff tours', as they are called, are a necessary evil in the RAF. It was an education though, and, after two years, I was promoted to wing commander and sent off to the residential Advanced Command and Staff Course in Wiltshire. This was twelve months of studying leadership, operational planning and procurement with 300 officers from across the armed forces of fifty different countries.

The move to staff college came at the end of what had been a tough thirty months for me personally. My father had died suddenly just before the Afghanistan deployment. I had prioritized work above everything else and, with the constant pressures, my relationship with Kate had suffered. After Afghanistan, I had felt more detached, which I was aware of without being able to resolve. We had grown more distant those past few years. I had not communicated properly. I had buried my concerns and focussed on work to the detriment of our relationship. Ultimately, we separated. I blamed myself for all of this. It was a hellish thing to have to endure with everything else, although we remain friends, which is a huge blessing, and very united in raising our daughter.

Back at staff college, the months passed in a blur of study, which in itself provided a coping mechanism of sorts. Towards the end of the academic year, on a bright, sunny June afternoon, I was called into the office of the divisional director. He was at his desk, staring at a file, and I briefly glanced out of the window at a groundsman mowing a cricket pitch. It was Friday and I was ready for the weekend.

'I've got some news, Mike, the postings have come through. Grab a seat. Just finishing this; with you in a sec.'

It felt like another one of those moments that had become far from unusual, where a short email or a statement relayed by an officer you barely know determines your fate for the next few years of your military life. I was desperate to get back into the air again, but it was far from guaranteed. There were any number of headquarters I could be posted to, a seemingly infinite quantity of staff jobs and only a handful of positions flying.

Play the game, Mike. Pretend you're going to be pleased with any 'challenging opportunity'.

The director rose from his desk, picked up a sheet of paper and walked over to me.

'It says here you are off to command a Typhoon squadron. 1 (Fighter) Squadron to be precise. Congratulations.'

I had stood as he walked towards me and now felt as if I needed to sit down again. I wondered if I'd heard right.

'1 Squadron?' I repeated. I needed to hear him say it again.

'Yes. Lossiemouth, aren't they? You're off to Scotland in a couple of months. Good luck.'

We shook hands. I walked down two flights of stairs, holding the handrail in case I fell. My knees were shaky. The posting was totally unexpected. In the Royal Air Force it did not get any better than 1 (Fighter) Squadron. I felt humbled and unworthy and proud to be put in charge of such an illustrious unit. Proud, and just a bit terrified.

My knowledge of running a squadron was limited to watching other, more experienced pilots in the role, and privately wondering whether I would ever be up to the job.

Before I drove north to the base at Lossiemouth, I did a refresher course on the Typhoon and spent every moment getting back into the tactics. In over three years out of the cockpit, the procedures and equipment had evolved.

Wearing the colours of 1 Squadron was more than significant. It meant everything. The entire team on every level was proud to be in the squadron and become a part of its history: the oldest military flying unit in the world and one that had been involved in just about every conflict Britain had faced since the beginning of manned flight.

Since being commissioned at Cranwell, I had spent almost every working hour in training, studying and, without my knowing it, being prepared for the challenge I now had ahead of me. I had rarely been responsible for giving orders, just following them. From the moment I got my feet under the desk at Lossiemouth, I was on the steepest learning curve of my life.

I had always seen parallels between fighter squadrons and professional sports teams. Both require training, focus, teamwork and camaraderie; all essential ingredients to achieving a common goal. I had studied and tried to absorb the concepts of marginal gains advanced by Sir Dave Brailsford, the coach who had brought home a hatful of Olympic medals for British cyclists, and Sir Clive Woodward, the coach and former rugby player who took England to Rugby World Cup victory in 2003.

Mike Seares had managed his squadron like a rugby coach, focussed and disciplined, but always fair. He was a good role model. So was the US Air Force general Robin Olds, a triple ace, whose book sat on my desk. He had fought in the Second World War over Europe, and he was considered the best air force commander of the Vietnam War, with more than 150 sorties under his belt. In 1949 he was made the boss of 1 Squadron, a remarkable achievement for an American-born pilot. He remains, to this day, the most revered fighter pilot in the US, on account of his fearsome reputation in air combat and as a passionate wartime leader.

One important principle of leadership was reinforced for me by Bertie Beddoes, a Tornado navigator I'd met in Afghanistan.

'People don't mind the crap,' he told me. 'As long as someone takes the time to explain why it's happening, and why it's important.'

Servicemen and women are trained to follow orders. On an operation, it's crucial that people trust that what they have been told to do is appropriate. On occasions, there may be no time for explanation or discussion. However, in my experience, there normally *is* time to explain, to answer questions, to listen to feedback. Just because someone holds senior rank, it doesn't make them any more insightful than those under their command, and they certainly do not have a monopoly on good ideas. In fact, the best ideas often come from the youngest members of the team.

The junior engineers of 1 Squadron were no exception. They were incredibly enthusiastic and astute, and they often possessed impressive university degrees. The squadron's newest pilot, the outdoorsy and fair-haired Tom Hansford, had gained the callsign 'Rainman' due to his insanely good memory. He had a first-class degree in astrophysics from Oxford and had written his thesis on something so esoteric involving satellites that no one else had any idea what it involved.

From the outset, I decided to explain my decisions and welcome discussion and criticism from all the pilots. They deserved candidness. I wanted to shape a team that would live up to the squadron motto, *In omnibus princeps* – 'first in all things'. To be the best, we had to get the tactics right *every time* and maintain detached honesty with every mission debrief. By not micromanaging, and by providing empowerment across the unit, I would gain the headroom to deal with the challenges ahead, not just the daily firefight.

One of the risks of single-seat tactical training is that much of it is self-contained within the aircraft. As a formation, or even a squadron, you are often left to mark your own homework. Peer judgement and fear of failure are important motivators, as is performance during international exercises. The pilots of 1 Squadron were well aware that our focus was on multi-role tactics. With openness in debriefs and the cockpit TV screens on full view, there was nowhere to hide from errors. I was not immune from making mistakes and had bad days, the same as everyone else. I would invariably feel disappointed in myself, that I had somehow let the side down. Exactly the same gnawing feelings of underperformance I had experienced during flying training would emerge once again from the shadows. Flying is a great leveller and needs constant focus.

To respond to a tactical situation in the best possible way, you have to know the disciplines inside out. Novelty in the air was not encouraged. We thrived on knowledge, automotive skills, trained responses and repetition. This might appear counterintuitive for such a dynamic environment but, on the contrary, we had learned to be extremely disciplined when flying and to instantly select the ideal action to tackle a constantly changing scenario. This was not dogmatic – far from it – but the execution of a carefully constructed game plan. As with athletes, so much of performance is in the preparation.

We placed a premium on thinking and mission analysis. For millennia, surprise has been one of the key components of warfare, and innovation was at the heart of our closely guarded tactics. But this had to be mapped out in great detail on the ground with clear heads – at one G – with the aim of being able to deploy our skill sets ruthlessly during the confusion of a dynamic mission.

A specific missile threat was best countered with *this* type of manoeuvre. A target of a certain construction would best be struck in *that* manner. The ideal speed and angle to intercept a low, slow-flying target were *such* and *such*. All were precisely rehearsed many times.

Any scenario that demanded an original response in the air was seen as a failure of forethought or planning. When we had reason to evolve our tactics, the experts would analyse the options, the documents would be reviewed, amended, learned and – like a flock of starlings – the whole force would adapt to the new pattern. That was the theory.

Fighter pilots have to be able to operate under severe pressure, at night, in massive formations, and at immense speeds and G-forces, countering threats, employing weapons and working through an electronic attack that would degrade onboard systems. This requires a calm, composed mindset engendered by constant training, mission rehearsal and debriefing on a daily basis.

Good pilots are made in the air. There was a constant push to offload training onto the simulator. This was cheaper than live flying and had benefits, but also limitations. The simulator did not reproduce the sentient experience, the same psychological pressures, the physical sensations and resilience earned by time carving through the skies at nine G. Synthetic training has its place and will continue to evolve and improve. But a squadron that flies more is invariably tactically better than a squadron that leaves the end-to-end system gathering dust in the hangar and focusses on synthetic training. The simulator is good for training the mind, but performance is not gained through thought alone. There has to be a balance.

We needed to develop swing-role tactics, bring the new Paveway 4 precision weapon to frontline service on the Typhoon, train daily with our peer squadrons, deploy on exercises throughout the world with our NATO allies, and hold readiness for global air operations. The key to all of this was tactical proficiency. The rest was secondary.

The tactical side was run by the weapons instructor, Alex Thorne – Thorney – a gifted pilot in his early thirties who was incredibly tactically astute and hated the banality of admin with a passion. Jonny Anderson, the former Parachute Regiment soldier, was always a discreet, stabilizing influence. Together with the other pilot flight commanders, Bobby Winchester and Chris Wright, and the senior engineers, they ensured I was freed up to concentrate on running the squadron – although, even then, some things remained beyond my control. Pilots were weighed down by base admin, the endless flood of emails, and the other military requirements which were intrinsic to being in the RAF but which had little to do with the primary role of tactical flying.

What seemed bizarre to everyone, and particularly those pilots seeking promotion to squadron leader, was the requirement to prove their talents by completing so-called 'additional duties', such as organizing a formal dinner or doing charity work. Without these boxes ticked, they would stand no chance of advancing in rank, regardless of their abilities as a fighter pilot. I doubt that the NHS chooses consultants in this way: 'Dr Smith, you've been very good with all the brain surgery this year, but as you haven't helped with the crèche or organized a charity cake sale, we're sorry to tell you that you haven't made the grade.'

Dealing with personnel matters like postings, career development and personal issues was an enjoyable part of the job. I wanted people to feel supported. The days also filled with risk and flight safety meetings, endless report writing, the constant hosting of visitors ranging from air cadets to HM the Queen, media liaison, deployment planning and the continuous drumbeat of supporting military tasks, which varied from taking part in local parades to ensuring that the priceless Squadron Standard made a safe appearance at a retired officers' dinner half the country away. I often wondered what Robin Olds would have made of it all.

My intention was always to lead the squadron from the front: to fly as much as everyone else and continue to teach airborne tactics. It wasn't always possible and I regretted losing time to the paperwork. I recalled a friend at South-ampton University, who was doing an IT course, and who told me computers would save the world's forests by increasing efficiency and doing away with our constant need for paper. I don't know about the rest of the planet, but in the RAF the opposite seemed to be true.

General Olds was again full of wisdom when it came to working with engineers and ground crew; in 1 Squadron, 130 men and women from all walks of life, with their own ambitions and differing experience:

> Get to know those people, their attitudes and expecta-tions . . . Don't try to bullshit the troops, but make sure they know the buck stops with you, that you'll shoulder the blame when things go wrong. Recognize accomplish-ment. Reward accordingly. Foster spirit through self-pride, not slogans . . . Only your genuine interest and concern, plus follow-up on your promises, will earn you respect.

Genuine interest. Follow up on promises. Recognize accomplishment. Olds's biography *Fighter Pilot* told of a bygone era, but many of the lessons endured. I set clear priorities and boundaries. I was open to adapting our pro-cesses when needed. But when it came to the engineering, I'd had no training whatsoever and had to completely rely on the expertise and judgement of the ground crew.

I considered myself lucky to have Tim Lowing, the senior engineering officer, a slightly unconventional and highly intelligent squadron leader who was never afraid to roll out in a tweed jacket, and Warrant Officer Dave Bowman, Mr B, the man with the broadest shoulders – metaphorically speaking – I have ever met. They were a superb combination, both providing different perspectives and experiences, their diversity making the team stronger. A trusting relationship with Tim and Mr B was critical, and we became friends more than colleagues.

No matter how much paperwork piled up on my desk, I walked through the hangar every day to chat with the engineers. I was dazed by the complexity of hydraulic snags and engine changes and impressed with the engineers' utter dedication to getting the jets serviceable and ready to fly. Maintenance requirements were extensive, with a ratio of about ten engineers per airframe on the squadron. An engineer spends just as long mastering his or her trade as a pilot does their own, and my respect for the technical skills of the men and women who kept us flying only grew through my time leading 1 Squadron.

One thing I set up that proved popular was a rank-less forum where groups got together over coffee and spoke freely about their concerns. These raised some surprising issues, such as a corporal's smashed bedroom window not getting fixed for two weeks, or the poor availability of food on base after a night shift. I then did my best to find quick resolutions to these small irritations.

As a result of my being open, it wasn't that long before people began to approach me to talk about more personal problems, knowing that it would be in confidence and I would help if I could. By the time we were on operations twelve months later, the most junior guys and girls on the unit felt free to express their views and knew they had a voice. This was something that would pay off many times over. The engineers produced serviceable jets and the pilots got the flying hours they needed to sharpen their skills. As the squadron progressed, I became confident that we had given ourselves the best chance of coping with whatever was thrown at us.

Outside of the flying there were other capabilities to be maintained. One of these was the annual refresher training with the Browning 9 mm pistol. After twelve months of neglect, it was always a clumsy affair. Mr B looked me in the eyes as he watched a pilot drawing a pistol from its holster.

'Nae offence, sir, but I'm always nervous when I see one of the pilots holding one of those things.'

'Me too,' I replied, trying to look vaguely competent, and he gave me a supportive but unconvincing laugh.

Generally, the pilots were terrible at handling small arms. They could hit a target with an aircraft cannon from over a mile away at 500 knots, but rounds from a pistol that landed on a large target at ten metres always came as a pleasant surprise.

On one occasion in Afghanistan, I was travelling back from Lashkar Gah to Camp Bastion, where I would need a bed for the night. A Welsh regiment had found a bunk for me in a tent, but my flight was delayed and I arrived at Bastion much later than planned. I was met in a makeshift wooden hut by a burly Welsh sergeant who seemed to take an instant dislike to the RAF pilot from southern England who had kept him up. It was the Six Nations season and I thought of the perfect way to ingratiate myself. As he was a Welshman from a rugby-loving nation, I thought perhaps we could bond over a shared love of sport.

'Did you manage to catch the rugby this afternoon?' I asked him.

His features stiffened. 'What? Which match?' He paused, and then added, 'Sir.'

'The England . . .'

'You beat us by seven. It was 19–26,' he uttered and looked down at the table.

'Ah, I'm sorry.'

My efforts to build a bridge had failed miserably. I apologized as if it were my fault.

From his desk, he pointed outside towards my accommodation, one tent among a hundred laid out in a grid on the flat, rocky ground. It was dark. Some portable lighting vaguely illuminated the shadows. I could hear a generator hum. My rifle was hanging by its shoulder strap across the front of my body armour. As I turned to follow the sergeant's gaze, the rifle butt swept across the desk and knocked over a glass percolator. Hot coffee spilled into his lap, scalding him in the worst possible place, before the percolator rolled off the desk and smashed to pieces on the floor. He jumped up and away from his desk to relieve the sting, then paused and gave me another long, despondent stare.

'My wife sent me that,' he muttered. 'It only arrived yesterday.'

I apologized again and hurried out. It wasn't quite up there with killing the station commander's cat, but it felt like a close second.

Back at RAF Lossiemouth, the pilots came through the annual shooting exercises without any physical injuries, which I concluded was something of a win.

The Typhoon is a warfighting machine and you can end up killing yourself or someone else if you make the slightest misjudgement. As a team of fifteen pilots working closely together in the extreme circumstances demanded of the job, we established a sense of unity that would be hard to achieve in almost any other walk of life. The guys on the squadron were motivated, capable, hard-working. The environment was informal and the relaxed professionalism created a level of trust and brotherhood that extended into the social life, where sometimes, as the boss, I often found myself torn between joining in and trying to put a lid on it.

'High jinks' is the wonderfully understated term for social misdemeanours. It is a phrase that features in guidance for military personnel: 'A reminder that officers should conduct themselves with decorum, and that high jinks are not appropriate at the ladies' guest night,' and so on. While service discipline for more serious offences can be harsh – and for good reason – the response to high jinks normally results in the offender writing a formal letter of apology, which usually smooths ruffled feathers.

The apology letter is a universal military currency. 1 Squadron had been obliged to deploy them on several occasions at home and once during a NATO exercise working alongside Spanish, Turkish and French air forces operating more than fifty aircraft from a base in southern Spain. It was a decent training opportunity with some tactical benefit, and it showed we were good NATO partners able to integrate and cooperate. Diplomacy was the watchword. I briefed the squadron accordingly.

On Saturday night, most of the guys made their way into Albacete, the nearby city, with its lively bars and seafood restaurants. I was awoken at 3 a.m. by the sound of loud, raucous singing – in English – in the accommodation corridor. I then heard some muffled Turkish and more shouting. I was about to haul myself out of bed to investigate when it suddenly all died down.

In the morning I learned that it was one of the squadron's pilots who had caused the carnage before being ably returned to his room by Andy Layton, one of the engineers. By chance I bumped into Andy as I made my way into breakfast.

'Thanks for last night. That was totally unacceptable. The pilot's on a dry det from now and will write to apologize.'

'No worries, boss, it was fine. The Spanish jockey was quite pissed off, mind.'

The disgruntled officer turned out to be Turkish, not Spanish, and not just any officer, but the teetotal air force colonel in charge of the entire exercise.

An international sortie involving numerous formations operating across multiple borders was scheduled for Monday morning. I walked into the planning room and it sounded like a bazaar at the time of the Tower of Babel, with everyone trying to communicate in a different language. The tasking order was inaccurate and it was unclear whether the Portuguese authorities even knew thirty fast jets were going to enter their airspace. I felt for Thorney, who was trying to coordinate the rabble. Unfortunately, he had a nosebleed, which he was ineffectively trying to stem with a flying glove, the only thing available. He looked like he had just returned from a seal-clubbing trip.

Into this disorderly fray, the apology letter was delivered and it appeared to do the trick. The Turkish officer seemed pleased by the pilot's courtesy and I was pleased his grasp of English was far from perfect. His name was unpronounceable, and for the remainder of the exercise he was privately referred to by the team as 'the Spanish Jockey'.

The RAF can be – and usually is – wrought with modest tribal rivalry between different aircraft types; it's not a commendable quality, but it is the way of things. We had worked closely on this exercise with a Tornado unit – 31 Squadron, 'the Goldstars'. We had struck up a good friendship and so we decided on the last weekend to go out for a meal together. Bobby Winchester, my deputy, had even asked his wife to delay her elective caesarean section – against the doctor's advice – so that he could enjoy the evening and head back to Scotland the following day.

His request was not well received, and he had to fly straight back to the UK.

The rest of us sat down at the restaurant table and a pleasant waitress with long dark hair and olive skin gave out menus, which we studied. She spoke good English and was patiently explaining what various things meant. We passed round the baskets of bread and poured glasses of Rioja.

When she returned with the plates, she looked momentarily confused.

'Who ordered the squid?' she asked, as she peered at each of us.

'That was me,' answered Joe Murphy, a sporty young pilot on his first tour.

'Ah, yes,' she said, putting the plate down in front of him. 'Sorry, you all look alike.'

I glanced around the table. The waitress wasn't wrong – except that Murph was the only one there with a disappointed look on his face. He had clearly not expected the squid to come whole, with eight arms and two tentacles attached to its elongated body, and two black eyes staring up from the plate.

'You all right, Murph?' I asked.

'It doesn't look very happy, does it?' he replied. 'I thought it would be chopped up or fried or something.'

'What do you mean it looks unhappy?' Jonny asked him.

'The poor thing looks sad. I can't eat it.'

'Well, just leave it then.'

'But then it died for nothing.'

'Fuck that. Give it to Rainman and he can take it home. Rainman, get the squid.'

'Me?' As the most junior pilot, Rainman knew better than to offer more than the weakest of protests.

'Yes. And make sure it gets back safely to the UK,' Jonny insisted.

Rainman took him literally, wrapped the squid up in a restaurant napkin and shoved it in his pocket.

Shortly after we returned to Lossiemouth, I was on quick reaction alert and going through the normal arrival process for the twenty-four hours on duty. I was surprised that the second pilot hadn't arrived at the designated time, but almost immediately the door swung open and Rainman burst in with his flying kit half on.

'Sorry I'm a bit late, boss. Rachel said the squid had started to smell and threw it out,' he explained. 'I only noticed when I was about to leave the house, so I had to go through the bins. I found it and put it back in the fridge. She's not very happy.'

The off-going pilots looked quizzically at each other.

'What's she unhappy about?' I asked him.

'The smell, I think. Maybe the whole concept. But it's safe now. She won't touch it.'

Later that day we were mulling over the problem.

'The truth is, it's seen better days,' Rainman said. 'I think it's starting to decompose.'

By this time, the dead squid was becoming something of a squadron mascot. Rainman thought through the problem until he found the solution.

'What we need is some formaldehyde,' he announced. 'But God knows where I can get it from.'

'Check online,' I suggested.

He turned straight to his iPhone. eBay did not disappoint, and he sent off £10 to buy a jar of formaldehyde from a seller in Birmingham. Rachel, his wife, received the purchase notification within moments and sent her husband a text: 'Why on earth have you just bought formaldehyde?' He read it aloud and looked worried.

'I think I'd better ignore this,' he said, and put his phone back in his pocket.

In August, I took some time off, picked my daughter up from Devon and flew to Sweden, where my brother Peter was living with his wife Elin and their three children. One evening we had a barbecue on the beach. Peter and I stood in the sunshine and watched the four cousins splashing around in the water.

'How's Kate doing? We haven't seen her for over a year now,' he asked.

'She seems well, actually. Teaching keeps her busy.'

He pointed at my daughter sprinting along the beach and smiled.

'Look, she's having a fabulous time. It's so great to have you both here,' he said, and turned towards me with a more serious expression. 'Can't be easy running the show and being a single parent all of a sudden?'

'We manage. Probably no harder than having to learn Swedish and eat rotten fish from tins at Christmas.'

'And don't forget their bloody Christmas porridge.' He grimaced.

'Trouble is, I always feel guilty when I have to go away. It's difficult to get the balance right in the military.'

'Don't think I don't know what the RAF asks of you,' he said, and changed the subject. 'Elin was chatting about ISIS the other day. The Swedish news is full of it. Do you think you'll have to get involved?'

'It's pretty unlikely. The west doesn't seem to want to get dragged in at the moment.'

He was about to continue when the kids came running up the beach with wet sandy faces, demanding ice creams.

16. Very High Readiness

The officers' mess is a great place to socialize on an RAF station but it is only for officers and that excludes 80 per cent of a squadron. Non-officers use the sergeants' mess or the junior ranks' mess. 1 Squadron needed somewhere that we could all get together as a team, regardless of rank, experience and trade, and so we decided to build a squadron bar.

A disused mezzanine floor off the back of one of the hangars was converted and it was named the Robin Olds Bar after our esteemed former CO. General Olds epitomized the qualities of a maverick aviator which we most admired. Even as he rose through the ranks, he had little patience with hierarchy and cared most about those under his command. He also famously loved a party and married the Hollywood actress Ella Raines.

Nights in the new bar raising a toast to General Olds followed long days of stringent, non-stop training. The Paveway 4, the most capable precision weapon in the RAF arsenal, had been integrated onto the Typhoon and we were impatient to show its capability.

Our chance came with Exercise Red Flag in January 2015. We set off across the Atlantic for Nellis Air Force Base – where the temperature would be twenty degrees higher than in Lossiemouth – with eight Typhoons in formation with a Voyager refuelling tanker.

The Typhoons were almost at idle alongside the tanker at 280 knots, so I used the time to practise with the Litening pod: tracking vehicles, generating coordinates, carrying out simulated target runs. As we cruised in cloudless skies at 20,000 feet across mainland USA, the pod provided a precise image of the ever-changing US landscape: boats lazily crossing the churning, murky brown Mississippi River, queues of pickup trucks at small town drive-throughs, the vast rocky expanse of the Grand Canyon.

Nellis sits among low ranges of sandstone cliffs, which provided a stunning backdrop as our two four-ships of Typhoons levelled along the airfield and peeled off, touching down one by one on the 10,000 foot runway. As we taxied past a pair of waiting F-15s, they raised and lowered their airbrakes, a huge flap of metal along the spine of the jet. *Welcome*. No pressure. I shut the engines down and, as I did so, the triangular foreplanes parked vertically. From the front, the jet looked like a cobra.

The RAF had returned. The last time I had been on Red Flag was in the Jag, a dying ember of the single-role, Cold War RAF. This time we arrived in nine G, Mach 1.8, 55,000 foot multi-role fighters.

Red Flag in the Jag had felt like we were involved but not necessary. The opposite was true in the Typhoon. The US Air Force put us right up front at the start of the fight, 'tripping the line', embedded with the newest jet in their inventory, the F-22 stealth fighter. The other US jets were still there – dozens of F-16s, F-15s, F-18s, and the B-2s. In the Jag we had hidden behind them. Now they were waiting for us to clean up the air picture. A few days after landing in the warmth of Nellis, we had our first mission.

I could feel the adrenaline building; 35,000 feet, holding steady at Mach 0.9. Just under the speed of sound. I gently banked the jet into a left turn to roll out pointing west towards a growing threat of aggressor jets. I glanced to my right. A Typhoon was sitting just off my wing, the airframe easing up and down gently in formation. I could see the dark visor and oxygen mask of pilot Dan Jones – Danjo – staring across towards me and occasionally glancing down into the cockpit, assessing the navigation, timing, and defensive systems.

With a quick wave, Danjo rolled away. The huge delta wing disappeared to my right, becoming a grey speck then vanishing from view into a tactical formation several miles away. Another pair of Typhoons were off to the south. I glanced down at my radar. Dozens of fighters appeared in the far distance as orange symbols against the black background of the display. Bright red radar jamming lines began to appear across the screen. My pulse quickened and I could hear the intake of my breath through the oxygen mask.

'Commit.' The codeword to commence the attack.

The mission leader's voice grated through the radio and I threw both throttles into full afterburner. Huge flames spiralled from the aircraft jet pipes and the sudden acceleration felt like a hefty shove between the shoulder blades. Simultaneously, all four Typhoons raced skywards. Outside, the temperature was minus fifty degrees Celsius and the supersonic air formed patches of grey mist as the shockwaves blasted over the canopy.

The voice of the fighter controller sitting at a radar display in a command and control aircraft fifty miles behind us broke into our headsets. The tone was urgent.

'Five groups, tracking 090 degrees, 30,000 feet, hostile.'

I kept the jet climbing, through 45,000 feet, easing above the highest of the clouds. Ahead, I could see the scratches of white contrail lines emerge from the horizon into the sky towards us. An airborne claw. The defensive aids computer shrieked to life with a warning siren. Multiple fighters ahead.

'One targeted. Two targeted.'

With my left hand on the throttles, I used my index finger to move a cursor across the computer's display, hovering it over a radar contact racing towards me. I held the control column lightly, flicked my thumb to select a radar-guided missile and checked as the targeting information emerged in the head up display. Good radar lock. The target was in range.

'Fox Three.' The codeword for missile launch.

I squeezed the trigger and racked the Typhoon into a left-hand turn and immediately pulled back hard on the control column to get the nose moving. I felt a bead of sweat slide down my forehead. The G-suit tightened around my chest and legs as the G-forces clamped me tight into the ejection seat. As the jet bit hard and buffeted in the airflow, thin wispy-white trails sprouted from the edges of the wings in contrast to the arid desert below.

Rolling out, I pointed away from the threat and pushed the stick forward to zero G. I felt another surge of acceleration and the speed increased through Mach 1.4 as my body weight rose from the ejection seat with my shoulders held tight by the seat straps. High and to my right, I glimpsed a supersonic F-22 race past a few thousand feet overhead, a closure speed between us of almost 2,000 mph.

186

The sleek black outline vanished behind me in seconds and was lost in the dazzling sun.

The defensive aids computer continued to squeal a chaotic melody of warning sirens in accompaniment to the fighter controller's hurried tones.

'Ghostman . . . threat . . . bearing 300 degrees, twenty-eight miles, 30,000 feet, hostile.'

The controller immediately called out another threat to a different group of friendlies. I heard a voice respond, straining under G and through the oxygen mask. The radios were non-stop, it was almost impossible to get a word in.

Suddenly there was an agitated radio call.

'Defending . . . !'

An F-18 had been locked up by a radar-guided surface-to-air missile. The pilot would need to manoeuvre violently in all directions, release chaff and transmit electronic countermeasures if he had any hope of breaking the lock.

'One away . . .'

A Typhoon from our formation flown by Lewis Cunningham – Lex – placed the cross hairs from his Litening pod onto a tank hull lying in the desert, fired the laser and guided the Paveway 4 straight through the turret. The high explosive bomb ripped through the hull, leaving a cloud of smoke and dust. Instantly Lex was targeted by fighters launched from an airstrip twenty miles to the west. Switching into air-to-air mode, he retaliated with a volley of missiles before hauling the jet away and accelerating back to the east.

All around, fighters locked each other up with their radars. Some merged together and turned in air combat, some evaded surface-to-air missiles, some sought out their ground targets. My helmet-mounted sight presented bright green digital cues showing where the rest of my formation were, some of them now twenty or thirty miles away. Most of the fighting was beyond visual range. Through the canopy, the serenity of the cirrus clouds and the desert floor miles beneath belied the chaos and intensity of the moment.

A Predator drone, piloted remotely from a cabin a hundred miles away, maintained an orbit 20,000 feet below, keeping overwatch for a couple of helicopters as they kicked up the dust while hovering twenty feet above the desert. To the east, several air-to-air refuelling aircraft waited patiently in their holds, while the airborne command and control jet continued a relentless radio transmission detailing the evolving air picture.

'Ghostman 3, you're dead.' The American controller's voice hung on the radio.

It was time to head home. Out of gas and, for one of our formation, out of luck. Pretend dead, 'shot down' by an aggressor aircraft. The Paveway bombs had been high explosive, but the missiles simulated. Dozens of fighter aircraft began to converge as they made their way out of the airspace. Above, a couple of silhouettes flashed past, probably F-16s.

I set a course back to Nellis with a Typhoon sitting in close formation on my left wing. Bobbing gently in the late afternoon air, it was a rare moment of calm. Ahead, a huge highway threaded a snaking path through the baked mountains towards the urban sprawl of civilization. We'd be down in twenty minutes, then the joy of a six-hour debrief.

It would be valuable, and every aspect of the mission would be scrutinized: long-range missile shots, electronic warfare, air combat, surface-to-air missile defence and precision strikes. It was exhausting, frustrating, compelling. I felt like I'd just been in a vortex. But it turned out we were barely out of first gear.

Abu Musab al-Zarqawi had founded the Islamic State of Iraq and Syria in 1999 and declared jihad – holy war. In early 2014, ISIS fighters drove Iraqi government forces out of key towns in western Iraq and seized Mosul, a cosmopolitan city of two million people on the banks of the River Tigris. As the jihadis marched on across vast swathes of Iraq and Syria, what had begun as a ragtag band of terrorists transformed into a self-proclaimed Caliphate, with its own flag, taxes and bureaucracy. ISIS forced religious sharia law onto a population that was now in the millions. The terrorists had seized the territory's oil wells, and the cash made by selling off black-market crude was being used to fund the onslaught and procure weapons.

US troops had already deployed to Syria. The UK national narrative remained uncertain. Having just withdrawn from Afghanistan, there was little political appetite to plunge back into the Middle East. But if that changed, I knew we would be the ones in the firing line.

From September, we assumed a state of very high readiness. This meant the squadron would be first out of the door if something kicked off internationally. All frontline units were on a rotational cycle of readiness blocked into four-month chunks, with training focussed accordingly. Low readiness meant that core skills exercises could be conducted, periods of leave taken and the general tempo marginally reduced. One in every four cycles was the highest level of readiness. In the run-up to this period, the high-end proficiencies needed for any conflict scenario were drilled and sharpened. These included day and night air defence, air combat, close air support, complex strike profiles, electronic warfare and defence against threat missile systems. The list went on.

If a training flight was below par, it would be analysed in forensic detail and flown again with guidance on how to do better. Sortie debriefs would last for hours. There was always room to improve the small percentages that, when added together, made a tangible difference. This was the most important thing for operating fighters: not the ability to fly, or the knowledge of tactics, but the desire that lay underneath all of that. By September we had fifteen fully qualified multi-role pilots and a fully manned and qualified set of engineers whom I was extremely proud of. The work rate was unrelenting. Everyone knew what was at stake.

Morale on 1 Squadron was high and, to keep it that way, shortly before we took over as the very high readiness unit, there was time for an official opening of the Robin Olds Bar. We invited the Typhoon Force commander, Air Commodore Ian Duguid, a shrewd and well-respected former Harrier pilot, and a group of officials from the US Embassy.

While music played in the background, I stood at the bar chatting with the US air attaché, Colonel Travis 'Flak' Willis, a charming and confident F-15 pilot most at home cooking Texas steaks on a barbecue with frosty cans in the chiller. He pulled a face as he sipped his pint of bitter.

'How's the beer, Flak?' I asked him.

'Excellent, man. Room temperature – just how I like it.'

We were both laughing as the force commander strolled towards us.

'Flak was just telling me how much he enjoys warm beer,' I explained.

'That,' he replied, 'is called diplomacy.' Then his expression changed. 'Can I have a quick word, Sooty? Do excuse us, Flak.'

We moved into a quiet corner away from the bar.

'How's it all going?' he asked.

'I don't want to tempt fate, but OK, I think. The last two pilots to join us have completed training and are signed off as combat ready. It's been a busy summer.'

'That's good to hear.' He paused. 'It might be about to get busier. You're probably tracking the disruption in the Middle East at the moment?'

'ISIS?' I replied.

He nodded, and lowered his voice. 'I know you've got to keep up all the skill sets, but it would be wise to focus on the air-to-ground. The mood seems to be changing somewhat in London since the *Charlie Hebdo* attack and recent ISIS activities in the region. There might be a call for UK forces to increase their involvement at some point. But it's all pretty uncertain.'

Ian Duguid had mentioned the *Charlie Hebdo* attack, which had happened in Paris earlier in the year. After the satirical magazine published cartoons of the Prophet Muhammad, two French Muslim brothers, Saïd and Ché-rif Kouachi, burst into its offices armed with rifles. They killed twelve people and injured eleven more. These were journalists and cartoonists exercising their freedom of expression; news of their bloody slaughter had reverberated across Europe.

'That's understood, sir,' I said. 'As you know, we're scheduled for a NATO exercise in Spain in about six weeks. It'll be difficult to do anything from there.'

'I appreciate that. We'd bring you home.' His shoulders went up in a shrug. 'You know how it is; it'll probably amount to nothing. I just want you to be aware that there have been some discussions in the Ministry of Defence. For now, just crack on as normal.'

'Yes, sir.'

'Nice evening, by the way, thank you,' he said, and made his way back to join Flak Willis at the bar.

The force commander had given a vague indicator, but false starts were commonplace in the military. I had been on XI Squadron when a purported push to deploy Typhoons to Afghanistan had amounted to nothing; instead, it was the Tornado Force that had replaced the Harriers as they were withdrawn from the frontline and then retired from service. More recently, 6 Squadron – now a sister Typhoon unit at RAF Lossiemouth – had revved up for a deployment to Iraq that was quickly turned off.

I brooded over the warning during the weekend, and then shared it on Monday with the flight commanders in strict confidence. I made a couple of phone calls to headquarters first thing that morning. They confirmed that, for the moment, it was little more than rumours and speculation, and, sure enough, we soon set off to the NATO detachment in Spain. Meanwhile, I listened to the BBC in order to follow what was happening in the Middle East.

In Syria, President Bashar al-Assad was fighting on two fronts, against the jihadis carving out their Caliphate and the opposition militias trying to shrug off the dictatorship Assad had inherited from his tyrannical father. Any chance of opposition advance had ended with the arrival at Bassel al-Assad Airport of a fleet of dozens of Russian aircraft, including attack helicopters, Su-25 ground attack fast jets, and Flanker multi-role fighters. Russian fast jets entering the airspace changed the dynamic, escalated tensions and posed a serious threat to US-backed Kurdish forces fighting ISIS.

Russian geopolitical interests were clear: a permanent base in Syria and the roll-back of US and western European influence across the Middle East. If anyone had ever believed Vladimir Putin was a man the west could deal with in order to bring about a safer, more harmonious world, they were wrong. The bloodshed created by ISIS had provided a strategic opportunity for Russia.

In response, RAF ground attack Tornados had been redeployed from Afghanistan to Iraq and were now being armed with air-to-air missiles. They had been doing all the legwork in the Middle East for years and were slowly being retired from service due to the age of the aircraft. The force was stretched and the dwindling number of crews had done massive amounts of time away. With the Typhoons we had, in my opinion, the best multi-role fast jet in the world being held at very high readiness – just sitting, unused, on the tarmac at Lossiemouth.

The regions occupied by ISIS had become savage, medieval. More than 1,000 unarmed cadets at Camp Speicher in Iraq had been massacred in a single day. A Jordanian

F-16 had crashed outside Raqqa. The pilot had been captured and burned alive. For the oppressed Iraqi people, all
freedom had been lost at the hands of ISIS. Adultery,
alcohol, dancing, music and social media were punishable
by the cane, the whip, the severing of hands, decapitation
and crucifixion. Executions were commonplace. Boys
were brainwashed and transformed into suicide bombers.
Women were bought, sold and raped.

Kidnapped western journalists dressed in orange jump-
suits were beheaded on film that was shared across social
media, attracting more recruits to the jihadi cause and
a wave of assaults across Europe. In June, thirty-eight
tourists – thirty of them British – were killed by a gunman
in a Tunisian beach resort. In August, a terrorist attacked
people on a train making its way to Paris and was subdued
by passengers. In October, suicide bombers ended the
lives of more than 100 people in Turkey, and another 224
innocent lives were lost when a bomb exploded on a
Metrojet airliner that had taken off from Egypt.

On Friday 13 November, nine ISIS gunmen in a series
of coordinated attacks across Paris killed 130 people and
injured 416. I watched it unfold live on television with a
pain in my gut, just like millions of others across Europe.

On 24 November, a Turkish Air Force F-16 fired a missile that brought down a Russian fast jet operating close to
the Turkish–Syrian border. This was the first time in a decade that a NATO country had downed a Russian warplane.
The pilot had ejected but was shot and killed by Syrian
rebels on the ground while he was still in his parachute.

A few days later, in response, the Russians deployed
their most advanced surface-to-air missile, the S-400, to

western Syria. This potent weapon system had an extra-ordinary range, allowing it to engage multiple targets simultaneously in an arc that included southern Turkey, Israel and the eastern Mediterranean. Russian and Iranian forces assisted the Syrian regime to subdue the uprisings from both ISIS and Syrian opposition forces, while Assad's helicopter pilots dropped barrel bombs on the civilian population in Aleppo on a daily basis. ISIS had marched south at pace, expanding their territory, and now controlled more than four million Iraqis. The Middle East was disintegrating.

17. The Road to Syria

The world will not be destroyed by those
who do evil, but by those who watch them
without doing anything.

Albert Einstein

On the walls of my office at Lossiemouth, I had three pictures that I often paused to look at. Every time, they
brought me a feeling of equanimity and pride. On the left
was a colour photograph of a 1 Squadron Typhoon dropping the first Paveway 4 bomb, about a year earlier. Hanging
in the centre was a dramatically lit black-and-white photo
of 1 Squadron as a Royal Flying Corps unit at Clairmarais
airfield, near Saint-Omer, during the First World War. The
third was a painting of a 1 Squadron Hawker Hunter skimming under Tower Bridge in 1968.

Flying the Hunter was Alan Pollock, a fast jet pilot who
made this solo protest against the politicians of the day
playing down the fiftieth anniversary of the RAF. He circled
the Houses of Parliament three times, dipped his wings
over the Royal Air Force Memorial on the Embankment
then swooped at speed under the spans of the bridge. He
went on to beat up the RAF airfields at Wattisham, Laken-
heath and Marham. He landed back at RAF West Raynham
knowing his flying days were over. The government wanted

to avoid the publicity of a court-martial, so he was placed on 'sick leave.' Some years later, he was exonerated, the announcement receiving considerable support from the public.

The three depictions of 1 Squadron reflected the depth of our history, the fierce loyalty and passion we all felt for our country, and – for me – the potency the unit had displayed over the past year.

On our return from the NATO exercise in Spain, we went straight onto quick reaction alert while simultaneously preparing for a small air policing operation that might or might not have been required. A few jets were armed in QRA fit with air-to-air missiles, and a group of pilots and engineers had their bags packed ready to go.

It was the end of another hectic week when I dropped down in my office chair and opened my inbox as the rain tapped at the window. How on earth could so many emails have arrived in the couple of hours since I had stepped away from the desk, especially on a Friday afternoon? As I started to write, 'Sir, with reference to the proposed amendments . . .' the red secret phone next to my computer went off like a jumping cracker. I grabbed the receiver.

'Sooty, is that you?'

Bloody hell.

It was the voice of the force commander. He seldom called squadron commanders directly and I assumed the worst, that we'd messed up in Spain and I needed to apologize for something.

'Yes, sir, it is. How are you?'

'Fine, thanks,' he replied and hurried on. 'Remember we spoke a couple of months ago about Syria?' He didn't wait for me to answer but continued. 'Following the Paris attacks, there have been further discussions in London about the UK forces needing to do more. David Cameron is going for a vote in Parliament next week to authorize air strikes. If he gets the support, you are going to deploy.'

'Understood. In what role?'

'We don't know yet. There might be an uplift in Tornado numbers to conduct more strikes, but they are already very stretched. You're aware of the Russian presence.'

'Yes, I saw they've deployed Flankers and the S-400.'

'You might be conducting air policing, or establishing quick reaction alert. Potentially working alongside the US F-15s from Incirlik. Another possibility – you could well move into an air-to-ground strike role, doing close air support. We don't have any details.'

'Copy. So potentially multi-role, but we could be required for anything?'

'Exactly. It's unclear at the moment,' he went on. 'But you need to get ready to deploy in case Parliament approves.'

'Do you know where we'd be based?'

'No decision on that. Somewhere in the Med. Maybe Turkey. Maybe Akrotiri. You'll need to get some recce teams out.' He paused, and his tone changed. 'This may well be very fast moving. On Monday, we are going to release some new clearances for the jet, which you'll need for the operation – that is, if it happens. Some new countermeasures and targeting pod capabilities.'

'Understood.' I thought for a moment and grabbed a pen. 'How long have we got to plan? What size of deployment are we looking at?'

'I don't know. Maybe a week. The political situation is

far from clear. You would need to deploy six jets. As of now, you have to hand over the air policing contingency you're holding. Give it to Jim Walls's team on 6 Squadron and get yourselves ready.'

I made notes as he spoke.

'You'll be away four to five months. I must have an understanding of your requirements by Monday – pilots, engineers, support staff. Finally, Sooty, this has to be done in complete secrecy. Understood?'

'Yes, sir.'

'It is imperative that this does not get out.'

He put the phone down. My mind was racing.

Stop what you are doing, and get your squadron ready for operations, right now.

It had been the most remarkable phone call of my life. I glanced at my notes. My heart pounded in my chest. My first instinct was to make some calls and rush into activity. I stopped myself from doing that and turned off the computer. From the dark screen, I could see a faint outline of my reflection.

This is what it had always been about. This is what we had all trained for. If this was going to happen, I knew every one of the pilots would put their lives on the line without a moment's thought, to do what was asked of them. We had seven days to prepare. Maybe less.

Slow down. Think first. Think clearly. The secret of getting things done quickly is not to hurry.

With an almost inconceivable amount of information to consider, I needed to get the tasks into some sort of order and priority. There was no playbook for getting a squadron out of the door in these circumstances. Typhoons had been on kinetic operations only once before, in Libya, but under very different circumstances.

As the thoughts tumbled through my mind, I wrote them down.

- What surface-to-air missile systems are on the ground?
- What are the rules of engagement?
- What will our mission involve?
- What are the campaign objectives?
- From which country, with whom, and whereabouts?
- What are the likely target sets?
- How is the airspace coordinated and organized?
- How will the new countermeasures work?
- What equipment will we need to deploy with: computers, escape maps, pistols, clothing?
- What critical briefs will we need to refresh in the coming days – escape and evasion?
- What about Russian military activity?
- What preparation do the aircraft need?

As the current high-readiness squadron, we were fully trained in all core multi-role missions and had refreshed the numerous skill sets in Spain. During the previous months, every pilot had qualified again in air combat, counter-air missions, quick reaction alert, pre-planned strike and close air support, by day and night.

I considered all the minor admin that might catch us out – such as passport expiry dates, inoculations and air-crew medicals. As far as I knew, that had already been taken care of, but I would double-check. The first task was to move from a state of generic high readiness, then narrow our focus onto a specific mission set and ensure that we were ready for those exact requirements.

It was not going to be easy to explain why a frontline Typhoon squadron had decided to cancel all training flights for a week, then shut the hangar doors for preparation work and get the squadron ready for a five-month deployment *in complete secrecy.*

With my adrenaline pumping away, I considered setting up a full planning session but again changed my mind. I needed everyone to be rested and thinking clearly. Instead, I called a quick meeting with the flight commanders to hand over the contingency to 6 Squadron and plant the seeds of our new task. The rest we would pick up on Sunday, when everyone had had time to digest it.

Bobby Winchester, my deputy, had already gone home for the weekend. He had the wonderful quality of taking the job seriously, but not himself. I called him on his mobile.

'Hey boss, what's up?' he answered.

'The force commander just called. We might be on. First we need to hand over to 6. Can you get the key players together for 7 p.m.?'

We had been watching the news and discussing possibilities over the previous days, and he knew exactly what I meant. Over mobile phones, we couldn't talk in any detail about our plans.

We met two hours later. Everyone was quiet, focussed, poised. Friday-night plans were a distant memory. I glanced from face to face. These were not just my work colleagues, but friends, my best friends.

The 6 Squadron flight commanders took the handover

extremely professionally, then shuffled out to do their own planning.

'We have seven days to prepare for a potential deployment to Syria.'

I summarized the conversation I'd had with the force commander and went over the key points.

The atmosphere was electric, but controlled. No one needed any motivation. It was like flicking a switch. This is what we had all joined to do. I knew everyone's brains had gone into overdrive. A few notes were taken, and questions asked.

'Take Saturday off. Spend some time with your families and try to clear your heads. If you can. We will need to meet again on Sunday to get this off the ground. Headquarters needs answers on Monday.' I thought for a moment. 'We're going to have to join the dots as we go. We'll need daily meetings and we'll have to make decisions rapidly. Communication is key. If you're unsure about anything, talk about it, share it.'

The week ahead weighed heavy on my mind and I wondered how on earth we were going to crack it.

18. The Busiest Week

An appeaser is one who feeds a crocodile – hoping
it will eat him last.
                                        Sir Winston Churchill

I spent Saturday morning trying unsuccessfully to relax as
thoughts swirled through my mind. When a fog of complexity descends, clarity and fresh ideas come to me after a
run. I shoved my trainers on and jogged through town,
across the rickety wooden bridge and onto the soft sand
of Lossiemouth beach. The skies were blue with chilly,
clear November air and the waves lapped languidly onto
the sand.

When I got home, I called my daughter on FaceTime.
She told me about her nativity play rehearsals and that
she was excited to be the Angel Gabriel. It stung that I
wouldn't be able to be there, again, and would miss
another precious moment of her childhood, one of the
small, everyday occasions in life that it is so easy to take
for granted. If this all started, then Christmas, too, would
be a write-off.

The day I was supposed to relax, I didn't relax for a
second; I felt the tension ease only early on Sunday morning as I drove back to base. The squadron car park was
coated in frost, and there were only four vehicles parked in

a line. I swung my car into a space and walked around the hangar to the offices. The wind bit into my cheeks as I paced across the tarmac. The cold was invigorating. I could see clouds of showers forming over the hills in the far distance. I bounded up the stairs into the welcome smell of freshly brewed coffee wafting from the planning room. Waiting for me were the four senior members of my team. Bobby Winchester, the executive officer; the senior engineer, Tim Lowing; Jonny Anderson, who was in charge of squadron weapons and tactics; and Chris Wright, the flight commander in charge of training.

'Here you go,' said Tim, passing over a cup of hot coffee.

We took seats at a large oval table, aware of the deep significance of this moment and what this very table represented. Around the edges, the wooden surface was etched with the 1 Squadron battle honours from the Western Front in 1915 through the Battle of Britain, Normandy and Arnhem to the Falklands, Kosovo and Afghanistan. The twenty-eight awards unfurled round the table like a Bayeux Tapestry, charting the squadron's life from its roots far back in the dawn of flying to the conflicts of recent times.

I kicked off by thanking everyone for handing over the contingency task to 6 Squadron so efficiently on Friday evening. I then recapped what the force commander had said.

'We need to prepare in total secrecy. If Parliament votes for Syrian strikes, we will be getting involved.'

'Do you know in what capacity?' Jonny asked.

'Good question. It's unclear,' I said with a shrug. 'It

206

could be an air-to-air role, possibly from Turkey, and operating close to Russian and Syrian forces near Aleppo. We
would be acting as deterrence against Russian aggression
and protection for Turkish airspace. Just as likely, we might
be required for air strikes, either hitting targets in ISIS territory or conducting close air support for troops on the
ground. We may need to do a mix of all of these tasks.'

'So pretty much any type of mission,' Wrighty continued, and the others nodded in agreement.

I explained that we would deploy six jets, for five
months, then hand over to the next Typhoon squadron.
'First thing tomorrow, we will be getting some new targeting pod clearances and countermeasures. This will mean
some more flexibility for the Paveway 4 and better defences
against the surface-to-air missiles ISIS have got their
hands on. Jonny, you'll need to grip this.'

There was a momentary pause as everyone processed
the ramifications. I glanced at Tim.

'Immediate thoughts?'

'How long will the sorties be?' He was considering the
logistics footprint and maintenance requirements.

'We must plan for seven to eight-hour trips. Six days a
week.'

There were a few swift intakes of breath. Normal sorties were about ninety minutes. Tim was jotting notes
down as he spoke.

'I'll run the numbers on what that means in terms of
maintenance and spares. But first, boss, if we're going to
get ahead of the game with prep and servicing, we must
stop flying.'

'Understood. Flying stops right now.'

'We'll need to prepare eight jets to ensure that six are definitely good to go. We'll need to check every threat detection and electronic warfare system and get moving with the servicing requirements. It'll take a team several hours per airframe.'

'That makes sense. Please just do what you need to do and let me know if I have to chat to the head engineer on the base.'

I turned to Jonny.

'We've got a video conference with the Typhoon test squadron first thing tomorrow. They're going to explain the new pod capabilities and countermeasures. We'll also need to talk to the Air Warfare Centre about the weapons clearances.'

He knew exactly what to do.

'Copy that. I'll set up a brief for the pilots on Tuesday, when we've had a chance to digest. Everyone will have to be fully up to speed with all the mission types, as well as defensive manoeuvres for both the radar-guided and heat-seeking surface-to-air missiles.'

'The boys are current,' I replied, 'but a refresher won't hurt at all.'

'We'll need details on the operational procedures out in Syria, airspace restrictions, rules of engagement and code-words.' He paused as we reflected on the growing list of tasks. 'I'll double-check that all next-of-kin details are complete and we'll need to develop and brief an escape and evasion plan. I'll get Thorney on the case.'

I made a note. 'Good thinking,' I said, and Jonny continued.

'I'll speak to the squadron intelligence officer and get

him to produce updates on Russian, Syrian and ISIS threat systems. In the last few weeks, the Russians have deployed the S-400, their latest surface-to-air missile,' he said, and glanced from face to face. 'This is a serious bit of kit, with a range of over 200 miles.'

'The strategic relationship with Russia is on a knife edge. Putin's supplying weapons and missiles to Assad's forces,' I said. 'As I'm sure you all know, the Turks just shot down a Russian fast jet. Probably a miscalculation, but it shows how complex the situation is out there at the moment.'

'As well as the potential for weapon systems to get into the wrong hands,' Jonny added.

'Exactly. It looks like Iran is shipping out the latest portable heat-seeking surface-to-air missiles to the area, and ISIS have captured stockpiles from all over Iraq. That stretches the threat right across the board, from soldiers with AK-47s to the most sophisticated radar-guided missiles.'

I turned to Bobby Winchester, who had been listening quietly. He was the perfect foil as a deputy, someone I hugely respected.

'Manpower?'

Bobby was unfazed. 'We're in good shape,' he said, with his usual reassuring smile. 'We've got fifteen pilots fully combat ready. One is currently deployed in the Falklands, and of course we've got some of the guys on quick reaction alert this week. I'll try to swap them out. A couple are due to be posted to new jobs off the squadron in the next few months. I'll come up with a plot. We may need to cycle a couple of people through, but it's workable.'

I looked across the table at Tim.

'How are we looking with engineer numbers?'

'I've put Mr B on the case,' he answered. 'We'll get names.'

'So, what's the total footprint going to be?'

'We're looking at about 100 people in all, pilots, operations, engineers and logistics.'

Bobby was thinking ahead, as always.

'I do have one concern, boss,' he said. 'I know we have to prepare in secret, but are we allowed to tell the engineers and pilots what's happening?'

'I know, it's a bloody quandary isn't it,' I replied. 'Officially, I've been told to reveal the absolute bare minimum, basically just the people at this table. But that would mean entering a sort of lockdown which, frankly, won't work. The problem is, we won't be able to *not* tell the rest of the squadron. If there's no information, the rumour mill will run wild and people will almost certainly draw false conclusions.'

We were quiet for a few moments. The coffee cups were refilled.

'I was thinking about this all day yesterday,' I continued. 'I'd like to get everyone together tomorrow, tell them what's going on and be really clear about protecting the information. They'll need to tell their wives and partners they might be going away for some months. It would be unfair on the families if we keep them in the dark, and we'll need their support while we're away.'

I took a sip of coffee; the second cup's never as good as the first. I wasn't trying to force my opinion on anyone. I knew if one of the guys thought it was a bad idea, he'd speak up. My suggestion wasn't without risk. They knew that, but there was little alternative.

'I think that's the best option,' Bobby finally said; 'buy everyone in.'

'I want to treat everyone like adults. To tell them the truth and ask them to protect the information. Besides, I don't think this could be covered up in any case. We've got a great team. We're about to ask them to work at an insane tempo next week, then probably deploy on operations.'

'Agreed,' Tim said, nodding slowly. He would need the engineers absolutely focussed on the mammoth task they were all about to undertake.

'OK then,' I continued. 'Tim, can you get everyone together in the hangar tomorrow and I'll talk to them. If the parliamentary vote is positive, I'll also write a letter to all the families to be posted on the day we go.'

'Copied. I'll get Mr B to sort it.'

It was the first time that some of the men and women on the squadron were being deployed on operations and the letter I was still preparing was a personal note from me to their families, thanking them for their continued support of the squadron and reminding them that the deployment was necessary for national security and that everything would be done to minimize the risk to their family members while away.

We broke up and went about our own tasks. The fact that I did not know our potential operating location was an immediate headache. Before you deploy fast jets, it is normal to send a recce team to explore the foreign military airfield you are going to be working from and plan accordingly. That team would then provide critical information about host-nation support, weapons storage and infrastructure, accommodation, communications, airfield equipment, security and logistics. I had three experienced pilot flight commanders who could manage such a task and no solid destination on the table. To add to the conundrum, the selfsame pilots that I needed out of the door on the recce I also needed on the squadron to plan the deployment. With everything the week had in store, I was trying to add two and two to make seven.

It was also frustrating that our operations officer, Sophie Ashley, wasn't around to assist with the plan. She was incredibly organized. The guys listened to her and her presence would have been invaluable. She had already been deployed to the Air Operations Centre in Qatar on an unrelated routine staff rotation.

The first time I had spoken to the entire squadron had been two days into my tour as CO, and I had been pretty terrified. The 130 unfamiliar faces had stared intently back, and I had seen from their expressions that they had no idea what was in store with their new boss. I was formal, stilted, scripted. It had felt unnatural, and I vowed after that to be more personable, to relax and just be myself.

On this Monday, with the sea of pilots and engineers gathered in near-silence, I felt none of that former stage fright. They were now familiar faces, friends. We had been through a lot already that year. The shuffling and muffled murmuring stopped as I walked across the hangar. I spoke from the heart.

'I had a call from the force commander on Friday night. The Prime Minister is planning to hold a vote in Parliament to authorize air strikes in Syria in the next week or so. If that vote passes, we will deploy.'

There were a few hushed whispers.

'Potentially for air policing,' I continued. 'Or close air support. I don't know yet. The flight commanders are already developing plans. We are getting new capabilities on the aircraft right now, and the priority is to prep the jets for operations. The hangar doors will stay shut. All flying has stopped. Finally, my priority . . . *your* priority, is complete and utter secrecy. I want you to protect the information and protect my trust in sharing it with you all. You can tell your partners, but no one else.'

I paused again to let that sink it. There wasn't a sound in the big hangar.

'That means no social media,' I stressed. 'One stray Facebook post could derail the whole political agenda, and you know what that means: I'll be for the high jump. What you tell your families should be minimal and, again, it is very sensitive. If we don't deploy, we're going to look pretty damn silly talking about it.' I broke off, then added. 'I probably don't need to say this, but the week ahead is going to be one of the busiest of your lives.'

The emotions on the faces staring back at me varied greatly. Some looked shocked, blank, expressionless; some were excited, some anxious. There were a few questions, the same uncertainties that had arisen during the meeting the previous day.

'What I can promise,' I said, 'is you will know as much as I know. That's it, let's get to work.'

The atmosphere was tangible, buoyant. I got the sense that everyone in the hangar that day was aware that they were going to be making history. There was an excited mumble of approval, but no cheering, no backslapping. The chatter rose as I walked back across the hangar floor with Mr B. I felt relieved, but already my mind was turning to another meeting starting in five minutes.

'Jeez, what a week we've got,' he remarked, and lowered his voice in case the walls had ears. 'Mind you, the force commander will have your balls if it leaks!'

'Don't I know it.'

'I'll be keeping my eyes and ears peeled.'

'Thanks, Mr B.'

Jonny Anderson was glued to my side as we spent every waking minute bouncing between secret video conference calls and planning meetings. Far from being exhausting, it was exhilarating putting into practice everything we had trained for and the next two days flew by like a rocket.

The pilots rushed from tactical mission briefs to learning the new countermeasures, from last-minute simulator emergency-training to completing pre-deployment admin. We were like the levers, sprockets and springs of a giant machine winding up ready for blast off. It is strange preparing for operations without the certainty of the final order to go and knowing, too, that your life and the lives of your pilots would be in jeopardy.

I stood in the planning room as the intelligence officer placed a black ink-pad in front of me. I rolled my thumbs, then fingers, along the pad, and then pressed them onto the paper lying next to it. We each took turns to have our fingerprints taken for DNA records. It was a grizzly thought.

Thorney sat across the room, facing a computer screen, preparing a brief. When I had first arrived on the squadron, an outgoing flight commander remarked, 'Thorney has zero interest in the admin and trivia. He'll evade it at all costs. But if it's genuinely important, he's your man. He's got a backbone of steel.' His analysis of the squadron tactics instructor was spot on.

It was a relief when we got the information that – given the go – we would be based at RAF Akrotiri in Cyprus. It was a base I knew pretty well, having been there several times before. A couple of the pilots rolled out the European airspace maps and the team began to plot the outbound flight. I left them to it: they were more than capable of planning a six-ship out to that part of the world.

I made my way back to my office. I had been informed earlier in the day that the Armed Forces Minister was planning to make a visit the following morning. I thought of this as a positive sign, that the preparations were not in vain, but I couldn't help wondering what she was going to think, arriving into the chaos of a squadron preparing for conflict.

As I moved files from one side of my desk to the other, the door burst open. It was Mr B, his face red as a balloon.

'Sir, sorry to disturb you, but fucking hell, my guys can't get any kit out of the base stores for the deployment. The fucking storemen aren't letting them have any boots or desert stuff or nothing. They say they don't know anything about a deployment.'

'Well, at least we know the secret hasn't got out, Mr B.'

I called the station commander, Paul Godfrey, to ask for help. He had only been in post for a few days.

'Leave it with me, Sooty,' he replied.

The next day, bags full of kit arrived. Desert boots, combat rucksacks, body armour, respirators, the lot. The military is nothing without good logistics, and the guys had done an outstanding job. The show was slowly coming together.

We were in the midst of unpacking when Penny Mordaunt arrived with her host, Air Vice-Marshal Gary Waterfall. The final decision on Syrian air strikes had still not been made, but the appearance of the Armed Forces Minister on the squadron on a cold winter morning turned what had, until that moment, still felt like a planning exercise into something very real indeed.

As a Royal Naval Reservist and the daughter of a former paratrooper, Penny Mordaunt seemed at ease, and accepted the frenetic activity around her. She asked perceptive questions of the pilots as we swooped through the planning room and moved on at a swift pace to the hangar, where a few of the engineers were buried in the aircraft making final checks before the jets were signed off one by one as ready for combat operations.

'Wow, they are fearsome machines up close,' she said.

We stood in front of a Typhoon chocked, fully serviceable and ready for action. The peacetime aircraft markings had been stripped off and the jet had just had its defensive systems fully checked. I could tell by the minister's body language that she wanted to take a closer look.

'Would you like to climb into the cockpit?' I said, and she turned to me with a faint smile.

'I thought you'd never ask.'

She climbed the metal aircraft steps and cautiously

lowered herself onto the ejection seat of a 1 Squadron Typhoon. I followed her and knelt on the platform next to the cockpit. She gazed around at the dials, switches, levers, the mystery of it all. From the height of the cockpit, we had a good view of the other Typhoons in the hangar, the fleet of fighters sitting ready to deploy.

'If the vote for air strikes is passed,' I told her, 'this very airframe will be carrying weapons over Syria. The next time it takes off, it will fly into combat.'

She thought about what I had said. She asked some questions about the aircraft and, as I spoke, her role as Armed Forces Minister faded away and we were just two people talking about something that was deadly serious but intangible, where feelings are indefinable and there aren't any words to express them.

As she stood up from the ejection seat, she reached forward and tapped the jet's cockpit window.

'Good luck,' she whispered.

It was a poignant moment that stayed with me.

With that, she climbed down the aircraft steps, rejoined the escorting party and disappeared out of the hangar and into a helicopter back to London.

A week had passed, and the parliamentary vote had been set for Wednesday 2 December. The debate took place in the House of Commons and raged through the day and into the night. Never before had a bunch of RAF pilots and engineers understood the nuances and implications of a political 'free vote' with such clarity.

The Labour Leader, Jeremy Corbyn, was a well-known pacifist and was against military action of any kind. His position had become more isolated as the daily reports of

ISIS horror and brutality struck a chord of disgust with the public.

The Labour Shadow Foreign Secretary, Hilary Benn, however, summed up the mood of western democracies with an impassioned speech that brought the Commons to its feet with applause. He referred to ISIS by its Arabic acronym, *Daesh*.

> In June, four gay men were thrown off the fifth storey of a building in the Syrian city of Deir ez-Zor. In August, the 82-year-old guardian of the antiquities of Palmyra, Professor Khaled al-Asaad, was beheaded, and his headless body was hung from a traffic light. In recent weeks, mass graves in Sinjar have been discovered, one said to contain the bodies of older Yazidi women murdered by Daesh because they were judged too old to be sold for sex. Daesh has killed 30 British tourists in Tunisia; 224 Russian holidaymakers on a plane; 178 people in suicide bombings in Beirut, Ankara and Suruç; 130 people in Paris, including those young people in the Bataclan, whom Daesh, in trying to justify its bloody slaughter, called apostates engaged in prostitution and vice.

He appealed to our shared historic values as a British people who should stand up to tyranny. There was, he said, no doubt whatsoever about the justness of the cause. He concluded by addressing those Labour MPs who shared Jeremy Corbyn's opposition to air strikes.

> As a party we have always been defined by our internationalism. We believe we have a responsibility one to another. We never have and we never should walk by on

the other side of the road. We are faced by fascists – not just their calculated brutality, but their belief that they are superior to every single one of us in this Chamber tonight and all the people we represent. They hold us in contempt. They hold our values in contempt. They hold our belief in tolerance and decency in contempt. They hold our democracy – the means by which we will make our decision tonight – in contempt.

What we know about fascists is that they need to be defeated. It is why, as we have heard tonight, socialists, trade unionists and others joined the International Brigade in the 1930s to fight against Franco. It is why this entire House stood up against Hitler and Mussolini. It is why our party has always stood up against the denial of human rights and for justice. My view is that we must now confront this evil. It is now time for us to do our bit in Syria.

They were still debating at 5 p.m. when I called everyone together for a briefing. The vote had yet to be taken, but I felt certain which way it would go. I looked out again at the sea of faces in the half-light of the hangar. I felt privileged and humbled to be standing there in front of 1 Squadron on the eve of an operational deployment.

'Thank you for everything you have done over the last week,' I began. 'We're a great team, and I trust every single one of you. We are going to be working flat out when we arrive in Akrotiri and we all need to pull together. The hours are going to be long and we will be working through the night. The sorties will be involved, complex and drawn out. There will be teething issues and logistical problems. But we will get through it all, because to the left and right of every one of you are members of the finest squadron I have ever known. Together we can achieve whatever's thrown at us.'

The anticipation was palpable. There was a passionate sense of unity and team spirit that would serve us well.

'Finally,' I said, 'watch the news at 10 p.m. If the vote is yes, I'll see you back here at 6 a.m. sharp.'

I had written up the last of the notes that needed to be written, and the letter that would go out to the families; I had made all the phone calls that had to be made. It had been the busiest week of my life, but I didn't feel tired in the normal sense. I felt wired but at ease – the calm before the storm, I assumed, and headed home to the stone cottage I rented a mile or so from the base in the town of Lossiemouth. It was Christmas in a few weeks. Mariah Carey was singing happy tunes on the car radio. The houses along the way twinkled with red, white and blue fairy lights in the windows. It all seemed hugely inappropriate, and it stung that I would not be able to see my daughter before I went.

I had to suppress my feelings of guilt for putting her through the uncertainty and fear she would experience while her dad was away. Saying goodbye on the phone was not going to be easy, when what I really wanted to do was give her a big hug, tell her how proud I was of her and how much I loved her.

The debate rumbled on. I heated up some leftover lasagne that I picked at while I watched the news. Shortly after 10 p.m., the parliamentary vote for air strikes against ISIS in Syria was passed by an overwhelming majority.

I turned off the TV. I felt an immediate sense of relief

that the preparations had gone well and that we were ready, that the pilots were up to speed with all the skills they were going to need. I felt proud that I would be leading 1 Squadron on an operation that was justified, was supported in the country, and in which we would 'confront evil', as Hilary Benn had said. I also felt a massive responsibility to the men and women who had put their complete trust in me and for whom I would do everything to bring them all home.

The moment my head hit the pillow, I slept without dreams.

19. Heading East

A pink-grey dawn rose over the airfield and I stood with a few pilots and engineers on the tarmac watching as six Typhoons spooled up their engines with a roar that shattered the morning calm. The huge grey hulks taxied out as if in a procession and took off one after the other. They turned to the south-west and headed towards the vague outline of the tanker that was holding in the distance, its shadow just visible through the morning mist.

A wave of adrenaline washed through my body. Every time a Typhoon took to the air I felt inspired, that opening day of the deployment more than ever. The machine was both severe and majestic, unpretentious yet futuristic, restrained and clumsy on the ground while taxiing, but once airborne it burst into life.

Bobby Winchester was in charge of getting the six-ship down to Cyprus. Having joined with the Voyager tanker sent up to us from RAF Brize Norton, they would make their way down the length of the UK, across France, over the Italian Mediterranean and land, after almost five hours, at RAF Akrotiri.

An A400M transport aircraft had arrived on base during the night. I climbed the ramp with the rest of the pilots, engineers and support staff. There wasn't much talking. There were no certainties ahead of us. No one wanted to fail. The success of the team was more important than the individual and I had a strange sense of being involved in something bigger than myself, something difficult to define. Few people in the military ever have the opportunity to be the first to deploy their aircraft to a new theatre of combat, and we were reassured by our belief in the cause we were fighting for.

Soon after the Typhoons had launched, the A400M rumbled into the air. As it turned south, through the window I glanced down at the news teams filling the public roads and filming our departure live on Sky and the BBC. I was sitting next to Kev Broder, a squadron leader in charge of standards across the entire Typhoon Force. The seats were a long line of webbing straps, hung from a metal bar along the side of the fuselage. In front of us was a heap of rucksacks and bags. After the tension of the morning, it felt something of a relief to be finally on our way. I turned to Kev.

'This is completely surreal.'

'It's great the Typhoon is getting involved.'

We were both optimistic but knew what was at stake.

'We've got a busy few weeks ahead,' I replied.

'Wouldn't want to be anywhere else in the world.'

We had a plan, but, as the old saying goes, no plan survives first contact. Everything that past week had been rushed and I was sure I must have forgotten something that would turn out to be vital. I had sent out my letter to the families. I knew the words would be wholly inadequate for the anxiety they would be experiencing, and I felt a paternal responsibility for every member of the squadron heading out of the door. We too were a family, and one thing I didn't have any doubt about was that every single one of them was going to give their best.

The land slipped away beneath us as the A400M climbed into cloud. With a long flight ahead, we used the time to talk through contingencies, phases, priorities, knowns and unknowns. Kev Broder had come up from RAF Coningsby, our sister base, and would deploy with us for a month. His role was to see how we bedded in and developed new procedures. He would then design a training syllabus based on the operation for new pilots to get up to speed before they deployed in the future.

We had to get the first missions underway immediately and had been told to expect a target within twenty-four hours. That meant becoming *very* efficient *very* quickly and adapting to new circumstances immediately as they arose. The learning curve on a new operation is always steep – a high climb up the mountain without the peak in sight. You deploy on day one with a tactical plan, but unidentified threats and countermeasures, as well as weapons employment, airspace and communications issues, would likely require its swift evolution in response to the actual situation.

We would need to analyse, make tactical decisions and disseminate information rapidly from the very first sortie. The visionary Colonel John Boyd had created the concept of the OODA loop – 'observe, orient, decide, act' – which he used during combat operations. If we were to succeed, our OODA loops would need to be tight.

As well as maintaining good links with the Typhoon Force headquarters and our home base in the UK, we also had to develop relationships with key organizations that we would be engaging with every day. These included the RAF Expeditionary Air Wing at Akrotiri, which would provide operational and domestic support, and the Combined Air Operations Centre at Qatar. This was the United States-led HQ running the air campaign with its ranks of targeteers and specialist aircrew officers employed to direct and coordinate our taskings. There was also a team of lawyers to advise senior decision-makers and ensure targets were legitimate and legal, in accordance with the rules of engagement.

Crucially, I wanted to build relationships with the US JTACs. As my experience in Afghanistan had underlined, close air support is a process that is greatly enhanced by a rapport based on trust and understanding between pilots and the controllers: when the two are of one mind, it works far better. We were new to the operation and few US JTACs would have conducted air strikes from Typhoons. We would need to demonstrate our professionalism and form a bond of trust with the battle-hardened US soldiers.

We landed into a warm, muggy RAF Akrotiri. As the A400M's propellers wound down, the ramp lowered from the back of the aircraft and the briny Mediterranean air rushed in to meet us. The six Typhoons were parked up in a line, with the sun glinting from their canopies.

We grabbed our rucksacks and jumped into a waiting truck which took us straight to the squadron operations building. The engineers split into teams, some swarming around the jets to start the servicing, others setting up computers and equipment.

It was incredibly exciting to finally be on the ground, and I am sure Jonny Anderson felt the same as he strode towards me with a wide grin on his face. We took a spin around the facilities. They were basic at best: an ageing single-storey building with a few small rooms for planning and briefing. The rooms were furnished with grubby desks and plastic chairs. Faded cream-coloured paint was peeling from the walls, with paler oblong spaces where pictures had once hung.

There was a small admin office with a couple of computers and a separate room for our flying gear: G-suits, jackets, night vision goggles and our custom-made helmet mounted sights. These projected critical flying information onto the visor, so the pilot had information about the aircraft attitude, speed and height, as well as the location of ground targets when they were looking away from the HUD. It was frustrating that they had no night vision capability. The Gucci helmets remained in their boxes when it came to sorties in the dark and it was back to basics with the ancient NVGs.

A short distance away in a separate headquarters building was a larger room that would double up as a combined aircrew and engineering operations room. This would become our control hub.

The hours passed in a tumult of briefings, video conferences and discussions with headquarters. We had two aircraft fit to fly and the absolute bare minimum of equipment to launch immediate around-the-clock operations. With that in mind, some of the team had to find the accommodation and bed down, while the rest worked through the night to continue the set-up. Spares would be arriving over the next two days.

I was in the brightly lit engineering operations room discussing with Mr B all the things we didn't have but needed when the intelligence officer hustled in with a look on his face which registered both panic and excitement. Euan McFalls, an enthusiastic first tourist parachuted in at the last minute, rushed towards us. I glanced towards Mr B as he silently and slowly turned to face Euan. This hardy warrant officer wasn't used to being interrupted and fixed him with a Glaswegian stare.

Euan rocked back on his heels, slightly away from Mr B.

'Boss, sorry to interrupt. The HQ called a few minutes ago. The tasking has arrived for tonight.' He paused for breath. 'We need to destroy an oil pipeline in Syria. In the Omar oilfield. The timings are extremely tight. Thorney's just beginning to look at it now.'

It was nerve-racking with so little time to spare and I tried not to show it. We had been told to expect to launch a strike within twenty-four hours of arrival, but expectations are often followed by delays. Mutterings about potential missions for the evening had been changing by the hour. The arrival of a target pack ended the rumours and meant a formal tasking. I glanced at Mr B.

'I'll need to get into this. All OK with the jets?'

'Ken's on the case already,' he replied.

Mr B and I parted and I went to find Jonny Anderson. Given the complexity and the unknowns of that first mission, I had put myself down to lead it, with Jonny on my wing.

Outside, the sun was just beginning to ease towards the horizon, and the air hung thick and heavy. A shower was lashing down. The rain rushed though the guttering, sploshing noisily into the drains. In the distance were flashes of lightning and a band of thunderstorms was slowly making its way towards us, the clouds looming high into the late afternoon sky. I dashed quickly through the rain and found Jonny in the planning room. He had been studying the target pack and handed it to me. He pointed out the target analysis.

At first glance, the target looked impossible. The pipeline was buried deep within the bedrock.

'I'm not even sure the bomb's going to crack it,' he said.

'If we can't get the weapon deep enough, the warhead will have no effect.'

He nodded in agreement.

Our only hope was to put two weapons into exactly the same spot. A bullseye into a bullseye, the second bomb flying into the crater caused by the explosion of the first.

The Tornado Force had been operating in Iraq for some months and had been ordered to fly in company with us from Cyprus. The requirement to launch together, though, was pointless and added unnecessary complexity. Jonny and I in our Typhoons would be flying at a different speed and height, and we had our own target and refuelling times. The radios worked well at long distance. Tornados are not the most reliable of jets, and if we had an issue, it wasn't as if we could just pull over on the side of the road and talk about it with the other crews. It would have been far easier to go as two distinct pairs of aircraft; I had protested as far up the chain of command as my voice would carry, but my objections had fallen on deaf ears.

An hour later I was strapped into the jet. I took a couple of deep breaths and adjusted my position in the narrow seat. We would start our engines in exactly five minutes. Everything had been planned to the second.

It was time to finish off the cockpit checks. I made sure that the last of the aircraft systems were all on and serviceable, beginning with the threat radar detection aerials, part of the defensive aids system. These were going to be my eyes and ears, silently watching and listening in order to identify enemy radar throughout the night. The datalink had connected successfully and the Typhoon was receiving information on the position of other aircraft in the area. Aircraft from miles around appeared as little grey squares on the navigation display.

The moving map, in the centre of three display screens, showed my current position on an airways chart. By 'bumping' the cursor at the top or bottom of the screen, I could slide and zoom the map, as well as change the type of map and the scale. I had a long transit ahead, and there was just enough time to check the route had loaded correctly.

I moved the cursor to the right of the map, to the east, to check the navigation points. After a hundred miles or so, the map suddenly ended and the screen went black. I slewed it left again . . . all working fine. Then back again in the opposite direction . . . no map. I zoomed in and out, changed scale and changed map. Nothing. The mapping in the jet ended as we left local airspace.

Something had not been loaded, or something had failed. Either way, I could feel the blood drain and I cursed under my breath. It was going to make the mission a whole lot harder, as we navigated across multiple countries in unfamiliar airspace, when it came to finding the tanker, identifying targets and deconflicting from other aircraft in the allocated grids of airspace – all in the dark of night, in a rainstorm.

The default plan was that, if the other pilot was suffi-
ciently qualified, they would lead the formation and I
would become subordinate, taking the wingman role.

'Dragon 2 from 1.'

'Go ahead.'

'I've got a map fail to the east. Nothing mapped in the
area at all.'

'2, same here.'

Bloody hell, Jonny had the same issue. No maps for the
places where we needed them most. We could put some
GPS coordinates into the kit and that was it.

'Copy.'

We didn't need further discussion. We would fly blind
and stick with the plan.

To start the Typhoon's two Rolls-Royce EJ200 engines
requires an auxiliary power unit, a small internal jet engine
housed in the airframe. With a circular waggle of my index
finger, I let Jamie Robson know I was starting up. He gave
me a thumbs up. I then flicked the APU into life and eased
both throttles to idle power. The reassuring rumble under
the cockpit canopy meant we were on our way. My nerves
had gone now. The sweat had dried. I was a cog in the
machine. Map or no bloody map.

The pilots and the operations team were probably
standing outside the squadron building, the smokers
smoking, hearts beating faster as they heard the haunting
noise of the armed jets wind up their engines. A squadron
is a brotherhood. Accidents and mishaps have diminished,
but every time you take off in a jet you are putting your life
on the line.

From inside the cockpit, the big EJ200s hummed softly

at idle. Each engine packed 20,000 pounds of thrust, enough to launch the Typhoon vertically like a rocket after take-off. Like a supersonic Formula One car purring on the starting grid. I released the park brake and the jet immediately nudged forward.

Once clear of the rubber hangar, I pushed the rudder pedals a little to the left with my foot, steering the nose of the aircraft onto the taxiway between the line-up of parked Typhoons. Jonny's jet followed close behind. There were bright flight-line lights to the left and right, a dark sky above. Ahead was the aircraft arming check. I softly squeezed forward on the pedals to brake. A couple of engineers dressed in fireproof clothing dived under the aircraft and pulled the final set of safety pins from beneath the jets. We then taxied away from the harsh lighting of the aircraft line onto the dark taxiway parallel to the main runway. I could see areas of the night sky flashing and glowing with lightning. The gusty winds rocked the tail of the jet to the left and right.

The taxi took five minutes. Air traffic control gave us departure instructions to head south, climbing to flight level 310 (31,000 feet), our transit height as far as Iraqi airspace. After we read back the departure clearance, we were instructed to contact the control-tower frequency and await clearance for take-off. I had stopped the jet a few feet from the end of the runway. To my left I could see the airfield domestic site, mostly closed up for the night, the cones of car headlights slicing through the dark.

Pinpoints of blue light like cats' eyes guided us along the route to the main runway with its white lights on either side of the tarmac meeting in the distance. I ran through the pre-take-off checks from memory. Ejection seat pin stowed, seat live, canopy closed and locked, master arm switch to live – that would ensure all the external fuel tanks could be jettisoned into the sea after take-off in an emergency.

The fuel gauge was already counting down in increments at eye level in front of me. It was an hour and fifteen minutes' flying time to the border, assuming the upper level winds hadn't changed too much. We had another twenty minutes' reserve to find the pre-strike tanker and complete a lights-out night formation join and refuel. Thirty minutes' fuel to make it to the diversion airfield if something went wrong.

It was tight. Extremely tight.

It was one minute to take-off when the radio buzzed.

'Dragon, this is Ultra.'

'Go ahead.' My heart sank. It was the Tornados calling. Very rare just before take-off.

'Dragon, Ultra 2 had a problem on taxi out and needs to go back for a spare.'

'Copy. Have you got a time estimate?'

'Quick as we can. About twenty minutes.'

I took a deep breath. If they were one minute over, we would need to abort the mission before we had even taken off.

20. First Strike

Headquarters had insisted – ordered – that we took off as a four-ship, two Typhoons and two Tornados together. Now we were stuck at the end of the runway, engines humming, while the second Tornado taxied back and de-armed before the crew bustled into a spare aircraft and went through the whole start-up process again. I hoped someone back at HQ took note.

Unlike a car, the Typhoon burns a lot of fuel sitting on the ground at idle; about half as much as it would flying at 35,000 feet. Fuel is the fighter's lifeblood. You never have as much as you want and you watch the gauge as if it holds the power over life and death. The transit across the Mediterranean into Iraq was fixed. We could fly a little slower and higher to save some fuel, but not much, and there was no routing shortcut to be had. The distance from the tanker to a diversion, in case of an emergency – such as the tanker not showing up or a refuelling probe not working – was also fixed. The only variable was the time it required to bring three aircraft together to conduct a formation join at 300 mph.

I took deep breaths as I calculated the absolute minimum fuel we could take off with and still complete the mission. If it went below that number, the first Typhoon sortie on Operation Shader wouldn't even get off the ground.

My eyes strayed over to Jonny's jet parked up on the taxiway to my right. The shiny wet tarmac around the Typhoon danced with reflections from its pulsing red strobe light. A metronome for decreasing fuel and increasing pressure. A red heartbeat. Rain angled down, driven by the wind, spattering onto the canopy. Inside his cockpit, Jonny would be making the same calculations and watching the fuel gauge numbers relentlessly reduce. I knew exactly what he would be thinking. In the distance the thunderstorm clouds groaned and heaved with flickers of light as they advanced towards the airfield. There was no moon. It was the blackest of nights.

The twenty-minute wait felt like two hours. The fuel had fallen to a level so precarious that I was seconds away from aborting the mission when the radio crackled to life.

'Ultra 2 ready for taxi.'

'Dragon ready for take-off.'

We were down to about five minutes of spare gas, a ludicrous amount of reserve with which to fly across several countries and find a tanker, but we'd had enough of being on the ground and were desperate to get underway.

I released the park brake and the jet pushed forward. I followed the blue taxi lights over the white piano key markings that signalled the start of the runway and lined up the nosewheel for take-off. With my right hand on the stick, I eased both throttles forward to maximum dry power with my left hand. Even with a full war load in summer temperatures, the Typhoon didn't need afterburners to get airborne.

As the engines spooled up, inside the cockpit it was quiet except for the hum of the pressurization system and the reassuring rumble from the engines as the aircraft acceleration thrust me back into my seat.

By contrast, the noise outside on the airfield would have been a deafening roar that sliced up the air like a chainsaw and vibrated through every bone in your body. I loved that booming, defiant snarl when I watched a jet take off. Every pilot does. It connects with something in your core, in your very being. The sound of freedom.

Every time I took to the air in a Typhoon was like the first time. The sheer power of the aircraft was exhilarating, life-affirming. It charged down the runway as if with a will of its own, as if it hated those hours spent earthbound, wheels locked, the umbilical cord of the fuel line jammed in its guts, the engineers crawling over its body. Now, she was free.

The HUD only starts to read the speed at 50 knots. With a jolt, it sprang to life and jumped through 70 knots, 85 knots, 105 knots. The squally crosswind caught the aircraft tail, pushing the jet to the right, and I made tiny dance steps over the pedals to keep the nosewheel pointing straight. I glanced across to the aircraft warning panel. It was a reassuring black. All good to go. The speedo kept rising as I raced towards the line of red lights that signalled the far end of the runway and the inky black nothingness beyond.

At 140 knots with the gentlest pull back on the stick, the jet soared into the air. The ground fell rapidly away as I gathered height, twenty degrees nose up and climbing at more than 8,000 feet per minute. I lost all visual references in the darkness and flew solely on instruments. The toy-town houses lining streets aglow with street lamps, the churches and football stadium had gone, replaced by the void of a moonless night. The sea below was a black sheet hazily glinting the reflections of a few dull stars, the imperceptible horizon merging into the night sky.

Shifting patches of shadow obscured towering thunderstorms in every direction. Lightning flashes zipped across the gloomy horizon. A strike wouldn't be fatal. But it could puncture holes in the fuselage and send the electrics out of kilter. Looking down from above, the entire thundercloud glowed brightly, as if alive, a giant churning cauldron of hail, icing and turbulence that would wreak havoc with the seekers on precision weapons. With no weather radar on the aircraft, I had to visually weave a snaking course left and right to avoid the worst of the storm.

With the jet settled in a climb, I attached my NVGs and felt my head dip forward slightly with their weight. That moonless night with little ambient light provided only a grainy green image that was difficult to decipher, but it was better than the dense waves of black outside the canopy. I could at least make out the outlines of clouds ahead and the fuzzy image of a coastline away in the distance. Occasionally bright flashes of green signalled lightning to my left and right.

Jonny's voice on the radio broke my stream of thought. 'Tied,' he said.

'Copy.'

This let me know that Jonny was now flying in a trail formation position, about one mile in my six o'clock. His onboard radar would indicate where I was, but he would still have to fly his aircraft manually, in and out of the cloud, in order to stay in position for the transit to Iraqi airspace.

A few minutes later, I heard the Tornados checking in with air traffic control. They were now airborne too. It was the last we would hear from them all evening.

It was calmer at altitude. Most of the thunderstorms were now below us. The fuel gauge ticked away and the engines hummed as the aircraft cruised at Mach 0.85, a groundspeed of about 600 mph. The radar screen was dotted with airliners cruising towards their destinations, passengers snoozing or watching films as the seas slipped silently away beneath them.

We curved east and coasted over Tel Aviv. From the streets below, people if they gazed up would have just seen a couple of white strobe lights flashing high in the night sky. From the cockpit, the starbursts of sparkling city lights were blinding through the NVGs. A few aircraft, lower over the water, were making their approaches into Ben Gurion, the international airport.

The teeming activity of Tel Aviv belied the unresolved conflicts that surrounded the city. To the north, the Golan Heights and Lebanon sheltered freedom fighters or terrorists, whichever way one wanted to look at it. Russian forces were established on the western shores of Syria with advanced surface-to-air missiles. To the east of Tel Aviv was the West Bank, where Israelis and Palestinians were locked in an endless cycle of violence and religious tension over disputed territories with names from the Bible – Jerusalem, Bethlehem and Jericho. We passed above it all in a matter of minutes. The lights faded into desert and darkness as we pressed on into Jordan. Iraqi airspace was ahead of us.

We had been flying for almost an hour. As we approached

the border, I prepared the aircraft for entry into hostile airspace. First, I checked the threat countermeasure systems and activated the electronic identification system. One by one, I monitored the weapons: AMRAAM radar-guided missiles, ASRAAM infrared heat-seekers, the 27 mm cannon, the 500 lb Paveway 4 precision bombs.

From the inky black at 30,000 feet, I selected the infra-red camera on the Litening pod and an incredible view of the Iraqi countryside stretching out below the aircraft burst into the cockpit. I could see clusters of houses, olive groves, fields tilled in ways little changed since Biblical times by people who didn't want war and didn't want to live under the iron fist of Islamic State. Like the people back in Akrotiri, the farmers and field workers scattered across the land were happy to be at home, safe behind locked doors, the politics of the Middle East as distant as the stars. As a pilot in the war against the terrorists, we were protecting these people as well as those at home in the streets of London and Paris and Berlin.

I killed the lights and against the night sky we were now invisible to the naked eye. I glanced at the fuel gauge. Our calculations had been pretty accurate, and we had about five minutes' gas remaining with which to find the refuelling tanker before I had to turn us about and divert to the nearest military airfield. I informed air traffic control we were en route and switched radio frequencies. It was time to change our aircraft electronic ID to the pre-assigned operational code and descend to meet the tanker.

The Typhoon cockpit has three television screens. The centre console usually displays the moving map with navigation information overlaid. The right screen is primarily used for the targeting pod information. The left screen shows the radar return. The aircraft you are flying appears at the base of the screen. In the centre, the view expands outwards in various range increments to seventy degrees to the left and right of the nose. It provides good information about what aircraft are ahead of you, their height and speed.

To my immense relief, the massive A330 Voyager tanker was bang in position and clearly visible on the radar forty miles away and turning towards us.

You goddamn beauty!

The secure radio crackled into life.

'Dragon, this is Madras. We're in a left turn slowing to 220 knots and rolling out heading 290. You are clear to join.'

'Copy that, cleared to join,' I said.

My heart raced. Night air-to-air refuelling is a controlled mid-air collision, visually flown in utter darkness with no horizon or depth perception, unaided by computers or night vision goggles and only a couple of shitty little LED lights for company. No sane pilot could possibly enjoy this. Those who claim to are either liars or madmen.

We were now twenty miles out. I could see the tanker only with my radar, which was critical for long-range situational awareness. Lights out, we were flying head to head with a closing speed of about 700 mph. The two Typhoons would maintain 1,000 feet below the Voyager until we were close enough to see the tanker with the naked eye. This would only occur when we had made the join and were almost touching distance from its wingtip.

With all the aircraft lights out, we would appear over the

desert as little more than a couple of shadows. I manoeuvred in a tight turn towards the tanker when we were about
twenty seconds from passing. The aim was to roll out just
below and behind the tanker's left wing. Using the radar,
some judgement and a little luck, the operation was always
something of a black art.

That night, fortune was on our side. It was straight out
of the textbook. With half a mile to close in the tanker's
six o'clock, I could make out a hazy shadow and switched
my attention from the radar to the tanker's wing, now my
primary guide.

Formation flying is pure hands and feet, without any
computer guidance. At night, it is doubly hard work. Once
alongside, I could look down the length of the Voyager's
wing towards the fuselage. The wingtip was approximately
twenty feet from my Typhoon. Slightly behind and to my
left, Jonny was waiting patiently in formation. I couldn't
turn my head to look, it would have been too disorientat-
ing. One hundred per cent of my attention was required to
maintain position on the tanker and I needed to make constant tiny control and power adjustments to do so.

At the worst possible moment, the Voyager hit turbulence. Its enormous wings flexed up and down as it climbed
and bumped around. The fuel hoses uncoiled from the
underwing into the darkness. When the wings jolted in
the turbulence, it caused a ripple all the way down the fuel
line like a whip, flicking the basket at the end up and down
like the tail of a rattlesnake.

I slowed by a few knots to ease back from the wing. The
unlit fuel line was just a black shadow against the black sky.
As I crept rearwards, I deployed the fuel probe, opening

Responsible for all the armaments, countermeasures and ejection seats, the armourers were fitting high-explosive weapons to the jets twenty-four hours a day. Ken Gray (*far right*), led his team brilliantly. Adam Wagstaff, Pete Gates, Dave Wilson, Gav Carey, Will Dean, Dave McAdam, Steve Jones, Ads Nicol, Richie Marfleet, Ken Gray.

hatting to Tim and Jonny after landing from a ission. The Tornado flight line in the ackground. News had just come through about e requirement to destroy an IED factory.

ave Bowman chatting to Prince William. The quadron Warrant Officer, Mr B, had lived fast jet perations for over three decades. I trusted his dgement completely.

Walking in after an operational sortie over Syria, February 2016. It was always nice to climb out of the cockpit and stretch your legs after eight hours.

Taxiing out to the runway at Akrotiri, with a long mission ahead. The jet is equipped with four Paveway 4 precision bombs, ASRAAM heat-seeking and AMRAAM radar-guided missiles, the Litening targeting pod, 27mm armour piercing cannon shells, and two external fuel tanks.

A Typhoon air-to-air refuels over Iraq. The aircraft can fly for approximately two hours unrefuelled, so on the longer sorties we would refuel three or four times during a mission. The tanker's wing would flex in turbulent air, causing the refuelling line and basket to whip up and down.

Echelon right – checking each other's airframes for damage after clearing hostile airspace.

The Secretary of State for Defence, the Rt Hon. Michael Fallon, addresses the squadron in front of a Typhoon at RAF Akrotiri, 5 December 2015. The first bombing sorties had taken place the previous night.

Typhoon returns from a night mission.

Air-to-air refuelling at night was an art as much as a science. The basket was dimly lit, and only really visible when illuminated by the flash of the aircraft strobe light. The huge Voyager tanker is faintly visible by its cabin lights.

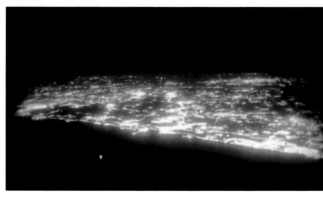

he frontline. By night, with no ectricity in ISIS held areas, the ostile territory appeared as a ark void with just the ccasional pinprick of light as idence of habitation.

Engines fired up, fully armed and ready to go. Engineers conduct last-minute checks to the avionics and weapons before it's time to taxi out.

The Russians deployed their most advanced fighter, the SU-35, to Syria, increasing the strategic tension between East and West.

Сирия

В | Вести в 20:00

Russia deployed the advanced S-400 surface-to-air missile to Syria in response to the downing of its SU-24 fighter by Turkish fast jets. This was a significant escalation.

A Typhoon banks away and releases infrared countermeasures. These flares were our defences against missile attack.

Typhoons in four-ship close formation en route to the US KC-135 tanker that would refill the jets, prior to their strike on the Improvised Explosive Device factory.

The sixteen-target strike required four weapons from each of the Typhoons, each aimed precisely at a different target. If all weapons struck, the entire factory complex would be destroyed in a single attack.

(1) Milliseconds before impact. A couple of the weapons are visible (with shadows on the roof of the building) just before they strike the target. (2) Direct hit on the first building. (3) The first two targets completely destroyed. The buildings to the right of the photo needed to remain untouched. (4) The remaining target, to the left of the picture, was destroyed moments later. Huge secondary explosions from the IEDs within the building cause an enormous column of smoke.

Tim, Heds, Kye, Harry, Ritchie (*back row*) Thorney, Spud (*front row*). The engineers are holding the four red Paveway 4 'Remove Before Flight' safety lanyards.

There were several noteworthy landmarks during the transit to Iraqi airspace. The high rises of Tel Aviv, the Dead Sea, the ancient cities within Jordan. And . . . what became known as 'c**k lake', which is in fact a hotel swimming pool.

Weasel wearing the helmet-mounted sight (official title the 'Helmet Equipment Assembly'). This projected critical information on to the helmet visor, meaning the pilot could see the target and get aircraft information without looking into the cockpit.

Callum catching some rays after an unplanned formation diversion following an air-to-air refuelling incident.

The end of the operation for 1 (Fighter) Squadron. Over 300 successful strikes conducted, with no civilian casualties. Megatron, Wrighty, Thorney, JT, Sutton, Cal, Jonny, Callum, Showtime, Euan.

Typhoon launches into the fading light for night mission over Syria.

Climbing out of a Typhoon for the last time, November 2016. A desk job in the Ministry of Defence beckoned!

ining in formation with the first British F-35s they head towards their new home at RAF arham. The F-35 is the first fifth-generation ealth aircraft in the RAF inventory. Between em, these two aircraft will make up the RAF ontline fast jet force for the decades ahead.

A Typhoon roars into the sunset.

the door to allow the metal refuelling arm to position itself out from the right of the cockpit. It made a rumbling noise as it interrupted the airflow. The Typhoon refuelling probe has no lights, and the Voyager basket contains just a few LED lights glowing around the outside of the rim. The trick now was to aim the refuelling probe into the basket to achieve a controlled connection. Over Iraq that moonless night, it required intense concentration.

From ten feet behind the basket, with just the vague outline of the wing as a horizon and height reference, I advanced the throttles a few millimetres and the Typhoon minutely accelerated. This required complete focus and precision. If you positioned too high, you could get caught in the turbulent slipstream behind the wing, the jet buffeting and potentially being thrown into the side of the tanker. I was nearly there. A few feet to go. The fuel gauge counted down relentlessly in front of me. All this time, Jonny was going through the same tortuous process until the three aircraft were just feet apart in total darkness.

Slowly, slowly forward, almost there.

Tiny power adjustments were required to control the closure. Counterintuitively, in order for this to work I had to aim the probe slightly to the right and above the basket. As the basket approached the aircraft canopy, it would be caught by the bow wave, and the air rushing at hundreds of miles an hour over the canopy would force it up and away like a leaf gliding off a car windscreen.

Luckily the turbulence had died down a little. At the last moment, the basket strayed up and away by a couple of feet, as anticipated. As I continued forward, I saw the probe disappear between the LEDs from the corner of my eye and felt a reassuring nudge from the airframe as contact was made. I had been tanking for years, but still I was as tense as a sheet of glass.

'Good contact,' called the tanker pilot.

With immense relief, I watched the gauge slowly rise as the aircraft gulped down fuel. Pilots are taught to hold the controls lightly in formation, and I realized I had been gripping the column with enormous pressure. I consciously relaxed and concentrated on maintaining position using just my fingertips on the stick. It would take ten minutes to fill up. I could just see the other hose rippling in response to a good connection. All three aircraft were now connected to each other.

Well done, Jonny.

21. One Away

We crossed from Iraq into Syrian airspace. The lights along the Euphrates had faded and there was a whisper in the back of my head reminding me of the pilot burned to death by the jihadis. I was imagining what might happen if I had to parachute into the stronghold of Islamic State. Could I walk out of the desert? Would local people help me? Or turn me in to ISIS? The only word I knew in Arabic was *inshallah*: God willing.

We were moments from commencing the targeting run.

Jonny was on my left in wide formation, a little higher and about a mile away. I could see him both on the aircraft datalink and as a speck of green light through the night vision goggles. I accelerated into a climb and swung the aircraft to the left, pointing up and behind Jonny as he flew north. As I did so, the G-suit automatically fired into life and gripped tightly around my legs and chest. Soon after, he swung his jet into a left turn as well. We were now flying on different attack axes in battle formation directly towards the target.

The doubt gremlins had gone. I was flying the most advanced multi-role military aircraft in the skies. Ahead was Russian-occupied Syria. Below was ISIS. My finger rested on the countermeasures switch. If I needed to, I could react instantly.

My gaze ran over the buttons and dials. The cockpit was

like a pinball machine with all its lights and devices. I selected air-to-ground mode on the HUD. This brought up the weapon aiming and selected the pre-determined strike package for the Paveway 4. The Litening targeting pod, sleeping like a cat, sprang to life, hungry for action.

The right-hand screen pinpointed the target: the pipe-line was buried somewhere deep into the metamorphic rock. I switched to infrared night settings and refocussed to clarify the image. We didn't expect to see anyone about so late at night, but it was essential to be absolutely certain. Islamic State fighters had seized the oilfield from the Syrian government, but it was unlikely that the engineers maintaining the facility were members of the death cult. Jonny, too, would have his eyes peeled; if we saw civilians, we would hold off or abort the mission.

We were thirty miles from our objective, cruising at almost 600 mph. The clouds had cleared. The night was black, littered with stars. I zoomed the infrared camera in on the target. It was visible and clear, but we were too far out to confirm. Turning my gaze to the left of the cockpit, I analysed the weapon system information to check that the Paveway was serviceable and ready for launch. Yep, she was good. I checked the target coordinates for the tenth time that night.

The countdown circle had appeared on the HUD to indicate the time remaining until weapon release.

The radio snapped to life and Jonny's calm voice entered my helmet.

'Capture,' he called.

He had acquired the target and was content to release. I zoomed in the targeting pod. It was critical to make sure, beyond all doubt, that we were looking at the correct point on the ground and that it was clear of people. The seconds raced.

'Capture,' I responded. 'Ten seconds.'

With five seconds to go, I opened the Late Arm, a protective switch covering the weapon release, then slid my thumb over the red button beneath. I pressed down firmly and waited for imminent bomb release.

The aircraft computers kicked into life and sent the coordinates to the Paveway. Its own internal battery fired up and confirmed that it was receiving a GPS signal. Half a second later, I felt a shunt from the bottom of the airframe as the bomb was ejected from the pylon. The aircraft aiming system then changed to confirm a weapon in flight.

'One away,' I called.

I took a breath.

'One away,' Jonny replied.

We maintained an exact height and speed as we manoeuvred away from the target, so as not to fly directly over it. My attention was fixed on the targeting pod in order to keep it pointed at exactly the correct spot to capture the weapon impact. The weapon's countdown continued.

Ten seconds to go.

My heart beat in my chest like a drumroll.

Five seconds to go.

. . . Three, two, one . . . pause.

There is always a delay of approximately one second between the countdown reaching zero and the weapon impact. Even in training it was a nervous moment that stretched like an elastic band before . . .

BOOM!

The ground erupted as the 500 lb Paveway burrowed deeply into the rock before exploding.

Another long second passed before Jonny's attack followed the track of the first into the crater and ruptured the pipeline. A massive cloud of dust and rock blew into the air.

We'd both hit the target bang on. I felt a tremendous wave of relief. It was the culmination of years of training. All the dots had joined. Oil financed jihad. That night we had struck a financial blow at the heart of ISIS. But still, stretching to the horizon, its forces continued to expand their territory and were engaged in a brutal struggle against coalition troops. The path to peace would be long and bloody.

22. Dragon Rises

It was day two. The first sorties were behind us. I glanced out of the Operations room window to see the huge hulks of C-17 and A400 aircraft arriving, carrying the spares and tools we desperately needed. The engineers were working non-stop setting up their procedures and prepping the jets. The Secretary of State for Defence, the Rt Hon. Michael Fallon MP, had just arrived for a briefing, hosted by the Chief of the Defence Staff, Air Chief Marshal Sir Stuart Peach. It was held in the hangar, with a few members of the squadron in attendance, along with the BBC – all good for morale back home. It had been interesting to report personally to the seniors on how the mission had gone the previous night, but there was still much to do. I was glad when they all set off back to the UK and we could focus on the business at hand.

Later that afternoon I sat down with our ground liaison officer, a secondee from the army, and went through a report sent from headquarters with the precise details of 1 Squadron's role in the coming weeks. James Murgatroyd – known as Megatron (because that's how an iPhone autocorrects his name) – was a young infantry captain from the Royal Welsh Regiment. He was bursting with enthusiasm and would establish strong links with the US JTACs. He confirmed that our callsigns would remain as 'Dragon', and that we would be conducting close air support missions across Iraq and Syria, by day and night, for the coming months. It would be a continuous operation, with the engineers working 24/7 to maintain and rearm the aircraft.

ISIS fighters had seized half of Iraq. The militias had subdued the population and slaughtered those who resisted as they made their way down the Euphrates river valley into Fallujah. Baghdad was now in their sights. If the capital fell, it would threaten the stability of Jordan, Iran, Turkey, Saudi Arabia and the entire Middle East. If you drew a meandering line back up the Tigris river valley from Baghdad to Mosul, then west towards Syria, that was the frontline between the jihadis and allied troops. They faced each other in deadly battles every day while we held in the fast jets deep over ISIS-held territory, ready to react when called on by the JTACs.

Sorties began in earnest. Junior pilots were thrust into the highly complex targeting scenarios with little time to bed in. The JTACs began calling in strikes by day and night with increasing urgency as ISIS commenced a major coordinated attack on the city of Ramadi.

Later that week I was back onto the night shift, and woke early to the noise of jet engines starting up. I was too wound up to get back to sleep; I climbed out of bed and pulled back the threadbare curtains as two Typhoons blasted off and turned to silhouettes against the morning sun.

At work there was admin to deal with and emails demanding a quick response. After a couple of hours, I stood and stretched my back, shaking off the desk. I went to get some fresh air and flopped down on an old picnic bench outside Ops. The high sun felt warm on the back of my neck. It was a rare pleasure to sit there in a moment of calm and watch the activity on the flight line. On the breeze was the faint waft of jet exhaust.

A couple of engineers hurried by carrying boxes of hot food. I followed the fresh oven smell back into Ops.

'Better grab one of these before they all go, sir,' one of them said.

I took his advice and put the kettle on to make a cup of tea to go with my halloumi and bacon baguette. The military had provided plastic spoons that were so feeble they folded in half when dipped in boiling water and I burned myself trying to hook the teabag out of the cup. JT – James Turner – wandered by and chuckled as I shoved my hand under the cold tap.

'It's you and me this afternoon. I've loaded the bricks. I think we're all set.'

'Nice one, thanks. We'll brief in fifteen minutes.'

'How's that going?' he said, pointing at the U-shaped spoon and my scalded hand.

'The cheapest bidder, of course.'

'Something the RAF knows all about.'

An hour later, we were airborne. Two hours later, we were deep over Iraq. It was a fine evening and the sun was going down over Ramadi, a few miles to the west of our position. The compounds in the village below formed long shadows across the desert, making the buildings appear to change shape as we cruised above.

'Dragon, we have reports of an illegal vehicle checkpoint in the centre of the village, can you see anything?' It was the voice of the JTAC over the radio.

'That's copied,' JT replied. 'We'll take a look.'

JT had been with the squadron for a couple of years after working as an instructor on Hawks. In the air he was laid-back and assured. Socially, he had no off-switch.

We circled the area for ten minutes and saw nothing suspicious. The roads were clear except for the occasional vehicle. I suspected people were already hunkering down for the evening. Most of the civilians had abandoned the area in advance of the ISIS advance. If there had been something happening, we'd missed it. In the waning sunset, the lights to the north flickering to life marked the frontline, the illuminations stretching like a loop of tinsel as far as the horizon. I doubted that the divide between enemy and friendly forces had been so clearly defined since the First World War.

During the day it was almost impossible to see the battle lines. At night, troops manned hastily constructed lookout posts with searchlight beams sweeping over enemy positions. In Iraq, small towns and villages glimmered in patches of ambient light. Without night vision equipment, as darkness fell over ISIS-controlled areas it looked as if a giant black wave was rolling over the landscape, with just isolated specks of light like quivering candles. There was no electricity in jihadi land, just a suppressed, opaque and miserable existence. The demarcation served another, more chilling purpose. We knew which way to head if the worst happened and one of us ended up on the ground.

'Dragon, we are moving you to Kirkuk. We need you to take a look at a suspected vehicle bomb.'

My ears filled with the slow, southern tones of the American controller.

JT acknowledged and we set a course to the north. The

sun had slipped below the horizon and, in the utter darkness, James's aircraft through the NVGs was just a speck of infrared light indiscernible to the naked eye. I concentrate on that little green glow, set the auto-throttle and we raced over to the potential vehicle bomb. The Typhoon groundspeed indicated 500 knots. I swung the aircraft into an orbit over the target area and focussed the targeting pod night-sight onto the ground.

'Special forces have reported an abandoned digger they believe has been rigged with explosives. It's a trap for civilians. The ground unit do not want to approach and would like it destroyed.'

'Dragon, copied.'

I could see the digger on an isolated dirt track outside a nondescript village where people lived a modest existence in mud-walled houses, with a goat, some chickens and a square of dirt sown with a few meagre vegetables. It was impossible even to begin to comprehend the extremists' malicious and misogynistic intent. Local men were bullied into their ranks or executed; their sisters and mothers dragged away to other parts of the country. The digger rigged with explosives was the cruellest of traps. At first light the villagers or children who came across it would nudge the tripwires and blow themselves to pieces.

The JTAC commenced the 9-line, the standard format for passing a CAS mission. As he spoke, I wrote the pertinent points down and entered the target details into the Typhoon's attack computer. The rules of engagement had been confirmed. It was a legitimate target. There were no nearby buildings, and no risk of collateral damage. Finally, we needed to ask the JTAC the most important question.

'Can you confirm the nearest friendly positions?'

'Only friendlies one kilometre to the north.'

'Copy.'

It was crucial to know the exact position of friendly forces: it's bad practice to release a weapon over their heads, in case there is a malfunction and it falls short. This meant we had to negotiate a target heading that would provide a clear attack path. We also wanted to be certain that they were well out of the way of weapon fragmentation at impact. There was the possibility, too, that multiple groups of friendlies were in the same area. We made sure the ones we were talking to were at a safe distance from the target and, at the same time, checked that there wasn't another group unwittingly in the vicinity.

If this process goes wrong and a pilot accidentally drops on their own forces – a so-called 'friendly fire' incident – it is known as a 'blue on blue'. For every CAS pilot, this is our worst nightmare. It has occurred multiple times in past conflicts, due to any number of reasons, including incorrect coordinates being passed, weapon inaccuracies, or an error with identifying forces on the ground in the heat of a battle.

With clearance to strike, I released a single weapon onto the target. I wasn't sure how much damage the relatively small Paveway would cause to a twenty-tonne steel digger. Forty seconds later, I found out and it was a surprise to us all: the digger had been so heavily packed with home-made explosives it vanished completely. The dust settled and there was nothing on the dirt track except a few scorch marks. Even the special forces guys on the radio sounded astonished. It was like the giant machine had not been

constructed from steel at all, but solidified petrol. If anyone had stumbled into that trap, they would have been
vaporized. They would have vanished as if they had never
existed: no bones to bury, no closure.

The targeting camera had, of course, recorded the
strike. A day or so later, I was flicking through the BBC
News website on my phone and saw the strike played back
to me along with the story of 'how the RAF had destroyed
an ISIS truck bomb'. Headquarters must have deemed the
imagery suitable for release to the media, but it felt odd
watching the attack at the same time as many thousands of
people all over Britain as they stirred their tea and ate their
cornflakes.

I was joined at a late breakfast by Mark Taylor – Phats –
a weapons system operator on the Tornados co-located
with us in Akrotiri. Phats was an old friend whose career
path had often crossed my own. We'd been on the same
course at Cranwell and he'd been flying Tornados out in
Afghanistan when I was there.

'How did it go yesterday?' I asked him. 'I saw you guys
crewing in.'

'Crazy busy. We had a number of strikes near Mosul,' he
replied, and put his cup down. His expression became
thoughtful, curious. 'It's funny the things that stick in your
mind. I've been doing this for years, but yesterday I was
involved in a strike that killed three. The JTAC reported it
on the radio afterwards and I could see the after-effects
through the pod. It was a direct hit, no civilian casualties.'

I nodded, and he continued.

'The thing is, as I was wandering back to the accommodation after landing I was thinking about them. How they

had got themselves into that situation, and whether their families would have been expecting a phone call later that night which never came.'

We both had children of our own, and that feeling of anxiety that families suffer when one of their loved ones goes missing was something we didn't even want to think about. Altitude provided a detachment from the immediate horror, an emotional filter of sorts. But sitting there with Phats, surrounded by others eating breakfast and preparing for another day, highlighted the stark nature that fortune and fate play in one's life. Where you are born, whom you meet, the choices you make. The conflict in Syria was about global power and politics, but it was being fought by individuals. With each contact, there was perhaps an imperceptible change to the overall strength of the forces and the campaign balance, but a devastating impact on the lives of the families involved.

'Still, best not to brood on it too much,' he added.

We sat quietly for a few moments with our own reflections and another long day stretching out ahead of us. Overthinking the human cost of it all was not good for a pilot's mental health. We knew what was involved, and defeating ISIS was a cause we and most of the people at home believed in. It was also wise not to think too deeply about shifting international politics. A few years before, Phats had been flying sorties over Iraq to suppress their armed forces. Now a graver danger meant that he was back in Iraqi skies, this time supporting that very same military.

Soldiers in battle endure utter chaos, unclear firing points, noise, smoke and physical exertion, with all of the associated fear and confusion such scenarios create. In fast jets, we had to be measured and clinical. Strikes had to be precise, well executed and within the strict rules of engagement. The cockpit screens, communications and targeting camera images were all recorded and sent after every sortie to headquarters as a permanent record. An error could be analysed in minute detail. With nowhere to hide, pilots strived for perfection. This added a huge amount of pressure, but I saw that as a good thing, one more prompt to be continually meticulous, vigilant and mindful of human life.

Countless reports during the Gulf War of 2003 had underlined the failures of so-called 'smart bombs', with civilians losing their lives in what was euphemistically called 'collateral damage'. The pressure for operations against ISIS to be an error-free conflict was acutely felt. We now had the technology to be precise and it was what public opinion in the west expected. Comparisons were made in the media with apparently indiscriminate Russian bombing over Syria using unguided weapons.

Snipers presented a target that was difficult to deal with in Iraq's crowded cities, where buildings were packed tightly together and the flat rooftops were a mishmash of water tanks, washing lines and lean-to shelters. They found hideaways among the clutter. They shot at civilians as well as coalition troops.

A few months before, the streets had been packed with market stalls, tailors, barbers, chai shops, all of daily life. Now, people had mostly fled, and those that hadn't were afraid to leave their homes. If they had to go out to find food or water or medicine, they ran the gauntlet of jihadi spot checks and marksmen with Russian-made rifles. They could not rely on their police or local security forces and had no ambulances to answer an emergency call. Life for them was utterly terrifying and hopeless. I felt extremely lucky to have been born in a part of the world where life was generally secure for the vast majority, and could see why we took it for granted. Back at home in the UK, away from the devastation, it was easy to forget what was happening across the Middle East.

I was in a formation with Bobby Winchester a few days after my chat with Phats when we received a call that a sniper was operating in a dusty town straddling the Tigris. We arrived overhead the target area to take over from a pair of American F-16 jets that had been on station for several hours. I watched their grey outlines flash past a few thousand feet above. They would be talking to the airborne command and control aircraft to organize their transit home, another mission chalked up. I heard a French accent on the radio, probably from a pair of Rafale fast jets. Down in the south of the country, US Navy F-18s were taking over from US Marine Corps Harriers. The multinational force worked harmoniously during conflict, which makes it even more of a pity that there is so much political wrangling in peace.

The sniper location was imprecise and we knew it would be hard to find from the air. We threw our targeting cameras over the sprawling town. Cycling between a television and infrared image provided different views of the same scene. Between us we scanned rooftops, windows, and arcaded streets with their crisscrossing shadows. It was the middle of the day, blisteringly hot on the ground. Most people were sheltering from the sun, the sniper too, no doubt, camouflaged amid the untidy rooftops.

A car approached from the west, kicking up dust as it darted at speed through the narrow winding streets and pulled up outside a house. Half a mile to the north, a few individuals dashed out of a ramshackle property and disappeared beneath some palm trees. Two small groups of people hustled along the main road. A snapshot of life in a town under siege. No surprises. No bursts of gunfire. The sniper was laying low.

We circled for twenty minutes until the silence was finally broken by the JTAC.

'Dragon, we've got reports of a mortar firing team in action to the west of Mosul. We need you to redeploy now. Standby for a grid.'

We immediately flew north, although by the time we reached the location, the intent to strike had subsided. By all accounts, the building had until recently been used as a school and there was some uneasiness about the potential presence of civilians. We held off, maintaining an overwatch. Half an hour later our tasking ended, and we returned to base fully armed and with mixed emotions from not having been in action that day. It felt a little like an afternoon spent on the subs' bench. That we hadn't struck any targets meant that ISIS activity must have been limited or contained, which was a success of sorts. Every tasking took its own form: an apparent crisis that amounted to nothing, or a quiet morning that suddenly exploded into action. It was impossible to predict.

We strode into the mess. With a no-flying day tomorrow for engineering maintenance, we ordered a cold beer and sat at a table outside, watching the sun go down. Bobby provided what was most needed at that moment, a bloody good laugh.

'Did I mention Jane's note-taking yesterday?' he asked.

Jane Smith was a flight sergeant, one of the most experienced engineers on the squadron. Bobby continued.

'I was on the auth desk yesterday while Mr B was giving the morning engineering brief to the seniors,' he began. 'I couldn't help but hear the whole thing. Jane stood to one side, looking very studious with her notebook. She was going to write down what Mr B was saying, but every other word started with the letter F and I don't think her pen ever touched the paper.'

'He's a great orator, Mr B,' I observed.

'I was chuckling about it, and wandered over to her afterwards to ask if she'd managed to get anything down. "No," she said. "F all."'

23. Danger Close

When flying sorties, one of the more experienced pilots would lead the formation, flying as Dragon 1. But if you had two experienced aircrew, then either could fly as the lead, and I was more than happy to be flying on Thorney's wing that evening. It was a beautiful calm night, with the moon low in the sky. Through the NVGs, bright shining stars on the horizon merged with the lights of towns and villages. The flashing white and red lights of civilian airliners cruising the airways were far behind us as we exited Jordanian airspace and set a course for Ramadi, just to the west of Baghdad.

We reached the outskirts of the city and the Litening pods provided a high-resolution infrared image of life in the jumble of narrow streets below. Broken cloud squatting at about 15,000 feet briefly blocked the view and forced us to manoeuvre. The tracking mode of the pod tried to maintain a stable view of the ground, but frustratingly, as the weather rolled through, it would sometimes snag onto the cloud image and drift away from the target. This needed some fast fingers to slew the image rapidly back over the search area and fly the aircraft to a point where a clear line of sight to the ground could be maintained. That particular night, as quickly as the line of cloud had arrived, it was carried away by the desert winds.

Unexpectedly, a dazzling elongated flash caused the

NVGs to momentarily bloom and we were unable to see anything in detail. It took me a few seconds to realize that the bright light was an illumination flare suspended from a parachute which slowly floated down and bathed the entire city in infrared light. For anyone using NVGs, the scene became as clear as day. Without the goggles, the flare was impossible to see and the area remained a pit of grim shadows and danger.

A moment later, the shrill wail of an emergency beacon screeched over our radios. The siren was triggered by an aircraft in distress, as a warning or a call for help. The tone repeated every second or so, a chilling sound, and was so loud I knew it must be nearby.

Another flare appeared almost instantly, followed by the bright sparks of automatic gunfire from rooftops and shadows across the city.

'Dragon, we've got a situation here.'

The JTAC's voice on the radio was measured. No matter how chaotic, the level tone remained cool and composed.

'Go ahead,' Thorney replied.

'An Iraqi army helicopter has been downed. We might need your assistance. Standby for a 9-line.'

'Understood. Ready to copy. We are eyes on the illumination flares. I can see multiple firing points.'

Like the JTAC, Thorney was the essence of calm.

From overhead the city, we could see RPGs flash across the skyline. The rocket motors appeared like streaks of gold thread that burned out before the flash of impact. Numerous automatic weapons were rattling out bullets. More flares arced into the sky like it was fireworks night. There was movement in the streets below as fighters dashed towards the crashed helicopter.

'Dragon, we need to strike an enemy firing point, under self-defence rules of engagement. The group is mobile. Danger close. I say again, danger close. Friendly troops are 200 metres away, to the north. How copy?'

'Copy, danger close,' said Thorney, reading back the rest of the detail of the tasking as he manoeuvred his jet to set up an attack.

Through the Litening camera, I could see both friendly and enemy firing positions with continuous rounds going out from both directions. The crew had pulled themselves clear from the wrecked helicopter. Friendly troops had reached them but were pinned down by crisscrossing gunfire. The scene on the ground was intense, like a movie set. With the opposing forces so close to each other in an urban location and at night, the potential to make things considerably worse with a poorly executed strike was colossal.

I swung the aircraft into a turn and zoomed the camera into the firing point. Three ISIS fighters were shooting relentlessly towards the downed helicopter. The launch of an RPG streamed overhead the city, leaving its tell-tale arc of spidery light and landed close to their position. This was going to be an extremely difficult attack. The friendlies were incredibly close, the enemy was mobile, and the contact was happening in narrow streets and shoulder-to-shoulder buildings. The weapon would need constant manual guidance, homing in on a laser spot that Thorney would have to continually adjust with one hand while flying the jet with the other. The attack heading would have to be perfect in order to minimize the blast risk to the friendlies and avoid the weapon catching the corner of a building on its way to the target.

Thorney was alone in the attack. He had one chance. He knew if he didn't get this exactly right, friendly forces could be blown to dust in a disastrous blue on blue. If he missed the target, the helicopter crew would likely be killed by the advancing fighters.

'One away, thirty seconds, laser on.'

My heart pounded in my chest. I counted those long stretched-out seconds until the Paveway slammed into the target. A rising cloud of dust and debris erupted into the air. Only as it settled did I hear the result from the unfussed and focussed response of the JTAC.

'Dragon, that's a delta hotel. Standby for BDA.'

Delta hotel – a direct hit. We waited for the BDA – the battle damage assessment.

Most of the automatic weapon fire ceased after the Paveway impact, and a fleeting moment of calm descended over the city streets. Another flare rose into the air and a vehicle rushed to the crash site to rescue the downed helicopter crew.

There was barely time to take a breath. I rejoined into formation with Thorney and the smoke and dust from the strike slowly thinned in the air as we changed course and pressed on to the north.

The evening's activities had barely begun. First, troops in contact near Mosul required immediate support. Then a coordinated strike against two mortar positions. Next, a move to Sinjar to deal with a group of jihadi fighters firing high explosive rockets. Dangerously low on gas, we made it to an American tanker for the third top-up of the evening. As we connected in formation, that blind dance requiring every ounce of concentration, the radio breathed to life once more.

'Dragon, once you are finished tanking, got another 9-line for you. Call ready to copy.'

The moment my tanks were filled, I eased rearwards from the basket, unplugged and inched the Typhoon over to the tanker's right wing. Sitting in loose formation, while Thorney completed his refuel, I gazed through the night vision goggles to maintain my spacing.

I now had to perform the tricky balancing act of staying in position a few feet off the tanker's wing with one hand on the stick and the other clutching a pencil. There was a miniature directional night light on the inside of the canopy. I aimed the thin beam at the sheet of paper clipped to my kneeboard and wrote down the 9-line's brief, constantly glancing down to write, then glancing back up and out of the cockpit again to make minor formation adjustments. I always used a pencil now. It was too frustrating to have a biro suddenly stop working during a mission brief because the paper was damp or the ink was too cold. More than once I had licked the end of the pen and scribbled wild circles to get the thing going. I never got over the irony that a pilot can get incensed beyond words in an £80 million fighter because a fifty-pence biro gives up the ghost.

We had destroyed the last two mortar positions and were out of weapons. I watched a shooting star, bright through the NVGs, approach overhead and vanish over the edge of the horizon. It had been a long night. I was tired. It was tempting to mentally relax but we had to remain vigilant. We were still bang over the most active ISIS stronghold in the region and needed to top up with fuel one more time for the long flight back to base.

Twenty minutes later we were tanking complete and set a course south-west to rejoin the airway. But before reaching Jordan, we had one more problem to deal with. The intensity of fighting those last twenty-four hours had drawn more aircraft into the conflict. The airspace over Iraq was completely chocka with ongoing taskings. Dozens of UAVs, fighters, tankers and intelligence-gathering aircraft were crammed in the space. An American airborne command and control aircraft was deconflicting the traffic jam. A voice from on board crackled over the radio.

'Dragon, we're gonna struggle to get you direct south-west. May need to vector you to the north around some traffic. Can you take a descent?'

A descent was the last thing we wanted. We were currently sitting at around 25,000 feet. There were aircraft both 10,000 feet above us and 10,000 feet below us. In the airway, about 100 miles ahead, I could also see multiple contacts on the datalink.

'2 from 1,' Thorney called.

'Go ahead.'

'Fancy a proper climb? See if we can get on top of all this lot?'

'Affirm.'

That was typical of Thorney and just what I wanted to hear. We were about to exploit the true performance of the rocket-ship Typhoon to get us out of a hole. We had dropped all of our weapons and were now full of fuel. There was only one thing for it.

'Dragon, request climb into Block 5.'

This was a climb above 50,000 feet. No other fighter could get up there. At that altitude, we could fly where we liked.

'Dragon – say again?'

'This is Dragon. Request immediate climb to Block 5 – 50,000 feet.' He paused, then added. 'Or higher.'

'Dragon, affirm, sir. If you can get to 50,000, it's yours.'

'Roger that,' said Thorney, and immediately called 'gate', the codeword for engaging afterburners.

I threw the throttles fully forward, releasing the full 40,000 pounds of thrust. Even at 25,000 feet the acceleration was insane and I was pinned back into the ejection seat. I needed to pull the aircraft immediately into a twenty-degree climb just to keep the speed under control.

I followed Thorney in loose formation, chasing his afterburners in a meteoric ascent, the huge flames like a NASA rocket blasting its way through the night sky. We raced through 35,000 feet, still pointing towards the stars. The lights of aircraft below and the distant flickers of villages and towns were falling away fast and merging into one. Through 40,000 feet, 45,000 feet. The scattered cloud layer at 20,000 feet was soon four miles beneath us.

'Dragon, levelling at 54,000 feet.'

Thorney cancelled the afterburners, and in an instant his jet faded once more to a faint green glow through the NVGs. I brought my throttles back to maintain our spacing and set the speed to Mach 0.97, just a few knots below supersonic. It felt safer and more serene at this altitude. No other jet was anywhere near us. We had escaped the carnage below. For the first time that day, I engaged the autopilot and set a heading back to base. It had been almost six hours since we took off.

The events of the evening quickly slipped into the past and soon seemed distant, unreal. A sortie of this kind demanded such focus that there was no time or spare capacity to process emotion or to reflect on what had just happened; it was too involved, too compelling. Every ounce of energy and attention goes into operating the jet and organizing the next strike. Then, sometimes, during the quieter moments, there is a strange loneliness that descends on black nights with nothing for company but the whisper of oxygen flowing through the mask, the land invisible below and the stars too distant to reach. A castaway in the desert universe.

Soon, the lights of the Mediterranean coastline glittered in the distance. Turkey to the north, Egypt to the south, the curvature of the earth plain to see. Millions of people were far below, dreaming and sleeping or lying awake and staring up into the darkness as we passed silently overhead.

24. Battle Rhythm

Bobby and I walked to the jets just before first light. The sky was dark, with the early signs of dawn rising in a faint glow over the horizon. The air was chilly and crisp. In England there would be birdsong at this time, but it was almost silent, except for the faint hum of the cicadas in the distance. I felt an involuntary smile appear and realized I was content. Basically, content. Work was unrelenting, but we were over the initial hump and settling into a rhythm.

'It's going to be an awesome sunrise,' I said.

'I love the Mediterranean air,' Bobby replied. It'll be roasting in an hour.'

We strolled on, carrying our helmets and the bags of flying paraphernalia we would need during the trip. Breakfast had been rushed. I never felt like eating at that hour but had to get something down with a long shift in the cockpit ahead. Hot, strong coffee during the mission planning always helped. We had scheduled an exact take-off slot but were early on the timeline; the process of sanitizing, collecting pistols and briefing was becoming slicker. It eased the pressure. I glanced down at my watch.

'No rush, twenty minutes until check-in,' Bobby said, and made his way towards his aircraft.

'Copy. See you on the radio.'

It was normal to walk in silence or talk about nothing much before climbing into the jets, in order to get into the zone. Bobby sounded just like his usual confident self, but he had a lot on his mind. Paternity leave had gone in a flash. His young daughter had been in and out of hospital since birth, and he had just learned she had briefly been taken into intensive care with bronchiolitis. He had been on the phone to his wife for a long time, asking at one point, 'But how serious is it?' If he tried to rush back to Scotland, by the time he got home his daughter would likely already be out of hospital.

He wanted to be there for his wife and children, but he was torn between loyalties. The operational pressures were acute but didn't relieve or replace the domestic pressures of normal life. The constant communication available with FaceTime and WhatsApp made chatting to loved ones much easier, but it also made all the problems at home that much closer. You could almost be in the room with family on a video call and mentally transitioning to an operational mission a couple of hours later.

Bobby didn't have a callous bone in his body. He would look back on this time with a different perspective, no doubt, but we were in a mindset where what mattered most was getting the job done and being there for the team. The fighter pilot role is so compelling and unforgiving that you have to be either fully in or out – a band of brothers.

The jets were under their shelters, the harsh portable lighting casting jagged shadows across the ground and under their wings. I felt my internal autopilot kick in as I began the routine walkaround of my aircraft, checking the brakes and the undercarriage, the missiles with their sharp angles and the bombs with their delicate precision seeker-heads, the intricate technology in stark contrast to the hard weapon-casing packed with high explosives. The cockpit checks flowed seamlessly, almost subconsciously, my hands darting around in a blur.

The jet hummed on external power, with a low drone like a bee dipping into a flower. I started the engines and Jamie Robson grinned up at me as he pulled the aircraft steps away. He was an excellent engineer and his smile and banter first thing in the morning were a huge boost. I held up the ten fingers of both hands and he gave me the thumbs up. We still had ten minutes to go until check-in.

I sat there calmly in the confined space with the clock ticking and the dawn rising. The working day had barely begun. The coffee had yet to kick in and I still felt only half awake. That would change as soon as I started to taxi out and my brain would automatically shift into gear. We knew from the brief that we would be flying east, probably towards Mosul or Fallujah, but had no idea what the day had in store. We could be re-roled to support any number of scenarios: a benign reconnaissance task along the Kurdish border, tracking enemy positions or vehicle movements; or working with unmanned aerial vehicles; or a troops-in-contact requiring an immediate danger-close weapon drop.

My mind wandered like a searchlight beam, picking out one thing and moving onto the next in the sort of dream-like sequence you can have killing time. Flying on operations means coping with the persistent, underlying pressure. After all the planning and training, no two flights are the same and you must be ready to react to surprises, emergencies and dangers which can change by the second.

In these brief moments of downtime, one topic that often came to my mind was the constant personal risk of flying a fully armed jet over hostile territory with SAMs on the ground and the uncertainty of Russian forces operating in the same region.

Every time I dropped a Paveway 4, some small gain was made by the coalition and, at times, people lost their lives. I had no sympathy for Islamic State, but the fighters themselves would each have their own story, and I had some understanding for their predicament. The majority, I suspected, were caught up in something that was not of their making, and through coercion, the need for cash or sheer desperation, they had ended up as jihadi terrorists. Where politics fails, conflict begins. ISIS activity, to my mind, was little short of genocide, and hard power was required to bring its vile doctrines to an end.

The conflict would have long-lasting impacts and I knew that, for some, the war would be with them for the rest of their lives. During my time in Afghanistan, I had witnessed first-hand the brutal aftermath of bullets and bombs. During my time in Afghanistan, I had routinely hopped around the country in the back of helicopters, Ospreys and C-130s, often sitting opposite injured soldiers or captured Taliban. The prisoners in their ragged clothes invariably looked dazed, drained, frightened. Despite the threat they had posed, it was impossible not to feel a pang of compassion for them. On one occasion, I climbed clumsily into a C-130 in the dead of night, a rifle hung over my body armour. A member of the crew stopped me before I slumped down in the first available space.

'Careful, mate, there's a medical team on board.'

In the dim light, I saw two Afghan army soldiers lying on stretchers on the floor of the aircraft, being nursed by medics. One of them, he wasn't a day over eighteen, caught my eye for a moment, then looked away with a vacant stare up at the ceiling. Both he and his companion were quadruple amputees from the battlefield. Bandaged and stable, they were barely alive. How they were going to cope in the future, without western healthcare, was hard to imagine.

On all of the coalition bases in Afghanistan, attacks from unguided rockets were routine. A siren would ring out and you'd dive to the floor seeking cover, if there was any, and lie prone, listening to your own breath as you waited, with a sense of dread, for the sound of impact.

God, I hope it's not me today.

A few seconds later there would either be a faint rumble in the distance, or a 'Kaboom!' if the munition landed close by.

Many coalition troops were killed in these indiscriminate attacks. The rockets were fired from the desert floor several miles away. They often came in volleys, and most were launched hours after their timers had been set and the perpetrators had withdrawn. Surviving them was just down to luck. There was a constant underlying threat, and little ballistic protection, but still the bases were a safer bet than the minute-to-minute hell the troops on patrol faced across Helmand Province. Most of the soldiers I met had assumed a fatalistic approach as a coping mechanism: there was little else you could do.

At staff college before I joined 1 Squadron, I attended talks given by soldiers who had lost multiple limbs and survived life-changing injuries. Others who had suffered long-term mental scarring spoke openly of the buried turmoil of PTSD, their constant nightmares and the demoralizing impact on their lives as well as on the lives of those close to them. Bereaved parents and family members did not hide their emotions when they spoke about their shock and anguish at the sudden death of a loved one – most of them young with their whole lives ahead of them – and of the gut-wrenching emptiness created by their loss.

Being shot down or having to eject over hostile territory were ever-present anxieties in the back of my mind. As a team, we barely spoke of it, except to cover the formal planning of what to do if it did happen. It was easier to focus on the drills, and trust that, by some perverse logic, by not shining a light on that particular tiger, it would remain quietly in the shadows.

News reports sometimes talk about hero pilots steering their planes away from populated areas before ejecting. There is some truth in this; but, more often than not, where the aircraft crashes is merely chance. In most cases, ejections are not controlled events. They are the last-gasp option after a few panic-stricken moments trying to regain control.

On operations over Iraq and Syria, an ejection near friendly troops might mean survival. An ejection into the hands of ISIS would risk brutality, torture and an ending that none of us wanted to think about. Pilots would attempt to escape and evade armed with their pistol, coping with whatever injuries they may have sustained during the ejection itself. Specialist search and rescue teams would be called into action, but time would always be in short supply, and for every second in hostile territory your life would hang by a thread.

All frontline pilots go through survival training, typic-
ally on rainy winter days on bleak moorland or in Canada's
frozen forests where it is so cold a boiling cup of water
thrown into the air vanishes in a cloud of ice crystals.
These experiences were useful, but they bore little resemblance to flying on operations over rocky wastelands
dotted with ISIS militias, criminal gangs trading in slaves
and arms, and the anachronistic sight of Bedouins on
camels living a way of life little changed for a thousand
years.

For me, the conduct-after-capture course lingers in my
memory like an old scar: seven days and sleepless nights
of escape and evasion training on Bodmin Moor, hunted
by Royal Marines with blackened faces and night vision
equipment. Everyone ends up getting caught. You then
spend twenty-four cold, wet hours intermittently in stress
positions or being grilled by interrogators who remove your
blindfold and shout inches away from your face as you
blink into the bright light.

The experience was exhausting, but you knew all along
you were in a phoney cell somewhere in Cornwall and a
recovery night out in Newquay was imminent. Psychological training would have been of some help against a
conventional enemy, but the brutality carried out by
Islamic State had shifted the paradigm and weighed heavily in the back of our minds on every mission.

While Bashar al-Assad continued to maintain 'domestic
security' by dropping barrel bombs on his own people, the
Syrian Civil War had become an absurd melting pot of foreign armies fighting on the same battlefield – purportedly
against a common threat, ISIS – but also spying on each

other and endangering the delicate balance of international relations. In September 2015 – three months before 1 Squadron touched down at RAF Akrotiri – Russia had deployed 4,000 ground troops in support of Assad's regime and, more to the point, to defend the seaport at Tartus. This key facility spared Russian warships the long voyage back through the Turkish Straits to their bases on the Black Sea and gave them a foothold in the Mediterranean.

Turkey remained an unpredictable risk, with its forces fighting against ISIS on one front and undermining American-backed Kurdish forces fighting ISIS on another. The Kurds, with United States patronage, saw this as their chance to create an independent state, something the Turks opposed even if it resulted in confrontation with their NATO ally, the US. Iraq, meanwhile, was all but lost to Islamic State. The wider region, too, was polarized, with tensions running high throughout the Middle East.

1 Squadron was operating in this region configured against one threat, ISIS, but mindful of the possibility of a miscalculation or unwanted escalation from another, Russia – as we were about to find out.

A couple of weeks later we were over the Jordanian capital, Amman – and well inside the country's airspace – when the defensive aids system blasted to life. This highly sensitive and extremely accurate piece of equipment jolts your survival instincts like an electric shock, and my pulse raced as I immediately scanned the electronic warfare sensors to assess what was targeting us.

A Russian early warning surveillance radar was taking a

look at us from the north. This was unwelcome but not wholly unexpected. I monitored the system and kept flying to the east on our planned route towards Iraq. Suddenly the aircraft picked up a modern Russian surface-to-air missile system in acquisition mode. Now this was interesting. It was likely that the early warning radar had cued the SAM. The missile had a very long range and we were well inside the heart of the firing envelope. After a short period, the SAM radar escalated from acquisition into tracking mode and locked onto our jets. One step away from launch.

I had taken off from Akrotiri with the sun glinting on the waves lapping into the bay. Callum Smith was on my wing, sitting slightly swept about a hundred yards out to the left-hand side. Tall and blonde, he was on his first tour, and a more motivated and dedicated pilot you would struggle to find. Socially, Callum was well intentioned, but he always seemed to end up in the middle of accidental chaos – he had recently attended a wedding at a Scottish castle and somehow ended up bringing down a chandelier while dancing, to the amusement of the squadron and the detriment of his bank balance. He, and I, were now facing rather more serious problems.

The SAM posed a clear threat. Inside the cockpit a loud audio siren sounded and the defensive aids screens alerted us to the countermeasure options available.

Since my earliest days as a fast jet pilot, I had been trained for this scenario. It had been drilled into us how to respond. A surface-to-air missile can arrive at Mach 4 and turn rapidly using tens of G-force, far more than any aircraft or pilot can withstand. To counter the SAM, you would normally jettison any external stores you were carrying – in order to make the aircraft lighter, more manoeuvrable – and throw the jet into a series of aggressive turns in an attempt to create inaccuracies with the tracking radar. You would also deploy physical countermeasures, such as releasing chaff – a cloud of small, thin pieces of metallized glass fibre which appears as a cluster of primary targets on radar screens – the aim being to confuse the radar operator or tracking algorithms. At the same time as you were employing simultaneous electronic warfare techniques to confuse the SAM radar, you had just a few precious seconds to manoeuvre the jet aggressively out of the threat area.

The combination of all of these techniques would either succeed in creating sufficient miss-distance, and you would survive, or they would fail and you would still be hit. SAM reaction training becomes repetitive, an instinctive skill. The alerts go off, and you immediately react. Modern countermeasures are good, but there is no guarantee they will be effective, and against the most adept systems, fighter aircraft remain vulnerable. The RAF has lost many aircraft to SAMs over the years, including the accidental shooting down of a Tornado by a friendly United States Patriot system over Iraq.

Back above Amman, the defensive aids system screamed into life again. The radar had gone into a mode that could support a surface-to-air missile in flight. If the missile operators wanted to, they could have fired. But there was no way of knowing.

Fuck.

I saw my wingman's jet twitch. Callum jumped onto the radio.

278

'1 from 2. Are you getting this?'

'Affirm. Standby.'

If we began a counter-SAM reaction right now, in an airway, it would involve violent manoeuvres and height changes, potentially threatening the safety of other aircraft. If we followed our tactical guidance precisely, we would now have to jettison our weapons and fuel tanks into the Jordanian urban sprawl beneath us. The overall consequences would be horrendous and the Russians would undoubtedly deny the whole incident. It would be a political disaster if ever there was one.

But if we didn't react, and there was a missile in flight, we had about sixty seconds to live.

Intelligence briefings had informed us that the Russians had no intention of targeting a UK jet. But they had form: one of their own fast jets had recently been shot down, and Russian missiles had recently brought down a Malaysian airliner in Ukrainian airspace, killing 298 people. It was also possible the SAM system had fallen into rebel hands and that this was an opportunistic shot.

My mind raced and spun. How on earth had we ended up in this situation? The defensive system continued to scream. Those sixty seconds were a lifetime of memories: days on the beach with my daughter, my first flight in a Bulldog with Daz Erry, the look of pride on my dad's face when I graduated from Cranwell. But I had to decide whether to react, jettison the weapons and risk a political disaster, or not to react, ignore the SAM threat warnings and pray that the intelligence had got it right.

Life, on occasions, presents diabolical choices. I opted for the latter.

'2 from 1. Don't react. Maintain course.'

'2.'

Callum stuck like glue in formation.

The radar lock indications continued to blare in the cockpit for six long minutes. I found the constant siren such a pain, such a distraction, that I switched the defensive system to 'off' to stop the incessant wailing. I had practised counter-SAM manoeuvres for more than a decade, and the first time the system screamed to life for real, it turned out the best course of action was to unplug it. This was not in the tactics manual. Just before we entered Iraqi airspace, I reselected the system to 'on', by which time the SAM had stopped tracking us.

Safely back down on the ground at Akrotiri once the sortie was over, it was interesting to reflect on this scenario. Fighter pilots are trained to respond quickly to information – there is often little time to mull over issues as they present themselves. That is why combat pilots have to live and breathe the role, assimilating information swiftly and training day in and day out to make the best choice at any given moment. A life could depend on it. Your own life depended on it.

Pilots love clarity. We thrive on least-risk options and binary, black-and-white actions: the right way and the wrong way. Yet life is rarely that simple. I remember the Chairman of the US Joint Chiefs of Staff, General Dempsey, giving a lecture at staff college and saying that everything is really 'just one big stew'. Just like Olds and Boyd, Americans often have a way with words that I admire.

When I was teaching the weapons instructor course, we used to force the students to try to think differently: the answer to most questions should, in fact, be 'it depends'. And this was a classic case. SAM reactions had been beaten into me and my wingman since we were junior pilots. There was only one correct, best way to tactically defeat that particular type of SAM. Yet in real life, when all the threat information appeared in exactly the way that we had trained for, my decision *on that occasion* had been to ignore it and trust that our intelligence was correct.

The whole episode highlighted the challenges that arise when ingrained training – the combination of technical knowledge and muscle memory – is faced with the strategic risks of employing air power in a congested and dynamic political context. Sometimes the two were at odds. What a bloody unpredictable world it is sometimes.

I made myself a strong coffee and walked into the planning room feeling more than a little relieved. The most difficult decision of the flight had turned out to be the right one. Through good judgement – or good luck – we had survived, and there had been no political fallout. The sun was angling through the window. Thorney was busy tapping away like a court secretary on one of the ancient computers. He was wearing his flying kit, ready to strap a fighter to his back later that evening.

'You'll make a great staff officer – just wait until you are promoted into a ground job in Air Command headquarters,' I said.

He spluttered out a cough and turned back to his screen.

The Typhoon had just been given a suite of new capabilities and clearances, and as we settled into operations, Thorney had been formalizing and writing up our procedures. Ordinarily, a squadron had months to integrate new capabilities and develop new roles. In action, we just had to crack on, evolving and learning in contact as we went along. This put a great deal of stress on Thorney and Jonny. There was no time to prove and refine a tactic, as in training. The process had to be analysed, written down, briefed and executed, all within a matter of days. An error on live operations using high explosive weapons could have disastrous consequences.

Thorney paused. 'How was this morning?'

'Oh fine, a couple of drops near Ramadi,' I replied. 'Looks like you're doing a great job. Any concerns?'

'We're getting there.' Thorney looked back at me. 'In all honesty, I'd rather it was like this, just being given the equipment and told to get on with it. It's a lot better than waiting years for clearances.'

'It's not too extreme?'

'Course it is. That's why I prefer it.'

I slumped into a plastic chair. I'd been up since 5 a.m. Outside, the sky had become orange with the setting sun. I had to summon up the energy to log on and start writing up the mission. These had to be good; poorly written sortie reports would get sent back by the Air Operations Centre for redrafting. I would tell Thorney about the SAM before he walked, and we would need to brief everyone else so they were on their guard. I tried to relax, and realized I hadn't really relaxed since that day when the red secret phone erupted with the force commander on the other end, all those months ago at Lossiemouth. In some ways, life before Akrotiri seemed distant, like a fantasy, a false memory.

'How's Lisa getting on?' I asked, changing the subject. 'I guess Christmas was a total write-off.'

I didn't want to pry, but when you were away for a long haul it was always good to check on people's personal lives. A short-notice deployment puts massive pressure on families.

He shrugged. 'There's always next Christmas,' he replied. 'We had a holiday planned for February, too. That's also ended up down the drain. But she understands. I just hate the thought of her having to go to all the get-togethers as the only person on their own, while everyone else is with their partners.'

'Yeah, it sucks.'

He went back to work. I strolled off to find the intelligence officer and get some mission reports underway.

Thorney's wife, like all the wives and partners and families, had to suffer in silence. They knew from the constant reporting of air strikes on the news that the deployment was dangerous, but the pilots were guarded when they chatted with their families and played down their sorties over Iraq and Syria. The missions were far too graphic and inappropriate to discuss in detail.

Compared to the daily life-and-death decisions of dropping weapons, conversations about family life could seem trivial, and they sometimes became strained as a result. Families could pick up on any such emotional distance, and the sense of not knowing made it tougher for those at home. For all that we worried about our loved ones, we at least had the distraction of a job to do and I was grateful for that. My thoughts turned, once more, to drafting reports.

25. IED Factory

Let your plans be dark and impenetrable as night,
and when you move, fall like a thunderbolt.

Sun Tzu

Thorney had been airborne for five hours when he finally had to give in to the call of nature – not easy in a single-seat fighter.

First, you had to make the ejection seat safe; ejection with your trousers down would not be good for life expectancy and would certainly raise some questions. Next, so you could actually move, you had to unstrap from the seat, unzip your flying jacket, and shuffle down your G-suit. Then you had to deploy the pee bag, which was similar to a freezer bag, with a plastic end. And with that, the business would be completed with a success rate slightly lower than the engineers would have liked.

Just as Thorney was at the *moment critique*, he received a 9-line for an urgent troops-in-contact. With his wingman unable to drop his weapon due to a technical failure, and no opportunity to delay, he had to engage the target with his pants down, literally.

A far more substantial challenge, however, was about to face the rest of the squadron.

After a spell of good weather, the thunderstorms had

returned. The previous afternoon, JT had been attempting to air-to-air refuel when a huge jolt of turbulence threw the tanker up and down. It caused an almighty ripple along the fuel line and slammed the basket at the end into the side of his cockpit. It smashed against the metal pitot pressure sensors that measure airspeed and altitude, and left him in a precarious state. Already on minimum fuel and now with some damage to the jet, he had to divert to the nearest airfield, which was in north-east Iraq close to the ISIS frontline. In response, we immediately dispatched an engineering team in a C-130; they would work through the night to get the jet airworthy again as soon as possible.

Late the next afternoon, the Mediterranean air was unusually humid as I walked back to Ops after a trip over Syria. I spotted Jonny Anderson and Tim Lowing approaching, arguably the two most critical and influential members of the team, responsible between them for the tactics, weaponeering and serviceability of the jets. I was surprised by their uneasy expressions and wondered if it was related to JT's Iraq diversion. I was in a good mood and tried humour.

'What's up, Tim, problem with your yoga class?'

'Boss, a tasking's come from the Air Operations Centre while you were airborne, so the Expeditionary Air Wing approached Jonny to discuss it. It's sensitive.'

'They want an IED factory destroyed ASAP,' Jonny explained.

This was interesting but not unusual, and if it was so urgent, I couldn't understand why we had not just struck it that morning. I had flown with James Harkin – Weasel – and we had returned with weapons to spare; we could have easily picked up an additional target.

'The thing is,' Jonny continued. 'It's huge. Several large buildings. They want it completely destroyed in a single attack to make sure none of the bomb-makers' stuff can be salvaged in the event of partial damage. And there's more. They think it will need sixteen weapons to destroy the target, with the strike happening simultaneously with US aircraft hitting other nearby targets at the same time. It will be a coordinated push, so the timeline is fixed.'

This was growing more interesting by the minute.

'For when?' I asked.

'Saturday, around 1400. They want to know whether we can crack this or not in the next hour.'

'No rush, then?' I said. 'What's the target construction?'

'Light materials. Single storey, bricks and wood by the looks of it. Thorney's looking at it now. Sixteen weapons should do it – assuming they all hit.'

Most of our work was close air support; it was dynamic and reactive, assisting soldiers during contacts and fire-fights. Pre-planned strikes were rare and would be against high-profile objectives that specialist targeteers would have studied and lawyers would have checked before sign off at the highest level of government.

'Destroying a bomb factory will be a huge blow to their capability,' I remarked.

'Sounds pretty important,' said Tim thoughtfully.

Hitting sixteen different targets from a single formation in a single pass had not been conducted for some considerable time by the RAF, and never by the Typhoon Force. Before precision guided weapons, this would have been an impossibility. 'Dumb' weapons in previous conflicts had only worked by saturation, often causing extensive collateral damage. During the Second World War, more than 90 per cent of weapons had missed their targets. When Churchill wanted to strike the Nazi experimental weapons factory at Peenemünde – a secret facility developing the V-2 rockets that would later terrorize London – the RAF used 596 heavy bombers for a 'precision' attack. Later, in the Vietnam War, formations led by Robin Olds needed sticks of munitions to create damage over a wide area. Even by the first Gulf War, smart weaponry remained in its infancy, and unguided rockets and bombs were still being used at the start of the Afghanistan campaign in 2004. Expectations had now reached the point that we would be tasked to strike within a few feet of accuracy, at a time and place of our choosing.

In a professional sense, I felt excited at the thought of the strike. We could potentially load four Paveway 4s per aircraft, fly a four-ship over the target and release all sixteen weapons at their different aiming points at the same time. We had trained for multiple targets, but sixteen different weapons delivered to sixteen different points was such an unlikely event that we had rarely practised anything like it, except to prove the concept was possible.

We were strolling slowly back to Ops. 'It's within the Typhoon's capability,' I said. 'But it's never been done.'

'As long as the targets don't require more than one weapon to get the effects we need, then . . .' Jonny paused. The wind was blowing his hair about and he pushed it back with his palm. 'Then, yes, it's workable.'

'The weapons have been amazingly accurate all detachment,' I continued. 'And the boys are up to it.'

He nodded his head slowly up and down. Jonny was cautious. He didn't jump to conclusions or make quick decisions.

'Both true,' he agreed. 'It will need some serious planning. I'll see how Thorney is getting on. If it goes, he could lead it.'

'That makes sense.'

'We've been flying only as pairs for weeks, but the boys did so much four-ship work before we deployed that I'm sure they'll be fine.'

We fell silent for a moment and nursed our own thoughts.

Launching four jets when we were only manned for pairs would put immense pressure on the engineers. Fast jets are not flown in the way we drive our cars, clocking up the miles then booking a service when the warning light flashes. The aircraft were checked daily. Engineering for every sortie had to be managed, programmed, planned for. The Typhoon was always hungry for maintenance and servicing.

Due to other ongoing commitments within the Typhoon Force, including quick reaction alert and exercises, we had deployed with the absolute minimum number of engineers for every airframe. Every aircraft component was tracked and subject to a strict maintenance schedule tied to the spares contract and a logistics chain reliant on an air bridge from the UK. This meant that the engineering and flying programmes were intrinsically linked. I could not even begin to understand the full complexity of keeping the aircraft in the air. Fortunately, Tim Lowing did.

It was Sod's Law that the mission was planned for Saturday. The jets flew six days out of seven. Saturday was a maintenance day which enabled in-depth servicing and time for more serious corrections and refinements. It was also useful to have some breathing space to sort the logistics and plan for the coming week.

It was Thursday afternoon. This gave us about thirty-six hours. What we would be asking the engineers to do was bin maintenance day, work around the clock and double their usual output. One of the aircraft had almost run out of hours and was slated to be flown back to the UK for a jet swap that day. The replacement would need prep on arrival in Cyprus and would not be ready to fly for a few days.

At that moment, we had three serviceable Typhoons plus JT's jet still stuck in Iraq.

We watched the sun dip down to the horizon. It was glorious, a palette of pinks, orange and scarlet. I turned to Tim.

'How are we getting on with the recovery from Iraq?'

'Should be home in the next couple of hours,' he replied. 'The engineering team got in there yesterday evening and worked through the night. It's launching any minute.'

'How does that leave us for Saturday?'

'Assuming there's no major snags between now and Saturday morning, we'll have four serviceable.'

Four jets for four task lines or, in the language of the RAF, four for four. At best. That was bloody tight for a critical mission. Ordinarily, to guarantee a successful launch, you would plan for 50 per cent redundancy, so six for four. Five at a pinch.

I looked at Jonny and Tim. I could almost hear the wheels and cogs spinning in their minds.

Given the constraints, timeline and lack of backup, I was sure most squadrons would have baulked at that request. But we were experiencing something unique and I felt deep down that we had momentum on our side. I had never seen a squadron synchronize and work so effectively. During the previous months, we had delivered on every single task. Day, night, good weather and bad, across multiple countries and in the most challenging of scenarios. We had endured the odd scrape and close call – like the damaged airframe stuck in Iraq – but the team had just rolled with the tackles and continued the flow. Every setback had just made everyone stronger and closer.

Since I joined the RAF, I had never seen such a robust and healthy relationship between the engineers, pilots and operations staff. The support and willingness to deliver were truly extraordinary. It was humbling to be a part of such a team. It was a moment in time with a set of characters that gelled and had formed an intangible and unbreakable bond. It felt like we were capable of anything.

At moments like this, when a task was demanding, I had learned not to put pressure on the engineers. The availability and serviceability of the aircraft were key.

The sun was setting. It was decision time.

'Tim, your call. I'll support you, whichever way you want to go.'

Jonny nodded in agreement.

Tim took a breath and nodded, too. 'It would be handy if we can delay the jet going back to the UK for a few hours and load it up. If it isn't needed, we'll strip the weapons off before it flies home. That'll potentially give us five, assuming the jet on its way back from Iraq is serviceable.'

Jonny and I listened.

'I can get Mr B to push some of the maintenance tasks into next week.' Tim paused and his expression changed, the calculations done. 'I think we should go for it.'

'And if a jet goes tech tomorrow?'

'Then it'll be four for four. But they're holding up well and the guys will be keen to make it work.'

Decision made. We were on.

We made our way inside. I wanted to see the Expeditionary Air Wing commander, Dave Burrows, and bumped into Chief Technician Ken Gray on the way. Ken was in charge of the weapons engineers on the squadron. For an operation as kinetic as the one we planned, he was a key part of the puzzle. He had cut his teeth on the Harrier Force and had huge operational experience in Iraq and Afghanistan. There was no bullshit with Ken. He spoke from the heart. I respected him and trusted him enormously. His approach and knowledge had been fundamental to delivering the new Paveway capability.

He had been watching the sunset from the old picnic bench in front of the Operations room, one of my favourite spots on base.

'Afternoon, boss,' he said. 'How was Syria?'

'Lovely weather for the time of year,' I replied. 'Do me a favour, will you. Get in touch with the bomb dump. We're going to drop sixteen Paveways on Saturday. They'll need to prep twenty, including the spare jet.'

He had been sipping coffee and practically spat it out. He wiped his lips and a large grin spread across his face.

'With pleasure!'

The need to annihilate the IED factory was absolutely clear and justified. The bomb-makers assembled suicide vests in all sizes, improvised explosive devices, and land-mines which they buried on roads and randomly in the desert. Nowhere was safe. They concealed booby traps in houses and in plastic toys that contained sufficient explo-sives to blow off the hands of the children who found them. The morning's intelligence briefing had been as dark as the night. ISIS had begun organ harvesting from pris-oners, and had hanged two teenage girls in the centre of Mosul for posting on Twitter. The suffering was unimagin-able, not acts of war but acts of sheer evil. If we could get it right and destroy this house of horrors in one fell swoop, it would not only be a huge tactical success, it would strike a significant blow to Islamic State's campaign of terror.

Jonny and Thorney were discussing the strike when I joined them in the Ops room. Jonny was down to fly the following day, leaving Thorney to run the day's operations while simultaneously sorting the plan single handed. The other pilots would either be flying or sleeping off nights.

'You all right with that?' I asked Thorney, knowing what he was going to say.

'I'll get it done. The secret phone has broken but the emails are working,' he replied. 'I'll do my best.'

'Easy for a man of your calibre,' Jonny remarked. 'Will you have your trousers on or off for it?'

We all laughed.

During the next thirty-six hours, the engineers worked with quiet obsession. The moment the absent Typhoon arrived back from Iraq, the team was swarming all over it, taking panels off and ensuring it was ready to go. As dawn was breaking on Saturday morning, the jets were fully fuelled and loaded: the cannon with its armour-piercing 27 mm shells, the long-range AMRAAM radar-guided missiles, the short-range ASRAAM heat-seeking missiles and four 500 lb Paveway 4 precision bombs.

Thorney was leading as Dragon 1, with JT, myself and Weasel making up the rest of the four-ship. I made my way to the briefing room, where Megatron was setting up the slide deck for the mission. He had been flying around Iraq in Black Hawk helicopters with the JTACs all week and had clearly enjoyed himself.

'You would have loved it, Weasel,' he remarked.

'Weasel would have hated it,' JT said. 'The rotors would have messed up his hair.'

Weasel rolled his eyes and shook his head.

I looked from face to face. Morale was high. They were happy. It augured well for what we had in front of us.

There was a warm, dusty breeze blowing across the concrete pan and the sun was high in the sky. It was roasting in the cockpit. Even before engine start I could feel the sweat slide down my back. All being well, it would be a short sortie, under four hours. The sunlight was glaring; after strapping into the ejection seat, I lowered the dark visor on my helmet to shade my face. I sat there for ten minutes, mind emptied of thoughts, arms resting on the sills, while I waited for the exact time to start the engines.

Two Chinooks returning from a dawn sortie flew low overhead, the dual rotor-blades making their distinctive thumping sound as the helicopters came into the hover and lowered elegantly onto their landing spots. I watched as a dozen or so soldiers climbed out of the back and disappeared into a couple of pickup trucks.

A shimmering heat haze bounced off the tarmac. To my left and right, the Typhoons stood armed to the hilt, poised and ready for action. Standing in front of each jet was an engineer whose job it was to supervise the engine start and conduct the last-minute checks: ensuring pylons were live, safety pins were removed, countermeasures secure and airframe panels all done up.

Precisely on time, to the second, the radio crackled into life.

'Dragon check.'

'2.'

'3.'

'4.'

We skimmed down the runway in succession, the fourth jet airborne just over a minute after the first. My thoughts turned back to the conversation with Jonny and Tim thirty-six hours before. The engineers had truly pulled off something remarkable.

We cruised at 30,000 feet. The aircraft bobbed softly up and down as we held in a loose formation for the transit out. An hour later, we crossed the Iraqi border and joined with the tanker, a United States KC-135. One by one we slipped behind the tanker's hose, gassed up with fuel, then crossed over to the right wing, where we reformed as a four-ship ready to head to our target. The IED factory was about fifty miles to the north.

Ten minutes later, we began running in for our attack. We had split the formation into two elements, spaced a few miles apart. This meant that our weapons in flight would be marginally deconflicted. It also allowed the pilots a little more time for looking at the targeting cameras during the run-up to the attack and for conducting the large number of weapon checks. We could maintain a good lookout under each other's aircraft for any surface-to-air fire as well.

About a minute out, I selected weapon aiming in the HUD. As this pre-planned strike had been authorized at the highest level, there was no requirement to make any radio calls to get permission to drop. We still, as always, scanned the target area and its surrounds for civilians or unexpected activity. In the heat of the day, there was not a soul in the enemy compound. The access road that led to a busy main thoroughfare off to the north was deserted. With the weapon aiming selected, I pushed the Late Arm to live.

The HUD symbols changed to show the four serviceable weapons on my jet and a countdown timer to release. The Litening pod tracked the factory perfectly. My heart thumped inside my G-suit. With a couple of seconds to go, I pressed and held the weapon release button, then waited for what seemed like an eternity for the weapons to drop from the frame.

With a thud the left outboard weapon released, with a small explosive cartridge firing it away from the wing. A few milliseconds later, another thud, this time from the right wing. Then another. Then another. All four Paveways were now in the air.

Forty seconds to impact.

I called my weapon release on the radio so the rest of the formation could hear a successful drop. At the same time, I could hear the releases from the other jets.

We sat through a tense waiting game, anxiously watching the targeting camera images in our separate cockpits as the precious seconds counted down to impact.

Twenty seconds.

Sixteen weapons were flying towards their separate targets.

I zoomed the pod out to observe the whole factory. There was no question about the importance of the attack. I felt the stress ratchet up.

Ten seconds.

Five.

I held my breath as the weapons slammed into the target. With an endless succession of flashes and blasts, the ground below erupted into flying debris. The initial blasts reverberated as the stores of explosives detonated in a series of secondary eruptions like cannon fire, and the buildings vanished into a swirling column of dust and smoke like a tornado which rose a few thousand feet into the sky.

It was an incredible and terrifying sight. The northerly wind slowly cleared away the smoke and we could see the result of the strike. Where an IED factory had been, nothing remained. The complex had been completely and utterly obliterated.

26. Close Aboard

Pilots are, in some ways, control freaks. You have to be. The environment is too dynamic and complex for things to run to chance. You are taught from the very beginning of training that, when airborne, you are the master of your own destiny. Without constant, positive action, fast jets become incredibly unsafe. Surprises are unwelcome.

I had already used up a few of my nine lives flying the Jag and a few more during my time on the Typhoon. These had routinely occurred during vigorous air-to-air training sorties where, in the heat of the moment, at extreme speeds and high G-turns, I had flashed past another jet close enough to hear the roar of the engines and the thump of the disturbed air.

During a busy tactical sortie, you aren't simply flying the aircraft, but constantly reacting to your electronic sensors, glancing at the radar screen, maintaining situational awareness and managing your weapons. A tactical formation consists of at least two jets, more often a dozen or more, that climb and descend at acute angles, by day and night, often passing each other at supersonic closure speeds. During two Typhoon near misses, I had spotted errors at the last moment and flinched away on instinct, missing the other aircraft by little more than fifty feet.

Such events are rare, but not that rare. As an instructor, you pass on your knowledge, but there is no substitute for the lived experience and hours in the air. In most cases, a blunder or impending situation could be picked up before it became critical, and sometimes a sort of sixth sense would kick in if something felt wrong; an awareness that something wasn't quite going to plan, but you couldn't quite put your finger on it. One problem is that you can believe you have perfect situational awareness right up to the point that circumstances show you do not.

Three months into the deployment at RAF Akrotiri, the close air support sorties had started to become routine. The most challenging weaponeering scenarios had been carried out with disciplined targeting and I was beyond satisfied with the skill with which all the squadron pilots were plying their trade. Every day, the guys returned with incredible stories after precision strikes in the most complex scenarios, often with friendlies and enemy just yards apart. They had tracked units of ISIS fighters as they moved through urban areas, cleared roads of IEDs, and seamlessly integrated with unmanned aerial vehicles and foreign fast jets. They were showing restraint, professionalism and tactical confidence. The most extreme circumstances had gradually become the new norm. We were thinking cleanly, unemotionally, ruthlessly about the task. That was a moment of pride. But if the dark sky that night was anything to go by, a fall was bound to follow.

We were over some godforsaken ISIS town in the middle of Iraq, the heavens gloomy, black and starless. Bobby had the tactical lead and I felt unusually relaxed as he organized the formation. Below, in the maze of mud-walled houses, there was little activity. A couple of people walking hastily along a back street; the odd glimmer of light from a window. It was zero degrees Celsius on the ground. As I passed my eye over the jagged shadows of the rooftops, I slipped into a moment's daydream and only snapped out of it when Bobby came on the radio.

'Dragon 2. We'll remain here for ten minutes then head to the tanker. My pod is playing up. I'm going to recycle it. You have the lead.'

'Roger that.'

I banked the aircraft towards the left and looked down once more. The infrared image on the pod camera provided a clear picture of the town's mosque and family compounds. I stared down out of the canopy through the NVGs to get a wider view of the overall area. A car meandered slowly through the empty streets with dulled headlamps like green cat's eyes.

As I glanced up at the HUD to check my altitude, something grey flashed through my peripheral vision and for a moment I could see nothing but a bright blurry haze, completely obliterating all sight from the NVGs. In an instant it was gone, the flash of blindness disappearing from right to left as quickly as it had arrived. I had that heart in the mouth, slightly sick feeling pilots get when something happens that you are not expecting and have no control over. Whatever it was, it had been extremely close, within a few feet. I felt disorientated. The blood drained from my chest and I felt a gnawing pain in the pit of my stomach.

What on earth was that?

My brain moved into overdrive. My entire sight had been momentarily drowned. Could it have been Bobby?

No, it couldn't. He was a thousand feet below and a couple of miles away. Then it dawned on me.

Fuck. I'm over Iraq. It must have been a surface-to-air missile.

It was confusing because I hadn't seen a launch, and the defensive systems on the jet hadn't picked it up either. My heart continued to pound. I peered into the darkness as I instinctively rolled the aircraft to the left a fraction of a second after the object had passed in order to look into its receding path. If I had narrowly escaped a missile attack, I didn't expect to see much at all, potentially the faint glow of a rocket motor.

To my horror, I couldn't believe what was there.

An A330 tanker was making an indolent left-hand turn as it rapidly receded before me – a view I was accustomed to seeing when about to plug in for a refuel. There was virtually no light, but I was so close that I could see it as clear as day through the NVGs, the giant aircraft illuminated by the faintest of infrared light. We had passed at precisely the same altitude with a closing speed of about 600 knots. I calculated that, from the position I was in, I must have missed the left wingtip by a few feet, if not inches.

Not for the first time in the last few weeks, my life had passed rapidly before my eyes. The thought of what might have happened if I had just nudged the stick even by a fraction in the moments leading up to that near mid-air collision was terrifying. I could have slammed into the side of the tanker, causing a huge explosion with the loss of both aircraft and their combined crew. Alternatively, I could have spun out of control and been forced to eject silently and alone into the arms of the enemy we had spent months fighting.

'2 from 1. I've just had a near miss. It was a pretty bad one. Get out of this height block right now. There's a tanker co-altitude.'

'Copy.'

We called it straight away on the radio. The airspace controller immediately responded that there had been an error with the other aircraft being placed into the same piece of sky and in the same altitude block as us. It turned out to be an Australian A330 from which we ended up refuelling later that night.

In the tranquil twin seats at the Airbus controls, the tanker pilots had heard the sound of the jet noise during the close aboard, the throaty roar of the Typhoon engines vibrating through their cockpit as we passed. Even for a couple of hairy Aussies, they sounded pretty shaken on the radio. That made three of us.

I struggled to sleep that night. I lay awake, unable to shrug off images of myself floating down under a parachute in the freezing air to my imminent death on the ground below. Before that moment, the flight had felt calm, almost benign. The intensity of close air support had become normalized: that night flight, with just a single weapon released, had barely raised my heart rate. How quickly things can change.

In the aftermath of Afghanistan and Iraq, the armed forces chiefs were beginning to acknowledge the potential impact from these asymmetric conflicts on serving men and women. Much of the stigma was beginning to disappear. The crippling effects of PTSD were now well known, and it was recognized that the symptoms could grow silently, like a psychological cancer, and occur years after a traumatic event.

I had no idea what the effect of guiding weapons onto enemy targets for months on end would have on the minds of the pilots – or, equally, the ground crew – but I was aware of the potential for lasting impact. The engineers did not strap those bombs onto the aircraft without thinking about the damage they were going to cause, and the pilots bore witness to the after-effects every time they conducted a strike. The implications for mental health were something I took seriously.

During the Afghanistan campaign, the military had introduced a system called 'trauma risk management' (TRiM). The psychology behind it was that an early, subtle intervention, with people talking openly about their experiences, increased the chance of mitigating the risks of a mental health episode later on. For the pilots, the preservation of their aircrew medical status is inexorably linked to their livelihood, and psychological concerns are not easily raised for fear of being grounded. We know now that suppressing emotions can be toxic.

1 Squadron had a TRiM specialist in John Greenhowe – DJ – an ex-Tornado navigator, who had a critical operational support role on the team. We had developed a strategy together that enabled us to monitor the guys through TRiM events masquerading as social gatherings during the weekly non-flying maintenance days. These were an opportunity to talk about complex sorties and weapon events and listen to the experiences of others. Through this method, we tried to normalize what in reality

was not normal, and those who took part came away feeling a little less isolated.

By the following morning, I'd shaken off the last traces of anxiety from the close aboard and sat down to a proper breakfast. Jonny wandered in looking down in the dumps. He had been back in the UK for a few days to do some emergency simulator training, a requirement that couldn't be waived even in the middle of operations. He grabbed a coffee and sat down next to me.

'How was the trip back?' I asked.

'Yeah, it was fine,' he said and glanced away momentarily. 'We had to have Honey put down, our boxer. Sylv and the kids are gutted. She's juggling a lot of stuff.'

'I can imagine. I'm sorry.'

I was reminded of the conversations with Thorney and Bobby. These were the toughest men I knew, but home life and psychological pressures affect everyone. For Sylv, the deployment had triggered memories of Jonny's time as a Para in Iraq. The weeks away, with zero contact and terrifying press reports of casualties, had left her feeling afraid and alone. Every time there was a casualty in the regiment, she worried herself sick with anxiety. When she learned that it wasn't Jonny, it made her feel at once relieved and then guilty for feeling that way. The run-up to Operation Shader had brought it all tumbling back. Incidents like the SAM lock-on, or the tanker near miss were never played back to families.

Jonny drank his coffee.

'We'll get another dog. It will all work out. It always does.'

'Sounds like a plan.' I knew my words were inadequate, but I didn't know what to say.

He stood.

'Right, I'm off to find Megatron and see what's on the horizon for the day.'

'Try to stop him jumping on any more Black Hawks will you,' I said, and he laughed.

27. Time and Eternity

The man who never alters his opinion is like
standing water, and breeds reptiles of the mind.
                                        William Blake

We had been in Iraqi airspace for less than two minutes
and were in the middle of tanking when the urgent tones
of airborne command and control sounded on the radio.

'Dragon, how quickly can you get to Fallujah?'

I looked down at the moving map. It was about eighty
miles.

'We can be there in ten minutes.'

'As soon as you complete your tanking, check in with
the JTAC. We need to prosecute a target as soon as
possible.'

'Copy.'

I was flying in a formation with Nick Callinswood – Cal.
He had been with the squadron for a couple of years, after
flying close air support missions on the Tornados in
Afghanistan. The diversity of experience he brought with
his crossover to the Typhoon meant we were able to operate effectively as a team, with either of us taking on any
role as the situation demanded. He knew what to expect
and it needed little further communication between us.

You learned to read a response by the tone of

someone's voice, judge their capacity by the length of the silence before they responded to a transmission. Sometimes you sensed what the other pilot was thinking, as you were on the same track. You didn't jump on the radio as the wingman, unless it was an emergency. You built your situational awareness, assisted as best you could and let the leader lead. Each formation position has a role. I remembered Mike Seares's gentle rebuke when I was an over-eager junior pilot on the Jag. 'When you're the monkey, be the monkey. When you're the organ grinder, grind like a good 'un.'

The priority right now was for both jets to maintain precise formation on the Voyager tanker with the hoses connected. I still had another ninety seconds to go before I was full.

Come on. Come on.

I watched the digital numbers slowly rise. I am not a naturally patient man. Patience isn't a gift. It is learned.

It was rare to get an immediate call to strike having barely crossed the border. Normally, other jets would be providing cover for that airspace. There was clearly something urgent – I had heard it in the voice of the controller – and my mind went into crossword mode trying to work out what.

The Voyager crew had been listening in.

'Clear to depart as soon as you're full,' one of the guys said.

This was useful as it would save a minute or so of admin and we could get on with the task. Sixty seconds is a long time on the battlefield.

My jet was full. I eased back from the basket, brought

the probe in and began to move across to the right-hand side of the Voyager. From the corner of my eye, I could see Cal's jet beginning to drop back as the probe disconnected. I called us to set heading 040 degrees, climb to 25,000 feet and accelerate to Mach 0.85. There was a decent tailwind at height. We would probably cover the eighty miles in about eight minutes.

'Good luck, Dragon. Catch you in ninety minutes – seeeyyaaa.'

As the Voyager checked out, we went straight over to the JTAC frequency.

'This is Dragon. Checking in as fragged. We're routing to Fallujah. We've got eight Paveway 4s, 27 mm cannon and Litening pods. Ready for tasking.'

An American voice, slow and steady, immediately responded.

'Hey, Dragon. We've got a situation here. There's an anti-aircraft gun that's recently been active. It's now hidden in a treeline. We need to take that out as soon as we can. We've also got an urgent follow-on task. Call ready for the 9-line.'

'Roger that. Go ahead with the data.'

The controller confirmed the target details and the rules of engagement.

'The anti-aircraft gun's an immediate threat and needs to be destroyed as soon as possible.'

'Copy.'

I entered the coordinates into the kit and selected the Litening pod. I wanted to try to see this gun. Cal would be doing the same. We were still about twenty-five miles out in daylight with good visibility. We'd be overhead in less than three minutes. I stared at the real-time video image in the cockpit and could make out some palm trees immediately to the west of a couple of two-storey buildings surrounded by scrubland. As we flew closer to the target, the site appeared with even greater clarity. I called the JTAC.

'This is Dragon. We've got the palm trees.'

I datalinked the image from our Litening pods directly to the soldiers coordinating the strike so that they could see exactly what we could. In this way we would be able to confirm the precise location of the target.

'See your image, Dragon. The anti-aircraft gun is beneath the two palm trees, twenty feet to the west of the northern building.'

'2. Capture.'

Great. Cal had acquired the target as well.

The JTAC continued.

'We're going to need you to generate a coordinate for that as the target just moved. It has recently been actively firing at aircraft. We have clearance to engage.'

'Copy that.'

'We also need you to destroy the ammo storage in the building to the south-east. But we want to restrict collateral damage. What weaponeering do you recommend?'

I put the aircraft into a gentle left-hand wheel, staying away from the immediate target area, and got Cal to set up a similar orbit 1,000 feet above me. We could now work as a pair, using both targeting pod cameras to get as much information as possible. Time was in short supply. It always is. I zoomed in on the pod and could now clearly see both targets.

As the weapons would create a damage radius from the blast and fragmentation, we had to be absolutely certain there was no one close to the targets and their surroundings during the attack *and* during the time of flight of the weapons. If we saw civilian cars, motorbikes or people approaching, we would hold off until the area was clear. Anyone seen operating the anti-aircraft gun was almost certainly hostile, but we couldn't rule out that people – potentially children – might be innocently using the artillery piece as a climbing frame.

I couldn't see any movement. Even the wild dogs were sleeping.

'Dragon 2, cover.'

This clipped communication meant that Cal would zoom out on the targeting pod and check the surrounding area again while I generated a coordinate for the anti-aircraft weapon and entered it into the targeting kit. He would also get ready to strike if I had a system failure.

'Copy.'

I now concentrated on the ammo storage facility. There was a building beyond the target that we didn't want to touch, and some additional buildings off to the east. By indicating a specific direction for our line of attack, we could make sure – to a certain extent, at least – that the weapon fragmentation fell into open land. I programmed the weapon to strike at a steep angle. Setting a long fuse delay meant the Paveway would corkscrew into the building before exploding. If the tactic worked, the blast would cause virtually no damage beyond its four walls.

It had been a little over fifteen minutes since we left the tanker eighty miles away and we were ready to strike. I relayed the weaponeering information to the JTAC in answer to his last question. The response was instant.

'Dragon. You're cleared live.'

I set the aircraft up exactly on the agreed attack heading, engaged the auto-throttle and again checked the weapons. Always. Time after time. You check and double-check and check again. I had allocated two Paveways, one for each target, with different fuse settings. I triple-checked the coordinates. Fifteen seconds to release. The countdown circle in the head up display now showed a decreasing quarter circle.

The dry dusty landscape drifted by in my peripheral vision. The pod image was steady on the target. Still no people in sight. Cal was out to the right, slightly above my altitude, looking into the target area and scanning the ground for the threat of surface-to-air missile launches or civilians passing near by. On the hot, sweaty throttle, one of my fingers rested lightly on the defensive countermeasures switch. If Cal called a missile launch, I would break off the attack, send the engines to idle to reduce the heat signature, and push down hard on the switch. This would release a plume of infrared countermeasures designed to seduce the missile. One way or another, it would all be over in a couple of seconds. I scanned the instruments.

Altitude good.

Speed good.

Weapon aiming steady.

Pod tracking nicely.

Areas still clear.

Five seconds to go.

Four. Three. Two . . .

I flicked the Late Arm open and committed the attack, squeezing down with my thumb. The short pause lasted an eternity . . . this is what purgatory must be like, I thought . . . and then thump, thump . . . The airframe trembled.

Both weapons in the air.

'Two away. Forty seconds to impact.'

I banked sharply to the left of the target and moved the Litening pod over the exact strike position. The weapons were guiding autonomously towards their coordinates, but if the anti-aircraft gun had been shifted to a new position, I was ready to move the pod and switch the weapon into laser-seeking rather than GPS mode. That way I could track the moving target and keep the laser spot on the gun so that the weapon would home in on it.

Ten seconds to impact.

Five seconds.

The ground erupted as both weapons smashed into their targets and exploded. For a moment the pod image was shrouded in a swirling blanket of dust. Smoke rose into the air from where the storage facility had stood, the secondary detonations from the ammunition throwing up towers of ash.

The breeze chased off the dust cloud and I had a clearer image of the target site. The weapons had done their job. The storage building had a clear hole in the roof. Some internal walls had fallen in, but zero damage had been caused to the surrounding area. Just a few stumps remained where the palm trees had stood and the concealed gun designed to shoot aircraft out of the sky was nothing more than a tangle of metal like a twisted coat hanger.

Normally, we would have remained in the area to

conduct an additional battle damage assessment and get as much recorded imagery of the strike as possible. But not today.

'Dragon. High order detonation seen on both targets. We need to move you north immediately. We have reports of a sniper.'

'Dragon 2, yours.'

On the radio, I gave the tactical lead to Cal.

The JTAC came back on the air.

'We've got an ISIS sniper reported on a rooftop. He's got a long-barrelled weapon and he's shooting at civilians in the area. We don't have an exact location, just a district. We need you to find him. This is a self-defence mission. As soon as we locate the target you will be cleared to engage.'

We spun north and set the speed to almost nine miles a minute. We could be overhead the location in about 180 seconds.

The JTAC had been given an updated threat location that was accurate to a few hundred metres, a reasonably narrow area to search. We threw our Litening pods down and began to scan methodically across streets lined with houses that looked half built or half demolished, derelict compounds, an abandoned car: the habitual waste and chaos. Many families had evacuated and those which had remained were now being shot at by a solitary zealot hidden from view. We circled overhead like birds of prey, and went from house to house, zooming in on anything that looked suspicious.

Nothing. Nothing. Nothing. The gunman may have been aware of us circling above and was keeping his head down. We were playing a game of patience. Not my strong suit.

The radio popped back into life.

'Dragon 2. I can see something. A man is lying prone on the south-east corner of a building.'

Cal datalinked the image to the JTAC.

'Affirm. That is the sniper with a rifle. We need to prosecute as soon as possible. Dragon, you are cleared to strike with a single weapon.'

Cal set up his attack as I scanned the area. The fundamental first steps, as always, were to avoid civilian collateral damage and to maintain a constant lookout for surface-to-air missiles. The pad of my finger rested on the radio transmit button. Cal's safety was my responsibility. If I observed a threat of any kind, I would call him to break. He would react instinctively, automatically, no questions asked.

Aside from the sniper, the streets were clear. Everyone must have been driven inside to hide. I would have done the same.

Cal was ready. No hesitation. Totally professional.

It was all over in less than sixty seconds.

He released an airburst, detonating the weapon in the air in such a way that the energy and the fragments from the explosion were distributed evenly, taking out the sniper and doing minimal damage to the building.

As soon as the smoke cleared from the attack, the JTAC was back on the airwaves.

'Dragon, how much fuel have you got?'

I glanced at the gauges. We needed enough to make it to the tanker, allow five minutes to plug, and carry enough spare to head for the nearest runway if there was a technical failure during refuelling.

'About twenty minutes,' I replied.

'Roger. We need you to head to the tanker now. There is something else kicking off to the east. Gas up and call me back on this frequency as soon as you're done.'

We tanked for the second time.

'We've got multiple enemy in a trench system. They're equipped with heavy machine guns and rocket propelled grenades. They are engaging the Iraqi army at this time. We need to prosecute as soon as possible.'

'Roger that,' I replied.

I wriggled about in the seat to stretch my back. I was physically tired, mentally drained. My throat was dry. I lifted the dark visor and squinted in the brilliant sunshine. At the same time, I released the oxygen mask. It fell away on its metal clasps and I savoured the momentary relief from the sweaty sting of the rubber which had been glued to my face for hours. I reached behind me into the little flight bag I had shoved next to the ejection seat and grabbed a Gatorade, which glowed bright orange in the sunlight. I squeezed the juice through the drinking cap and I gulped the fluid down in one go as the plastic collapsed under my grip.

Mask back on, visor down, we headed north-east to Ramadi. We could be overhead in five minutes. From the scenario brief, this sounded like it was going to be one hell of a scene. I double-checked the aircraft's weapon systems and countermeasures again. We had been airborne for more than four hours, in the jet for almost five.

Using diggers robbed from somewhere or acquired on

the black market, Islamic State engineers had constructed multiple trench lines to provide ballistic shelter. In much the same style as First World War defences, the zigzag cuts into the desert were wide enough for fighters to move along in relative safety.

Just under the speed of sound, we raced over streets lined with rubble piled up in vast heaps like tombstones, a scene of dystopian devastation. Soon we were over the battlefield. Iraqi infantry were bogged down in a huge contact on the outskirts of the city, facing an enemy firing RPGs and automatic weapons as they dodged in and out of the trenches. Soldiers were running in all directions. It was an inferno of explosions, men screaming and dying in the continuous crossfire. We needed to keep emotions under control and understand who was who.

'Dragon, we are overhead. We can see the trenches.'

28. First Strafe

Whilst shooting, think of nothing else, brace the
whole of your body . . . concentrate on your sight.
'Sailor' Malan, 'Ten of My Rules for Air
Fighting' (Rule 2), 1940, during the
Battle of Britain

An unarmed drone was on station with the capability to identify and highlight the targets with an onboard laser. Using the Typhoon's laser spot seeker, our Litening pods could search for and acquire that particular laser spot, cuing us in. Working together, we could maintain a high level of situational awareness and rapidly identify targets between aircraft.

The good fortune that the UAV was in our piece of the sky was offset by bad weather closing in. The cumulus clouds popping up would make target identification that much harder. If we flew through the clouds, we would lose sight of the ISIS trench system. The alternative was to set up a flexible racetrack that would weave around the clouds in such a way that we kept a line of sight with the targets.

To keep the Litening pods pointing in the correct direction required turning the jets to the left and the right every few seconds with one hand, while moving the targeting camera with the other. In a few moments, we were overhead the close quarters struggle between the friendly forces and ISIS fighters. We set off on an orbit between the clouds. I called the UAV, callsign 'Godfather', on the radio to confirm our position.

'Godfather. This is Dragon. We are ready for laser handover.'

'Roger that. Laser on.'

It was an American mid-western voice as clear as day from somewhere thousands of miles away, in all likelihood the mainland United States.

The UAV operators would be sitting in a cockpit, with all the displays and screens of a conventional aircraft, relaying data via satellite to the airframe. The reaction to drones in the press had been controversial – at best – and it was sometimes forgotten that a UAV always has a pilot at the controls. Drone attacks are subject to exactly the same rules of engagement and restrictions as any other aircraft.

'Unmanned' does not mean 'autonomous'. Drones can fly for extended periods, some in excess of twenty-four hours. This enables crews to be swapped out while the eye in the sky maintains continuous vigilance over an area. For targets that are difficult to identify, multiple intelligence specialists can gather around the cameras to assist with the image analysis and discuss different visual angles and requirements directly with the system operators.

Drone crews face no physical risk. But the mental pressures are similar to those of other combat pilots. Operators spend eight hours at the controls, striking targets and witnessing the aftermath on high-definition screens right in front of them. At the end of the day, they drive home, collect their kids from nursery, make dinner with their partners, and try to live a normal life, with the battle still playing through their heads. There is no geographic separation between conflict and home life, no space to process or reflect, no means to detach and reintegrate. For UAV pilots, this would be their life, day in, day out, year in, year out. A shift at the office would mean a commute to a windowless room no bigger than a shipping container for a long virtual flight in Iraq or Syria, with all the mental tension and violence that it frequently brought. I didn't envy them.

The UAV had found the target and switched the laser designator on. I zigzagged the jet to avoid the cloud and put the pod into laser search mode. During the interminable wait for the software processing to work, you have no idea if the laser return is strong enough for the pod to see it. It was not completely reliable. On occasions, you would not pick up the return and would have to reposition and try again, always at the cost of valuable minutes.

Suddenly the pod jumped location and indicated a good laser spot.

Thank God for that.

I selected a tracking mode, wrote down the GPS location it presented and zoomed in. I could clearly see the trench line running east to west and an ongoing firefight. ISIS soldiers were attacking Iraqi troops a few hundred metres away to the north. The scene was frenzied and fast moving. Combatants were running along the trench, climbing out, letting off some rounds, and returning again to the trench or darting forward towards the city. Others were in open fields, with RPGs over their shoulders, moving east towards Baghdad. Fighters were advancing or retreating in ways that defied logic, as if there were no overall command, just a general order for mass attack.

It was hot with the sun burning down, and it must have been deafening for the troops on the ground as large calibre rounds sailed through the air and exploded in mushrooms of rock dust that sailed off in yellow-tinted streamers. Into this mayhem, we had to place high explosive weapons – released at high speed and high altitude – into precise, bullseye locations. If we didn't get these attacks inch perfect, we could easily kill the very people whose lives we were there to protect.

The JTAC came back onto the radio.

'Dragon. Are you visual with three ISIS fighters running to the east?'

'Affirm.'

'Roger. They have been engaging friendlies and are now repositioning to attack the flank. They pose an imminent threat. We need a strike on these targets immediately. How long will it take you to set up?'

'Copy. About sixty seconds.'

Three ISIS fighters were sprinting across a field, hidden from the Iraqi forces' sight by a scrub line. Two of them ran north and took up a new firing position. The third headed down an irrigation ditch, then turned and attacked the friendlies once more from a different angle.

'Dragon 2, are you visual with the individual who just broke from the three?'

'Affirm,' Cal answered.

'Your target. We'll prosecute simultaneously. Deconflict laser codes. We'll strike on a heading of 060 degrees from battle formation.'

'Dragon 2. Copy.'

We struck both targets. The earth heaved and the three fighters were dead. Their motionless bodies were clearly visible.

My breathing raced in the oxygen mask.

God, I've just killed someone again. How can this be allowed? How on earth did I end up doing this? They were killing us all over Europe. Now here we are killing them all over the Middle East. It all seemed terribly wrong, a huge failure of humankind. I felt no satisfaction; I was just numb.

There was no time to dwell further. There never is. Just act and react, scan the systems and defensive computers, fly the jet, avoid the clouds, monitor the weapons, slew the cameras, assess the fuel burn, watch for the restricted airspace, stay visual with the friendlies, track the enemy, ensure the rules of engagement are met, keep communicating with the JTAC, keep monitoring for collateral damage, work out where I need to be in one minute, guess what could catch me out the next. Relentless.

Cal was immediately retasked onto another group of ISIS fighters directly engaging the Iraqis. He carried out his second direct hit, then a third.

We were running out of weapons after striking multiple targets across the region. But still the fighting raged on beneath us. Then the JTAC asked me to confirm our jets were armed with the 27 mm cannon. He was about to talk me onto the first gun target in the Typhoon's operational career.

This was heady stuff, with significant risk. A few days earlier, I had been on the auth desk when Jonny walked in visibly shaken up. He had been flying near the Syrian border, preparing for a strike, when he spotted through his NVGs the tell-tale bloom and corkscrew of a surface-to-air missile launch directly towards his jet.

'I just froze,' he said. 'For a moment I was mesmerized. I couldn't believe what I was seeing. Then I snapped out of it. I threw the throttles to idle, broke the jet onto its side and smashed out the countermeasures. The missile streaked past behind me, and bloody close.'

As I took the laser spot handover from Godfather, my heart quickened. I wanted to get us all back to the UK in one piece, and now, late in the deployment, we had experienced a few close calls. We had been lucky so far, but you only needed to be unlucky once.

During my first fruitless interview at Cranwell, I had told the two starched officers that I wanted to join the RAF because I was patriotic, that I wanted to serve my country. I was simply doing the job I had signed on to do. I was calm.

I now had to fly at 500 mph, descend at thousands of feet per minute, and squeeze the trigger at the precise time to hit the target. If I fired too early, the rounds would scatter during the flight and likely miss. If I fired too late, I would potentially fly right into the fragmentation from the bullets, or worse, into the ground. I needed to aim the aircraft, not the gun, and if the sight was just a millimetre away from the target, the bullets would miss by hundreds of feet. I would get one chance only. My intention was to fire a long burst of two to three seconds. The rounds were armour piercing and supersonic.

On strafe training sorties, the targets were set up on dedicated ranges so that they were distinct and obvious. It was nothing like that now. Flying away to set up for the attack, I craned my head over my shoulder to remain visual with the target as it turned from a sizeable bush to a tiny speck vanishing to almost nothing.

Things happen fast in a fast jet. In twenty seconds, I was ready to turn and roll back on my target. The JTAC pressed for an immediate attack.

I stared through the HUD in search of the target. I made it out after a couple of seconds. Ten seconds to go. Adrenaline was coursing through my veins. I tried to brush aside thoughts of the recent missile attack on Jonny. Through 400 knots. I selected some pre-emptive counter-measures with a switch on the throttle and fired the radar to start ranging to the target.

Do. Not. Fuck. This. Up.

My heart felt like it was going to burst through my flying suit. Sweat stung my eyes.

Five seconds to go. 450 knots. Speed increasing.

Bloody thing.

The radar ranging was suddenly jumpy and the sight bounced, just a fraction, but enough to need a correction. I eased the jet nose down a minute amount, settling the aiming point of the sight in the HUD back onto the target. All my effort, all my concentration, all my focus was on that aiming point. With my thumb I flicked the Late Arm up to live, and rested the index finger of my right hand on the trigger.

Three seconds to go. Almost 500 knots.

The whole airframe pulsed as I started to fire.

Bang bang bang bang bang.

The 27 mm rounds were in the air travelling at 4,000 feet per second. The desert scrub was rising up fast around my ears. The aircraft ground proximity warning was screaming.

PULL UP.

I was in the threat envelope of every ISIS weapon on the battlefield.

I felt very alone.

Suddenly a red caption appeared on the central warning panel, and the red attention-getters flashed before my eyes.

GUN FAIL.

Fuck.

Instantaneously I released the trigger, pulled back on the stick and started climbing at thirty degrees nose up. At this moment I was at my most vulnerable. If the ISIS fighters hadn't seen me approach, a few hundred feet above them, they would definitely see me now. I sent out more infrared countermeasures to decoy any missiles and rocketed into the sky, initially pulling five G.

With the ground falling away fast, I slammed the throttles forward. The Rolls-Royce engines kicked to life with a roar that bounced across the flat desert landscape, propelling the jet skywards like a rocket. I loved those engines, the sheer raucous power. Through 10,000 feet, through 15,000 feet and climbing. I levelled off and breathed again.

'Dragon. Looks like we've had some effect, but some rounds went slightly long. Need an immediate re-attack.'

'Roger.'

It would have been madness to try and strafe again. I still had one Paveway left in the armoury and remained visual with the target. I circled the aircraft straight back onto the release heading and dropped the last weapon the formation had.

'One away. Thirty seconds.'

I fired the laser and kept the cross hairs fixed on the

target. Thirty seconds later, the weapon slammed precisely into the stretch of bushes and left nothing but a plume of smoke and a deep scar in the landscape. The ISIS firing stopped.

We were out of weapons. Out of fuel. After another trip to the tanker, we set a course to the south-west. I was exhausted. I was sure Cal felt the same. In a formation there is teamwork without glances or smiles, with no mutual frowns of perplexity. It was all done by sticking to the tactics, the plan, and listening to the restrained changes of tone in your wingman's voice on the radio.

An hour later, I caught the first glimpse of the hazy Mediterranean sea-line on Israel's coast and the beginning of a pale sunset. I consciously relaxed my shoulders and stretched as much as the limited space would allow. The tension eased. We had walked to the jets at 0800. It was now approaching 1600. In those eight hours I had barely paused for breath.

Mission reports would have to be written on landing, weapon write-ups and intelligence to feed back to HQ. There would undoubtedly be a lot of questions about the strafe. I had a lot of questions myself.

For now, it was a simple transit into the setting sun and I tried not to think about the operation. The first thing I wanted to do after I'd finished the reports was FaceTime my daughter and find out how her day had been at school. Maybe a holiday in the early summer would be nice. No doubt the email inbox would be full. It would be a brief pause. We were due back into Iraqi airspace again in thirty-six hours.

29. Distractions

When I landed and taxied back, I was surprised to see Ken Gray waiting at the de-arming pan. He was wearing bright yellow ear defenders and a broad grin. It was rare to receive a welcoming committee after a trip.

I shut down the jet and opened the canopy. The warm Cypriot air filled the cockpit and I gulped it down like a tonic. I was physically and psychologically drained, relieved to be back on terra firma, and just a pinch satisfied. It had been the longest mission to date and we had done our job as well as it could have been done. I climbed out of the jet and down the steps. Ken was passing some 'Remove Before Flight' weapon tags to another engineer, and their red straps flapped in the breeze.

'What a day you've had,' he said.

'You could say that. Good to see you, Ken.' His smile was infectious. I felt better already. 'Bloody hell, I'm knackered.'

He nodded eagerly. He wanted more. News of the strafe attack would have run through the squadron like a virus.

'We had to support some huge contacts, about the biggest I've seen,' I continued. 'Cal dealt with a sniper and we destroyed some anti-aircraft artillery.'

He looked up at the aircraft. 'So, I can see – you've cleaned the jets off. How did the strafe go?'

I shrugged. 'All good to begin with. Then the bloody

gun failed after twenty-six rounds. Hugely frustrating,' I said.

'I'll take a look. I bet I know what it is.'

'This isn't the first time. The damn thing has been unreliable for years.'

We walked back across the baked tarmac towards the Ops room. I knew about some of the 27 mm issues, having been involved in the development of the Typhoon strafe since its inception a decade before. It had been suggested that the Typhoon would never need an internal gun in the first place. This showed a total lack of foresight after the selfsame experience with the Harrier and Phantom: designed without a gun system, then needing one. In the end we had been spared that particular fiasco, but manufacturing issues had followed alleged manufacturing resolutions: 'the gun wasn't a priority', apparently. Well, now the 27 mm cannon had been needed on operations and had been found wanting.

That aside, the Typhoon had performed superbly overall and the Paveways had been incredibly accurate. By this stage, we had conducted hundreds of strikes. Every single one had been a DH. Crucially, this meant there had not been a single report of civilian casualties.

This remarkable achievement was, to a huge extent, due to the way that Ken made sure his team was meticulous in fitting and securing the weapons to the aircraft, then checking and rechecking all of the sensors and connections. He had always been personally supportive and we'd often found the best solutions by bouncing ideas off each other.

'You should wear those ear defenders more often, Ken, they suit you,' I said.

'I know, and it's much more enjoyable being around the pilots when you can't hear what they're saying.'

Cal was waiting in the Ops room with the army liaison and intelligence officers to begin the debrief. With the mission recorded on the cockpit video tapes, we were able to review the sortie and construct a detailed mission report for headquarters. As always, we then studied the attack in slow time – frame by frame – to draw out tactical lessons, make sure we had followed procedures correctly and to ensure that we had not unknowingly caused any accidental damage.

The debrief took two hours. I went through the mission chronologically, how we had identified the rooftop sniper, how we had to liaise with the American UAV and split our attacks to cope with the rapidly changing firefight on the ground. Jonny was around and had joined us in the debrief room. He was keen to review the strafe attack footage.

'Mind if I take a look?' he asked.

He leaned towards the computer screen and with the mouse inched the video forward to look at the weapon aiming and attack in millisecond segments.

'The profile worked fine. The target was a bastard to stay eyes on,' I said, slouching back in my chair. 'But the bloody radar was jumpy. The pipper was bouncing around and then it jammed mid-burst.'

'They said that issue had been fixed.'

'Exactly. We've been here before.'

'The group captain wants to see you, and headquarters have already asked for a full report about what happened.'

'Can't wait.'

I finally grabbed some food. Flying fighters is the perfect diet. When I was really tired, I lost my appetite. I forced some chicken and rice down, drank a lot of water, then headed back to my bunk to crash out. I was too tired to sleep and lay there like an old clock slowly unwinding. The airfield was quiet. The jets on the night sorties wouldn't be in for another few hours and I wondered if I would be woken later by the engine rumble as they landed. Not that I minded. It was always good to know the guys were safely back.

The sun slowly faded from the sky, the room darkened and the sound of the cicadas drifted in through the open window. My thoughts turned inevitably back to the long eight hours we had spent in the aircraft that day. We had been right in the thick of it, and had caused one hell of a lot of casualties – the distress over this loss of human life offset to a certain extent by knowing we had saved the lives of many of the Iraqi soldiers on the ground.

Cal and I had come away unscathed. But my primary emotion wasn't relief, or shock at the nature of the day's events, it was exasperation that the cannon had failed during the attack. This was a known problem. Why hadn't it been sorted out? Tomorrow I would write a full report and it was my hope that the operational evidence might put some pressure on the manufacturer to fix the issues that they should have resolved years ago.

The fact that my reactions were more about aircraft reliability and mission efficiency than the extreme violence we'd left in our wake did not concern me at the time. Only with hindsight did I come to recognize this disparity. Where had the emotional impact of the events gone? Where was my empathy? Where was my compassion?

We were becoming machines. The shock and exhilaration of the first weapon drops had subsided into a ruthless, professional efficiency. We were completely focussed on delivering precise air support in highly complex scenarios. I had constructed a hard emotional shell, and I suspected that most of the team had done the same.

After an attack, the JTAC would give a quick mission report. If the tasking had gone as planned, it would be as clinical as: 'DH, high order explosion seen, target destroyed.' When there had been casualties, it would simply be reported as: 'Two enemy KIA.'

We would scribble down the JTAC's words on a scrap of paper to help generate an accurate mission report from the cockpit notes. I would routinely write '2 KIA' with no more emotion than I would have written a shopping list. Maybe the emotional detachment was a necessity, a form of self-defence. Hours later, at the end of the mission, after multiple separate attacks, the intensity and the information overload meant they often merged and became hazy. It was only during the video debriefs that the detail of each event could be fully recalled.

Within the protective shell, I nursed my deepest feelings: I missed my daughter. I chatted to my family, but they felt distant, detached from my reality. I could appreciate the beauty of a sunset when I went for an evening run along the cliffs, and was moved by the astonishing sight of the world as each day I cruised over the Dead Sea and watched as it gave way to the rocky, rugged expanse of desert.

When I awoke every morning, I wondered what surprises the day had in store – aside from flying missions, writing reports, dealing with the email tsunami and the welfare and discipline expected from me as the squadron boss. The House of Commons Defence Committee had visited the previous week as part of the Iraq Inquiry. They had asked tricky questions about whether we had targeted ISIS in support of the Kurdish militias in Syria. We hadn't. But the questions had felt intrusive. They had softened a little when we sat them in the cockpit of a jet.

That particular morning, as the early beams of sunlight streamed through a gap in the curtains, I shaved, clambered into my flying suit and remembered: oh, yes, we have a royal visit today.

This would ordinarily have been a huge honour, but its taking place in the midst of what we were doing meant my main feeling was ambivalence. Princess Anne was making a whistle-stop tour of British forces in Cyprus and was visiting the base for an hour to see the Typhoon and Tornado squadrons. On my way to meet her, I checked in with the engineers and pilots who were about to walk for a mission. They had been briefed to expect to support a special forces tasking in Syria. I wished them luck. It was going to be a tough one.

The headquarters had managed to find some china coffee cups and posh biscuits, but the small gathering was informal, and I was far too immersed in the operation to feel nervous meeting a member of the Royal Family. Anne – in tweeds, despite the heat – turned out to be incredibly warm and personable. She showed authentic interest in what we were doing, her questions were informed and she had a great sense of humour. We chatted as a group politely for about fifteen minutes, then she turned to me.

'Are you flying out here yourself?'

'Yes, Your Royal Highness,' I replied. 'We're flying around the clock. The pilots fly long missions every other day. In between we are debriefing, doing some mission analysis and planning. The engineers are fixing the jets twenty-four hours a day.'

'Are you flying today?'

'No, I was up yesterday. It was a busy trip.' I spared her the gory details and added, 'The jets are getting caned.'

This made her equerry snort for some reason. A few minutes later, the meeting was over and she was ushered out of the room.

The royal party and headquarters team left to continue their tour and I stood there for a few minutes eating the last of the biscuits with James Freeborough – Freebs – the boss of 31 Squadron, who operated the Tornados. We had become firm friends and our squadrons had formed a close bond. The banter and connections among our crews had allowed us to share experiences and learn from each other.

'It's bloody weird,' Freebs said. 'Last year we were in Spain together on that NATO det, and look where we are now.' He glanced around at nothing in particular. 'Then, all of this. Dropping weapons one minute, hoping a Russian SAM doesn't have a pop, striking targets, not wanting to fuck up . . .'

'. . . and Princess Anne turns up on base.'

He nodded thoughtfully. 'I thought she was great. Fantastic tweed.'

One morning when I was in the office working, I paused to listen as Ben Spoor went through his debrief with the intelligence officer. Spoory and I had been mates since our training days at Cold Lake in Canada. He'd gone on to fly the Tornado F3, and then Reaper UAVs in the United States, before crossing to Typhoons. The way he was speaking so naturally now, as if talking about a game of golf – he was a keen golfer – struck me as vaguely surreal; all the more so because it could have been any one of us providing the same report in the same tone of voice. He was describing an attack over Fallujah.

'Six KIA reported by the JTAC from that strike. The mortar was also destroyed.'

'And what happened next?' asked the intelligence officer.

'We tanked. It was pretty tight, as the basket was bouncing up and down with all the thunderstorms in the area. I plugged with one minute's worth of fuel remaining until I had to divert.'

'What happened after the tanking?'

'We conducted surveillance on a marketplace and saw some fighters carrying machine guns rounding up villagers in a group. There were about five of them and about twenty civilians, including some children. The JTAC noted that ISIS had been conducting public beheadings in that location the previous day, so they might have been getting ready to do it again.'

He paused as he thought about the next phase of the sortie.

'We then routed to support a troops-in-contact. It was danger close, the friendlies were just fifty metres away. We then completed a pairs simultaneous strike against two more snipers, then destroyed two stolen Humvees identified by a drone, which provided the laser spot for the Typhoons to use to guide their weapons.'

'Have you got all the coordinates from the attacks and the ROE?'

'Yep, I've written it all down and teed up the Litening footage.'

Spoory was sipping tea and talking as the intelligence officer typed. The mission had been as tough as they get. Listening in on the debrief made me appreciate even more how well the squadron had performed and how tight we were as a team. A smile crossed my lips as I remembered one night during flying training in Canada when we went as a gang for a curry. Spoory fell asleep for some reason. As he lay there with his head on the table, next to a basket of naan, we crept out and left him to pay the bill.

It was the camaraderie that kept us sane and kept us going. We had put up emotional walls to protect ourselves from the reality of the operation. But at some point, I thought, the feelings we harboured would come bursting out and those walls would need to come down.

Thirty minutes after hearing Spoory's debrief, I received a call from the department on base that controlled the local vehicles. The squadron had been issued with a few cars and a knackered old minibus. The person on the other end of the line ranted at me about the pilots who had taken the minibus off base without filling out the paperwork correctly. An official complaint had been made and I was now being warned that if there was to be a repeat, the vehicle would be removed from the squadron.

It was these petty things that ground you down and this particular conversation irritated me more than the enemy had managed to all week. We were under relentless pressure, day in, day out, and, truth be told, the minibus paperwork was not high on my list of priorities. My first instinct was to tell the official to sod off, but I reluctantly engaged my remaining diplomatic brain cells to come up with a resolution.

As the boss, I did not want my pilots distracted by this utter trivia. They needed to focus 100 per cent on their missions. A poorly executed attack could cause an immediate loss of life to friendly troops or civilians. We went to extraordinary lengths to avoid that happening. It exasperated me that the RAF expected pilots to perform in these extreme circumstances for months at a time, and then nibbed them with minuscule administrative tasks the exact moment they landed back from operational sorties.

Sometimes the Royal Air Force seems to lose its way with this sort of thing. It is probably the same in all large organizations when critically important and irrelevant tasks rear their heads at the same time. But in the context of operations the differences were acute, and the priority of combat missions seemed sometimes to get lost in the banality of paperwork and process. For those who had to strap a jet onto their back and get into action over the skies of Iraq and Syria, the juxtaposition defied all logic and common sense. The constant flip-flop between wartime and peacetime every twelve hours was draining and made it impossible to sustain a balanced mindset.

I was also beginning to feel fatigued in a way that was different from the tired feeling you get behind the eyes after a restless night. I was eating well, sleeping pretty well, and exercising. But the weariness was deeper. It was the end of March. We had not stopped since the NATO detachment back in October and had been on operations since early December. We still had a couple of weeks to go and I needed to maintain complete focus before handing the operation over in good order to the next squadron.

Midweek, I was flying a sortie with Rainman – Tom Hansford – over Hit, a small, ancient town in Iraq. Two snipers were hunkered down in separate places in the same low building. We were called in to conduct a strike on both snipers, two weapons dropped onto two different positions simultaneously.

'Dragon, confirm when you have got the target coordinates in your kit. We need to move on this strike as quickly as we can.'

The JTAC was doing his best to sound calm, but I recognized a clear sense of urgency.

'I've got the targets, I'm tally two,' I replied.

'OK. The building immediately to the south-west, right next to the targets, *that* is the city mosque. Under no circumstances can that be hit.'

'Roger that. I have the mosque. I am tally the targets, two sniper positions. I will need to use a steep impact angle on these weapons so they can clear the mosque.'

'Affirm. You are clear to strike. We need to get moving on this now.'

Paveways fall from their aircraft under gravity. Although they are capable of shaping their trajectory – impact angle – to an extent, there is still a risk of collateral damage. The consequences if they hit a Muslim holy site were too horrendous to even consider.

I turned the jet away, to set up on the correct heading. I was barely fazed about the strike itself, but it was midday and I was concerned about the mosque and the potential for there to be people praying inside. I got Rainman to provide cover for the attack, and it was now just a question of getting the weapons off quickly.

My hands darted around the cockpit completing the pre-strike inputs to the attack computer as if on autopilot. The past few months had been so unrelenting that the process had become second nature. I entered the target information into the aircraft kit, the weapon specifics about fusing, heading, impact angle – in all, there were dozens of switches and computer inputs required to get these weapons away.

Everything was ready to go in less than two minutes. I was moments away from turning in to conduct the strike when I made one final check through the targeting pod. Due to the line of sight from my aircraft to the snipers, all I could see was an unending line of compound rooftops leading to the mosque, which lay in the cross hairs. It was broad daylight, so I turned my head to look through my helmet-mounted sight towards the target. That was pointing at the mosque as well.

This felt uncomfortable but I convinced myself it was to be expected. I had planned to get the weapon to T-shape over the top of the mosque: in effect, to stay high, then arrive with a steep impact angle. I double-checked the target coordinates I had entered into the aircraft system, which all looked fine. I then rolled the Typhoon onto its side, turning in for the attack, and rolled out on the precise attack heading.

I was about to make the radio call to get final clearance to strike when I checked the targeting pod again. As I switched between the two targets, the image jumped location. Only marginally, but more than I was expecting. I switched targets, and the image jumped back again – just fractionally, but a little too far. I had become so familiar with the Litening pod I had a feeling something wasn't right. I double-checked and triple-checked. Maybe I was imagining things.

The radio snapped back into life.

'Dragon, how are we looking? Is there an issue? Can your wingman drop instead?'

'Standby. Just positioning for the attack now.'

I tried to sound calm but the pressure was building and I couldn't fathom what was amiss. With about ten seconds until release there was a growing knot in my stomach. Logically, all the boxes had been ticked. I had double- and triple-checked. I was ready to drop, but something held me back. I hauled the jet off the attack heading, rolled the aircraft onto its side and away from the target.

In the previous few weeks, I had done dozens of these strikes successfully: I was irritated that I had an *intuition* that something was wrong and that I couldn't work out what it was. Rainman waited patiently as the cover aircraft and maintained his scan for threats or civilians near the area. He said nothing. He would have known I was busy and I was grateful for his silence.

I opened up the attack system menu and reread the weapon coordinates again, for a fourth time. I compared them against the scribbled writing on my kneeboard. *Fuck.* From two sets of coordinates totalling thirty numbers, I had placed a single digit incorrectly, entering '42' instead of '24' into one of the weapons. This would cause a twenty-metre error and had triggered the larger than expected pod jump between targets.

The second weapon would have landed short and hit the mosque. I cursed myself as I fixed the error and released on the second run. I watched the aircraft timer count down to impact and my heart pounded as I observed the weapons skim over the top of the mosque's domed roof a few milliseconds before they struck.

'Dragon, good hit on both targets. Both sniper positions destroyed. High order detonation seen. Two KIA.'

It had been way too close. In my overly confident and weary state, I had entered critical target information incorrectly. I had been moments away from destroying a mosque. I had become so sure of the Typhoon's weapon system, I had ignored my own fallibility. The jet had worked perfectly: I had not.

During the flight back, I was angry with myself. We only had a short time left on Operation Shader and I vowed in the remaining days not to let my standards slip like that again.

30. End of Days

It was a clear warm day, the blue sky decorated with a few frilly clouds, and I was walking out to the jets with Rich Cullingford – Cully – a navy exchange pilot whose beard was the whimsy of the senior service. He was chatting about his old life playing football for Yeovil Town and how there was no better feeling in the world than scoring a goal on a Saturday afternoon then heading into town afterwards.

'It was always worth the hangover,' he added.

'We've all been there.'

With his laid-back manner, he assimilated the most complex tasks and carried them out with disarming ease. He had quit the football pitch to become a pilot and was equally in his element at Mach 1 or at 2 a.m. in a nightclub. I was never sure which was his more natural environment.

'See you in a bit,' he said as we parted, and I watched as he walked over to his jet, the engineers giving him a warm smile as he approached.

It was the sort of glorious clear day when life seems to have been renewed and you are starting afresh – although the very opposite was more appropriate.

The fighting had been intense those last few weeks, but the Iraqi army had reached a tipping point and was beginning to clear the region of isolated ISIS units clinging onto their strongholds.

We were directed to Fallujah to provide air cover for a column of advancing Iraqi troops. Visibility was good. I could see the jagged peaks of the Zagros Mountains in the distance and the Euphrates winding its way across the barren landscape. From the sky, the earth is multicoloured, ever changing, from the ice caps to the deserts, across the oceans with their movement and moods. At night, when the earth darkens, you can see at height a pale orange glow around its periphery, like a halo, and it is the sky that is multicoloured with its constellations and shooting stars.

On the ground, two soldiers on foot made their way cautiously forward. Immediately behind them were two Abrams main battle tanks with their gun turrets inching back and forth as the commanders surveyed the boarded up and broken houses. Behind the tanks, scores of troops primed for combat rode in silence in a convoy of thirty armoured personnel carriers which snaked around the hulk of an abandoned tank that had been struck by an IED earlier in the day. Overhead, drones provided a bird's-eye view with live high-definition imagery.

I saw smoke from a small explosion and the two soldiers at the front of the column darted back to the tanks. The house they had been checking had been booby-trapped by ISIS bomb-makers when the fighters withdrew. The tank commanders turned their turrets towards the building to provide cover and the armoured personnel carriers, as if in a ballet, paused in unison along the road.

At the same time, from the street behind, a motorbike raced away, and we were called to follow. Keeping up with a 60 mph motorbike in a Mach 1.8 fighter wasn't a challenge, but as it swerved through narrow alleyways and side streets it was difficult to maintain a good line of sight from the targeting camera. Whenever the motorbike vanished from view, I had to move the camera to where I anticipated it would reappear, while simultaneously hauling the nose of the jet around every few seconds to ensure we stayed overhead. After we had chased the bike for ten minutes, it pulled into a driveway and hid in a garage. We got the location and passed it back to the friendly troops. No doubt there would be a knock on that garage door later in the day.

We rejoined the column to find the military vehicles in an arc around another building, a hundred yards down the road. They were firing into a compound where they had obviously met resistance, but it was now under control.

After a meeting with the tanker, we were moved by command and control to another location, twenty-five miles to the east, closer to Baghdad.

'Dragon, we need you to look for suspicious activity between here and the river to the north.'

I swung the jet into a turn and my fingers automatically ran through the sequence of switches to get the Litening pod into the right space. The area had been quiet for the past few weeks and I wasn't expecting to see very much. I was controlling the jet subconsciously, barely thinking about flying control inputs. My fingers darted over the multitude of switches on the throttle and stick almost by themselves. Like mastering the piano, it was all instinct now.

'Dragon 2. You search to the west. I'll look to the east. Let me know if you see anything.'

'Roger,' Cully replied.

Soon I saw what looked like a people carrier and moved

the pod into position to zoom in. It passed another car and a motorbike, kicking up tracks of dust as it did so. The area had been abandoned for months and I couldn't work out why there was suddenly so much activity. I followed the vehicle, turned the datalink on and the JTAC reported receiving a good image.

The people carrier slowed and pulled up outside a house. The doors slid open and several people got out, including some women veiled in black. They didn't look as if they were in a rush. Two of the men opened the back of the vehicle and began removing some baskets and boxes. A dog ran over from the house next door.

The JTAC must have been reading my thoughts.

'Dragon, they're civilians. They are moving back home. We've started seeing this over the last twenty-four hours. The area is reasonably safe now. ISIS haven't been seen here for a while.'

Those few words from the JTAC were hard to take in at first. We had arrived in theatre in early December and been thrown into the middle of extreme combat as ISIS pushed south and threatened the outskirts of the Iraqi capital. The battle had raged week after week as the territory was reclaimed street by street, house by house, every small gain at the cost of blood and sacrifice.

Ramadi and Fallujah had suffered massive damage. No aircraft had landed at the nearby airport for years. It lay in ruins, scarred with bomb damage and potholes. The highway that passed through these small cities on the way to Baghdad was an assault course of boulders and burned-out cars. It looked like a scene from the end of days.

I felt a smile crack my face; that hadn't happened for a

while over this part of the world. After months watching ISIS advance, it was a relief to see the Iraqi army taking back control and refugees who had fled in terror from their villages arriving home to start again. It would take time to breathe new life back into those communities. There were still huge challenges ahead, but the fighting in this region had stopped.

To the north, further up the Tigris river valley, the picture remained bleak. But ISIS was in retreat. They were being squeezed upcountry, towards Mosul, where the next big battles would be fought.

My last sortie was with Jim Walls, the boss of 6 Squadron, who would be replacing us in Akrotiri. To help his pilots bed in and learn the ropes during the handover, we had scheduled a few formations with 1 Squadron guys leading. On my final flight Jim and I had been tasked towards Fallujah and mainly did overwatch, looking for points of interest with the pods and reporting any intelligence to the JTACs. We then flew north, up towards the hills northeast of Kirkuk. We were looking for enemy movement on the mountain roads, but didn't see any, and there were no weapon drops required.

That was it. The end of an era. Almost five months of operational missions and then a set of new names appeared on the Shader flying programme for the following day.

The relentless cycle of sorties – walking around the jets before take-off, taking 9-lines, wearing a pistol under my G-suit to defend myself in the event of an ejection, the four rounds of tanking in high winds and thunderstorms – was over. I made the final approach back to the runway in

Akrotiri. As the wheels touched down I felt a huge burden fall from my shoulders, to be replaced by an instant tiredness.

I climbed out of the jet as some of the pilots and engineers from 6 Squadron were on the flight line. They looked as we had looked when we first arrived in December, pale from the Scottish winter and with an unease lurking behind the bravado.

Jim strolled over. His hair was ruffled from his flying helmet and the tell-tale lines around his nose and mouth showed where the oxygen mask had sat tightly since early that morning.

'Well done, Sooty. You must be pleased?'

I was holding a mass of maps in one hand, my flying helmet in the other. It was a warm afternoon. I felt hot and sweaty.

'Good trip. Let's grab a brew and spin the tapes,' I said, dodging his question. I did feel pleased, but it was more complicated than that.

We strode back to Ops. Jim Walls was ready for the fight ahead. My fight was over. I felt somewhat at a loss and, at the same time, a paternal pride in how everyone had performed. Robin Olds refused to stop flying after his hundred missions over Vietnam and continued for dozens more. He didn't want to walk away. I understood that. It's difficult when you are completely bound up and emotionally involved in an operation.

The new squadron was well drilled and knew exactly what to do. Engineers began the handover process, signing documents, conducting inventories. The pilots were reading tactics manuals, listening to briefs, readying themselves. Tomorrow the routine would continue, but it would be them, not us.

With the new squadron in town, we weren't needed, and for the last few days it felt as if we were actually in the way. They were keen to get going. There were the usual hushed, corridor mutterings that this and that needed to change, and so on.

That was fine. It was their show now.

The days ran out suddenly. Pilots don't carry much when they go on ops, but what little we had would have to be thrown into a bag, and the next time I took off from Akrotiri it would be in the cabin of a transport aircraft, without a G-suit in sight.

Everything would change. I would miss the smell of the Mediterranean, the blue skies, the sun on my face as I sat in the cockpit waiting for check-in. I would miss the pressure, the routine of arriving at work, grabbing a coffee in the dawn light and studying the intelligence briefings for the day ahead.

That was over.

I would miss sitting with Ken Gray on the old picnic bench outside Ops, chatting about the weaponeering. Jonny and Thorney leaning across the table with intense expressions as they hammered out new tactics. The engineers with rolled-up sleeves checking the instruments and jacking weapons up onto the wing pylons. The sight of two Typhoons clearing the runway and turning into needles as they stitched a course south-east towards Syria. The palpable sense of purpose would fade. No one seemed exuberant, merely relieved.

1 (Fighter) Squadron had performed to its maximum

349

and conducted well over 300 precision strikes. Everyone who arrived with me on 3 December would be safely heading back to the UK. I was thankful for that. It was time to go home. We wanted to go home.

But still, there was a sense of loss as well as completion. We had grown attached to our baby and we carried an indefinable feeling of leaving the job unfinished. We were handing our creation over to someone else. I was happy to walk out of the spotlight and had no idea how I would feel going back to flying that was less challenging. I had become accustomed to the adrenaline, the pressure, the complexity; the energy of it all.

31. Home Fires

We looked different: tanned and confident, familiar with the stress of live weaponry, long sorties, constant risk. Racing around at 40,000 feet in a formation back in the UK felt strangely benign. I lacked motivation. The superfluous trivia of UK service life returned. Routine training felt hollow, even meaningless on occasions. It wasn't, of course, certainly not to the new pilots on their workups.

I missed the intensity of operations. I should have been feeling safe and secure, enjoying the lack of threat and doing a spot of training flying and a few socials. But it all felt empty, unsatisfying. If leading a fighter squadron on combat operations was the highlight, the pinnacle – what on earth came next?

I was off to a desk job at the Ministry of Defence, which would last for a couple of years. After that, if the RAF had its way, about twenty more years of desk jobs.

'It's a great broadening and growth opportunity for you,' I was informed by the military HR department.

It was a relief to see my daughter's huge smile when I returned to the UK. There had been moments when I'd thought I might never see her blue eyes looking up at me again. At least a ground job in London would allow us more time together.

The RAF moves squadron bosses up the ladder and

away from flying to work in strategy, procurement and aviation leadership. I had no issue with that, it was the way of things. They were important jobs and I understood the system. But I had already experienced military staff jobs and they held little allure for me. I knew that the next move would probably be my last in uniform.

Wearing a suit and tie one morning as I walked along Whitehall to the MOD, I passed a group of protesters. They were waving flags, and chanting slogans about 'the illegal war'. One man was shouting phrases into a megaphone for the rest of the crowd to repeat. The protest wasn't aimed at me, but still I felt as if I personally were being judged. A few days after I'd returned from Cyprus, my mother had asked me if I had dropped any bombs, and I said yes. She gave me a look that was at the same time both supportive and horrified. That was the end of the conversation. She didn't know what to ask, and I didn't know how to answer.

It was difficult to talk about the experiences on Operation Shader with friends and family. The actions had been too violent, and it seemed unnecessarily gruesome to be trying to paint a picture to describe the context. Again, I set out to compartmentalize and try not to think about it.

By contrast, it was easy to talk to those who had been there. There was no need to justify the context, explain the jargon, the complexity of the weapon systems, the absurd targeting scenarios. There was already an innate understanding before the words began to tumble out. You knew just by someone's expression what they had experienced, what they had felt, what they were going to say.

None of this came as any great surprise. Putting combat experiences in a box and taping it up went with the territory. Having never really opened up about my feelings during all the years I had been flying, it was perfectly natural that it did not happen now.

An American air force colonel named Lanny Geib gave a celebrated lecture in the 1970s in which he characterized fast jet pilots as invariably mission focussed, thriving on control, good at compartmentalizing, poor at discussing emotions, and predictable. When I watched a grainy recording of Geib's talk as a brand-new pilot during some aviation medical training, I saw none of this in my 21-year-old self. I saw all of it in my 38-year-old self when I watched it again the second time. Fifty years after the talk, the themes endured.

Perhaps these qualities are essential for making the most effective fighter squadron. Cultures are important for delivering set outcomes. In the same way that Prince Harry has described leaving military life as like being on a bus with all of your colleagues and then getting off in the middle of nowhere on your own, being on a fighter squadron is a roller coaster ride with your best mates – everyone with similar personality types, experiencing the same tremendous highs and plunging lows. You are all too busy, too focussed, too honed and sharpened to stop and reflect. You're in it up to your eyeballs and you can't do anything else but hang on for the ride. It is joyful and shattering, intense and benign, frightening and reassuring. I wouldn't have changed it for the world – but still, it's difficult to recognize when it's time to reach for the stop button.

Leaving the squadron was a wrench. It felt like leaving your family, and a big part of me ached to put on a flying suit and get back into the skies. Not just into the cockpit, but back into the environment, the culture – the brotherhood.

One of the last events I attended on 1 Squadron was the annual Battle of Britain dinner. As always, it commenced with a moment of remembrance outside the mess, where everyone gathered in formal dress uniform. The sun had begun to set. The whole team was there. I walked out of the mess towards the parade with Jonny and Thorney.

'What a year. Who would have thought it,' Thorney remarked.

'I know, it came out of nowhere,' Jonny said poignantly. 'I hope we got it right.'

We turned in unison to face the Union flag as it began to lower and the military band struck up the moving notes of 'The Last Post'. The crystal-clear sound of the trumpet hung in the air and heads lowered in a moment of private reflection.

As the music drifted to a close, the silence was shattered by the roar of a Typhoon as it thundered overhead. It was flown by Cully, our navy exchange pilot. He was precisely on time, to the second, and flew perfectly over the parade at 250 feet and 500 knots.

As the jet raced past, he lit the afterburners. The two engines glowed bright orange and the huge flames thrown out of the back gleamed brightly in the fading light. To the chorus of car alarms triggered as always by the scream of the Typhoon, Cully hammered across the rooftops towards the horizon. He eased the jet nose high into the evening sunlight and climbed higher and higher before finally disappearing into the wispy cirrus clouds. The end to a perfect day.

Come on, boys, it's time for a beer.

Acknowledgements

My story recorded here in *Typhoon* started off simply as the cathartic process of writing up and trying to understand the feelings and thoughts hastily scribbled down in a diary during an intense period of air operations. With the encouragement of friends and family it has become much more.

In particular, I would like to thank Alex Tennant, Andy Booth, Peter Dickson, Nick Egan, Iris Gioia and my brother Peter Sutton for their advice, suggestions and support, and also my mother Helen, for her uncanny ability to spot a typo from a thousand yards. My sincere thanks, as well, to my agent Andrew Lownie, the editor Rowland White and his team at Penguin Michael Joseph, and of course to Clifford Thurlow, my co-writer, for his enduring patience and wisdom, and for managing so brilliantly to bring the whole thing to life.

The events of *Typhoon* are all true. Some names have been changed, and real names have been used with permission.

Like all the best journeys, writing this book has turned into something of a voyage of discovery. I've met new people, made new friends, and I have gained a fresh perspective on my own feelings and, unquestionably, a better insight into the impact that these events have had on others, too.

Most starkly, I have a new-found respect and understanding of the effect that operations and deployments have on the loved ones left behind. The brothers, sisters, mums, dads, partners and children who have to cope – often with a forced, supportive smile – with all of life's pressures and dramas while the pilots, engineers and all the other members of the armed forces disappear, yet again, at short notice and halfway around the world.

This book is dedicated to the families who have to cope with all of that.

Instagram: @typhoonbook

Glossary

9-line: the format used to convey a CAS mission to an aircraft

27 mm: the armour-piercing rounds carried by the Typhoon cannon

A400: transport aircraft

AAA: anti-aircraft artillery

AMRAAM: advanced medium-range air-to-air missile (radar guided)

APU: auxiliary power unit – a mini jet engine in the aircraft fuselage which starts the main engines

ASRAAM: advanced short-range air-to-air missile (infra-red guided)

C-17: transport aircraft

C-130: transport aircraft

CAS: close air support – air action (strikes) against hostile units that are in close proximity to friendly soldiers

chaff: bundle of aluminium-coated glass fibres, dispersed from an aircraft as a self-protection measure against radar-guided missiles

crypto: cryptographic data; secure code for communication

danger close: friendly troops in such close proximity to the enemy that an air strike poses a risk to them, but the situation is so serious that it needs to occur regardless

DH: direct hit

flight level: a measure of altitude, based on units of 100 feet

G-LOC: G-induced loss of consciousness

GPS: global positioning system

HUD: head up display – a fixed display unit in the pilot's line of sight which presents critical information about the aircraft's position, navigation and targeting

IED: improvised explosive device

JTAC: joint terminal attack controller (controls CAS missions)

KIA: killed in action

knot: unit of measurement for aircraft speeds; one knot is equivalent to 1.15 mph

LATE Arm: launch and trigger enable – the final safety switch made before releasing a weapon

Litening pod: targeting camera and laser designator system

Mach: A number (speed) relative to the speed of sound, which varies according to altitude. Mach 1 equates to the speed of sound; greater than Mach 1 is supersonic

MOD: Ministry of Defence

NATO: North Atlantic Treaty Organization

NVGs: night vision goggles

OCU: operational conversion unit – a training squadron for a frontline jet

Ops: Operations / Operations room

pan: aircraft dispersal area; the flight line

Paveway 4: a 500 lb laser- or GPS-guided precision bomb

PTSD: post-traumatic stress disorder

QRA: quick reaction alert – jets on high-readiness standby to launch and intercept aircraft in UK airspace

QWI: qualified weapons instructor

ROE: rules of engagement

RPG: rocket propelled grenade
SAM: surface-to-air missile
strafe: aircraft gun used in an air-to-ground role
TRiM: trauma risk management
UAS: University Air Squadron
UAV: unmanned aerial vehicle (a drone)

Jon Egging Trust (JET)

Founded in 2011 by Dr Emma Egging following the
tragic death of her husband, Red Arrows pilot Flt
Lt Jon Egging, The Jon Egging Trust (JET) supports
vulnerable young people to get back on track and
realize their potential.

JET is an early intervention organization – working in
partnership with schools, to support young people with
low self-esteem whose futures are jeopardized by life
challenges which put them at significant risk of dropping
out of full-time education.

JonEgging
Trust
Helping young people achieve

Index